Resident Alien

For Nick —
Best wishes from

Resident Alien

The Hilarious Adventures
of a Public School Man
in Wildest California

by
Ian Whitcomb

Ian Whitcomb
July 1. 1992

CENTURY
LONDON SYDNEY AUCKLAND JOHANNESBURG

Published in Great Britain in 1990 by Century
An imprint of Random Century Ltd
20 Vauxhall Bridge Road, London SW1V 2SA

Century Hutchinson Australia (Pty) Ltd
20 Alfred Street, Milsons Point, Sydney, NSW 2061, Australia

Century Hutchinson New Zealand Ltd
PO Box 40-086, 32-34 View Road, Glenfield, Auckland 10, New Zealand

Century Hutchinson South Africa (Pty) Ltd
PO Box 337, Bergvlei 2012, South Africa

Set in Linotronic Times by SX Composing Ltd, Rayleigh, Essex

Printed and bound in Great Britain by Mackays of Chatham Ltd, Chatham, Kent

British Library Cataloguing in Publication Data
Whitcomb, Ian
  Resident alien.
  1. United States – Description & travel
  I. Title
  917.3'04927

ISBN 0-7126-2266-7

Part One
A Night Fight in June

Part Two
Home in Altadena

Part Three
Into Hollywood!

'Courage!' he said, and pointed toward the land,
'This mounting wave will roll us shoreward soon.'
In the afternoon they came unto a land
In which it seemèd always afternoon.
All round the coast the languid air did swoon,
Breathing like one that hath a weary dream.
'The Lotos Eaters',
Alfred Lord Tennyson, 1832.

Delight is to him – a far, far upward, and inward delight – who against
the proud gods and commodores of this earth, ever stands forth his own
inexorable self.
Moby Dick, Herman Melville, 1851.

Too much have I travelled topographically, detailing the flying buttress,
breathless vista, painted hill. For one's proper study should be mankind
and, in particular, modern youth in action. Without either rhyme or
reason, these golden children of the West are leading us, pointing like
Tadzio, away across the exotic margin. And I will follow, notebook in
hand, to the outer limits of this Last Frontier.
In Darkest Teenland, an unfinished travel book,
L. M. S. Farquar, 1978.

Part One

A Night Fight in June

I live in Los Angeles.

'Bad luck!' said the pale, naked old man in a fruity accent. We were in the changing room of the Putney Leisure Centre, drying off after our early-morning swim. The man was a stranger to me.

'Bad luck to you too!' I replied, as best I could muster at that time of day. In a few hours I was to fly back to my home town, after the usual lovely Christmas holidays amidst family and friends.

The very next week, as luck would have it, I was fed some ammo for future use against such brackish creatures. I was invited by a wealthy old Pasadenan oil man to a brunch-and-speech at the Town Crier Club in downtown Los Angeles. After fresh Dungeness crab and coleslaw, all heads at our round tables turned as a rich and radio-phonic voice announced the guest speakers:

'Meet Martinski and Journeymann, celebrated "Think Tankers". They're going to deliver an address on Los Angeles, city of the future – so let's surge them a warm Southland wave!'

Two bright-eyed young men, white shirts crackling, leapt on to the rostrum and, taking turns like a vaudeville double act, presented the following:

'Let's face facts head on: L.A. is happening – it's the gateway to Pacific growth, an entrepreneurial economy comparable to turn-of-the-century New York. Ride the wave! Forget the usual myopic East Coast view. . . . L.A. as the city without shame or embarrassment. . . . a place to find the perfect wave or thigh . . . a home for Spandex and the macrobiotic sprout. . . . A Bimbotown with a Vaseline Alley and Wannabee stars on every corner. A paradigm of the epicene soaked in solipsism. Sure, you can turn right on a red light – but so will the rest of the world when they catch up with you guys!

'L.A. is the model imitated by every city in the U.S.A. We're talk-ing serious money. We're talking finance and manufacturing; we're talking high-tech and aerospace and autos and garments. We're also talking gastronomy and culture. And we're talking PEOPLE – a humungous rainbow of races, shining out of a hot new world on the highly-happening Pacific Rim. Mark our words – L.A.'s gonna be the

1

World Nation, in a carnival of nations, all butting and biffing and busy. And PRODUCING!

'Let's be specific: serious money is moving west; major banks – not only our friends the Japanese – are putting down permanent roots – concrete ones – in Los Angeles. When the century turns, this city will be the financial and manufacturing centre of the world. The Occident will join with the Orient here on the hub of the Pacific Rim! OK – so we're excited! Shouldn't *you* be? Already 75 per cent of downtown is owned by foreign interests: they realize that L.A. is the world's eleventh largest nation in terms of gross national product; they're building towers to make their point. Their money sees growth in many industries: in aerospace, in autos – eight Japanese companies have headquartered here – in microchip and silicon, and in motion pictures. Management sees the replacement of middle-class whites with immigrants, particularly Asians, as a boon.

'*Space*. You got lots of it. You're four hundred thousand-odd square miles and still you're expanding! Where is the epicentre of L.A.? No special place, but everywhere where there's people and productivity, within this charmed desert garden. Los Angeles, spider woman, you are a model of decentralization: sixteen urban cores at last count. You are laid out to meet the demands of the auto and thus you are spun with freeways into a wondrous web of urban villages – *dispersed centres*, if you will. The perfect post-industrial city. Face, accept and *love* your car. Make her both comfortable and comforting. You will spend a great part of your waking life in her. Float – or bask when in jams – in your boat to the soothing sounds of New Age radio as you cruise to the isle of your choice, whether it be Simi Valley or Orange County. Forget town squares and moot halls.

'There is still space, nebulous space, out here, for the setting up of small businesses, keys to the future. L.A. is a happy hunting-ground for entrepreneurs and consultants – provided the bait is right: this is a moving feast, seasonal and cyclical. Sometimes downright faddish: one day croissants are the thing, next it's fluorescent neoprene surf-wear. But for management L.A. is a gold mine! First World management sees Third World labour and loves the sight: this population is becoming predominantly Hispanic and Asian. Take note: by 2010 the Anglos will be the minority here, but don't despair – seize the ladle of this bubbling hot-pot of disparate cultures! Stir the Old World out of its complacency! L.A. is the new Ellis Island, the new centre for the realization of the dreams of huddled masses. Muddled in language they may be, but all of them understand *the vision of the hauling of the*

2

green! And, of course, these immigrants bring a smorgasbrod of cuisine which is a gastronome's delight. . . .

'Sure, you got problems – smog, drugs, gangs, raw sewage in Santa Monica Bay, choked freeways, long waits in your favourite new restaurant. But problem-solving is second nature to Angelenos, a fine old tradition. You brought the water to this semi-desert, didn't you? And L.A.'s problems today are the Old World's problems tomorrow. Watch us run!

'In the final analysis, we – I'm Martinski – and I'm Journeymann – envision our Angeleno of the future; world citizen, master of destiny. This person is colourless, odourless, nebulous, weightless. This person needs no boosters, no "think tankers" such as ourselves. This person is self-starting. This person, in fabrics of washed silk and high fashion sportswear of soft construction, doesn't know or care what the rest of the world thinks of Los Angeles. Let the rest of the world go by! Or . . . let it come visit Disneyland and the remodelled Hollywood.

'*We have a dream.* A dream of a cottage industry nation, far-flung from the towering conglomerates of downtown and yet deeply attached to Los Angeles. We see a climate-controlled unit – a cottage of tomorrow, a little star within the constellation of suburbs that constitutes the galaxy which is L.A. And inside this unit-cottage, as robot servants attend to dishes and carpets etc, we see a person kneeling on an S-shaped surgically-approved chair and scanning a computer screen as suggestions for lunch roll up. A desk-top power breakfast for tomorrow is in the planning stage. For the rest of the day life can be planned and executed from such a computer terminal in such a cottage unit: business, pleasure, shopping, viewing, sex and food.

'Meanwhile, outside – there stream ribbons of freeway, glimmering and pulsating, ready to welcome you and your recreational vehicle should you desire time out to play at the ocean or up the mountain, or simply to cruise around the L.A. galaxy for the sheer fun of it all!'

*

I meandered home in my Honda Accord feeling much better all round for having attended that talk. To hell with the naked old man at the Putney Leisure Centre!

Welcome to my Los Angeles. People work hard for their money down here, this is a working town. Dressed for sports, perhaps, but always trying to meet the market head on. Only yesterday I caught a striking line from a black rap number blasted from the depths of a pick-up truck as it thundered past me and my dog:

'DON'T BUG ME MAN, I CAIN'T STOP HERE!
I GOTTA GET ON WITH MY CAREER!'

I've lived in Los Angeles on and off since 1965, when I arrived as a 'British Invader' with a smash-hit record and a desire to stick around as a star. The desire didn't materialize but I stuck around, doing a bit of this and that. Nowadays I'm known as a specialist in Tin Pan Alley songs, playing them on my radio show and at clubs, festivals, weddings and barmitzvahs. I'm often asked if I'm Australian, but in fact I'm English, attending a semi-progressive public school called Bryanston in Dorset. I now live in a 1947 frame and stucco house in Altadena, a leafy little strip in the foothills of the San Gabriel mountains, almost twenty miles from Hollywood and thirty from the Pacific. I like it here on the whole – I get more work here than in England – although life can sometimes be frustrating. But I try to keep my nose clean, because I'm not an American citizen, therefore they could deport me if they so desired.

I am a 'Resident Alien' with a number on a laminated blue plastic card. Why haven't I become an American after all these years? Something to do with betrayal and a stinging healthy sea breeze as my father plays golf on a bluff near wartime Scarborough and I watch from above. Besides, I might want to return home when I'm old and incapable.

*

Ocean Avenue, Santa Monica; up on the cliffs and facing the sea. But this sea is really an ocean, wide-screen and grandiose, sliding off the far horizon to lap in the Far East, end-of-the-line, distant to us. At this moment the water is halcyon and as for the sunset – it's magnificent: a reddish-pink has been squirted all over the sky by the sinking sun. Jumbo jets to our left, moving Indian file and lightly droning, are of burnished gold; to our right the Malibu mountains are milk chocolate; and on the horizon lies like a leviathan the mysterious island of Catalina, haloed by the racy sunset.

Suddenly, and with great confidence, a tall figure hoves into our Cinerama view. A vagabond in jeans and cape. He stops right in front of us to stand proud and erect on the well-trimmed grass of this clifftop park, Palisades Park, a gift to the people by the City of Santa Monica. In a successful gesture, and with all the panache of a matador, the vagabond whip-flourishes open a Navajo blanket. For a moment we lose our panorama of this Bay of Smokes (an old Indian description – even then they had their smogs) as the ocean breeze holds the filthy blanket in its tremulous grasp. In the blackness we catch a flash from the fellow's full set of fine teeth. He is smiling with something, perhaps gall.

I know this gypsy! I have given him my spare change while on my way to my club just down the way, loaded with ukuleles and accordion. Sometimes he has grunted and pocketed the coins, other times he has thrust up close, hissing and demanding more. One night I donated a second-hand tuna-fish sandwich and, after a swift inspection, he hurled the thing away with a phlegmy roar. His name is Dooley and he makes a sort of living as a guinea-pig for medical researchers. But, he says, no one may touch his bone marrow. He is also an activist in the growing army of homeless persons. 'We have a lawyer,' he told me.

The blanket settles on a patch of thick, rich grass in a grove of succulents close to the clifftop. With a laugh of steely gaiety Dooley descends to his camp-site.

Some hundred feet below the crumbly cliffs of these Palisades is Pacific Coast Highway, where all ages love to drag-race their autos at madcap speeds, hellbent on going places and doing things, same as their ancestors in the teen years of the century. Take a peek. Where are they all going and why so fast? Even *I* ask that sort of question once in a while, and tonight's the night. Near Dooley's camp is a stone bust of a stern lady, a memorial to Arcadia Baker, wife of one of Santa Monica's founders. Carved into a fat old cactus nearby is recent history: 'Hector Y Rosa . . . Christine & Mofu . . . I Gave Up Sex Drugs And Rock & Roll And It Was The Worst Fucking Twenty Minutes Of My Life.'

Cross over Ocean Avenue and amble down the sidewalk, noting the abundance of different kinds of trees in the park we have just left. Stretching to many crazy angles and twisted by wind, these sea trees might be termed 'grotesque' by other, safer cultures, but they are enjoyed and tolerated over here. One of the trees is growing parallel with the grass, like a homeless person sleeping it off.

Turn left and admire the Shangri-La Hotel – hunky, creamy, compact – a gift-package shape with sexy round edges. Gleaming tubular railings curve up the entrance stairway and into the dark but twinkling lobby where once were chromium cocktail shakers, white tuxedos and easily-snappable legs. Running along the outside wall is a wavy blue line, interrupted at intervals by little antique cypress trees cling-

5

ing so tightly. This is Thirties architecture: Streamline Moderne, Ocean Liner, Zig-Zag. There's not a lot left, so enjoy while you can. This is a city on the move. In the Twenties, on the same site, stood a row of 'Good Queen Bess' cottages, and before that there was a hacienda of mud and wattle. Before that – Indians.

Santa Monica's founding fathers were full of progressive zeal. British-born Senator Jones, a real-estate man who launched the city as an investment (in partnership with Colonel Baker) was fond of reciting to his plot salesmen at platting* meetings:

> 'Paint the town azure, paint the town tawny,
> Picture the landscape as September Morny,
> Give them some romance and give them some guff,
> But sell, sell, sell, sell, sell or I will get rough!'

*

Watch out! Here comes a squad of black boys. Bent low, careering down the sidewalk on bicycles. Keep moving, eyes front, then step lively to the side. Their cycles rear like stallions, their little eyes with laughter shine like moons.

As the last cyclist whizzed past me he spat. And I'm relieved to feel the juice run down my cheek and not yours. I live here. I understand. Now the juice has plopped on to the shoulder of my white tuxedo, and there it rests.

To the left: identical one-roomed bungalows of white lath and stucco, with red Spanish pan-tiled roofs, dinky and charming, visible to each other and open to the road and the sea breezes. Typical of old Los Angeles: a bungalow court, with communal garden in the centre, a sort of village green. This Twenties development inspired the motel of the Thirties. I can imagine a summer morning, 1930, when zephyrs are racing off the ocean to caress the courtyard and whisper that it's wake-up time. Soon all bungalow doors open synchronistically and apple-faced men, women and children greet the morning with a chorus of 'Bye-Bye, Black Bird' or something similarly chirrupy. And out on the blue water of the bay our all-year-round California girl is swinging the tiller of a dipping yacht as porpoise and flying fish dance around. If only that could be my recurring dream instead of the usual one: a dusty track in an arid wasteland leading up – after many miles trudge from the safe city – to the newly purchased house that is

* Plat: a plan or map of a plot of ground.

6

and isn't my real-life one; a dark crooked house of many levels and many rooms, and often I stumble upon some undiscovered room crammed with crapulous, scrofulous strangers who barely acknowledge me. . . .

I saw the sign announcing that this bungalow court is to be demolished next month, making way for condominiums. At the corner of Ocean Avenue and Santa Monica Boulevard, waiting for our orders to cross the street (there are loudspeakers in the traffic signals), observe the palm trees. So many varieties. And, like almost everything else here in the Southland, the palms are not native. They were imported by the original city founders. You'll find no fruit up them, but at least they're clean. Underneath, at their sides, are their brothers: parking meters with very short time allowances. The traffic police watch them closely and, at the first second of an infraction, whizz out from the shadows in their little chariots. Santa Monica is extremely civic-minded and the City Council is ever watchful. If you're interested you can listen to their deliberations every Tuesday by tuning into radio station KCRW – where, by the way, I host my own show every Wednesday at 1 p.m.

Cleared to cross – the picture of the sloping hiker is flashing in the signal box, and the cuckoo is calling.

There used to be a gas station on this side when I lived down here years ago, back in the Seventies. Corner gas stations are having a hard time these days. Now we have yuppiedom: 'La Dolce Vita Frozen Yogurt'. The other day when I was here I noticed a glass dome encasing scalloped madeleines. Impressed, I called the counter boy and told him how Marcel Proust had dunked such a plump, squat little cake into his tea, been transported back to childhood and written a classic which I was at present trying to read. 'Hey, I'll check that out!' said the boy excitedly. I said Marcel was French. 'Then I'll read it in French!' Southern Californians are never craven, always enterprising!

On your left. Up the street a block. See the sign painted on the side of the wall? 'The Queen's Knees – British Pub'. The place rather frightens me. Not a pleasant spot. Along the standard American flat-faced frontage wall are heraldic devices – all dubious; inside, decorating the walls, are pictures of Churchill at his bulldoggiest, London flaming behind him, and Raj officers and Edwardian cricket teams – the plunder of junk-shops – and these gentlemen are steadfastly looking straight ahead, while below them whale-bodied Americans hurl darts indiscriminately or guzzle British ales and guffaw.

7

Where are the British? Some airline personnel and a few Australians may be up at the front bar. My research tells me there are 350,000 British expatriates living legally in Southern California, many organized into clubs such as Thistle, Leek, Turnip, Mayflower. An awful lot make their home in Santa Monica, attracted perhaps by the bracing air, morning mists and later sunshine, and smells that are reminiscent of Bognor or Brighton.

You'd be hard pressed to find a public school man – especially the old-fashioned pre-war rover type: jutting-jawed, firm of step, all alone and liking it, outfitted in corduroy, knapsack on back containing a pocket edition of Palgrave's *Golden Treasury*.

A guttural voice from the upper bar: 'So I said to Engelbert, but I call him Gerry. . . .' A knot of expatriate Britishers, tabloid journalists, are enjoying a story from a man with a face the colour of fresh-killed beef (this is the same face we can see on the surrounding walls sharing jokes with Cary Grant, Alan Whicker, Tom Jones and Prince Philip).

But mine host's voice is trumped by a louder and more strident one. Why did you force me here? I know this idiot too – an American, a local restaurant writer who also lectures for the University of Southern California on 'The History Of World Cuisine'. The man is calling his class together: 'OK, gang – time to eat! Let's graze on the famed Brit dish of beer-battered Icelandic cod – fried so skilfully you'll be greeted by a hiss of steam as you fork open your fish. Mmmmm! And wait till you sample the chewy chips – truly a gourmet experience!'

Proceeding along Ocean Avenue – as we were – notice that all dogs are on the lead. No animals are allowed in any green area, and certainly not on the seashore. This is a pity. In England I can remember them entertaining in pubs, up at the bar. But, you see, drinking in America is for the most part a straight-faced business. We are now passing a bar: a stucco nondescript block, windowless, but relief is provided by a small porthole of rusty green metal. The entrance, on a corner, has wrought-iron trellis work and grilles, which makes the place jail-like. Inside seems soupy gloom, but serious drinking is being conducted there by ratty men, hunched and unsmiling, nursing and sipping and sucking and philosophizing. 'Soper's Wind & Sea' says the weathered sign outside, and 'Cocktails' winks the neon, backed up by a jaunty tipped cocktail glass with its maraschino cherry.

Now past a string of rough-edged motels of 'Late Fifties Functional' design – The Breakers, The Pacific Sands, The Surf Rider –

and quickly past a gamut of panhandlers. Sorry – no spare change. I only carry a credit card. One panhandler, a skinny man in dark glasses gripping his home – an overloaded supermarket shopping cart – has just collided with another cart heaped with old clothes, pushed by a tiny old crone. Now the old-clothes heap rises and, revealing itself as a bigger old crone, starts berating the beggar man. And yet they are laughing.

At this point we can escape from all this. For we are approaching my club, where life will be gay in the old sense of the word.

*

My home port. From atop the flat asbestos roof, an intermittent yellow light pierces the evening mist to spell out in the Gothic lettering of the Old West: 'Sterling's Steak House'. Architecturally, I suppose, my club isn't worth a preservation order: a standard block (once a car repair shop) faced in ski-lodge rustic flagstones fitted crazy-paving style, and front-moated by a wooden trough filled with black loam and slimy shrubbery. The thick and greasy front door, of Fifties Spanish Colonial design, is at present being guarded by two upright Great Danes. Around them lie other dogs, not so well-bred but all jolly and smiling-eyed, typical of Sterling's members. Hanging to the right of the front door is a welcoming hand-drawn poster depicting a twinkly old sport in an open-neck plaid shirt who is cradling a silver saxophone: 'ROSY McHARGUE & HIS DIXIELAND BAND'.

The great wooden door is ajar, and floating out to embrace us is a warm glow and some hot sounds. The Great Danes bark us through and next we are confronted by a partition of printed wood grain and a stencilled warning that 'Only Regulars and Friends of Regulars may use our Rest-rooms!' Bubbling from behind the partition comes the sound of rickety-rackety jazz at its most jovial, accompanied by the smell of fried onions and cleaning fluid. Walk right in!

The lights are low – it's darker than the street – the room is filled with blue streaks of tobacco smoke and a strange but appetizing drizzle-mist that anoints us as we steer a passage through coves and bays, to a long and wavy bar. Behind this bar is Jonny, a pert and compact woman in, I would guess, her late thirties, well-rouged and sheathed in leathers, commanding with glittering eye her many rows of multi-coloured liquor bottles and her ever-on television (from which, as usual, silently flickers a ball game). The bar drinkers, not strictly speaking my kind of Sterling's member, are grizzled varmints and

9

they sit on their stools facing Jonny and the front window, determinedly ignoring the rickety-rackety jazz tickling their backs. Their talk is sporadic, but usually it is of weather and current affairs; some stare out of the window, dreaming of a world that could and should have been. When I sit up at the bar every now and then I like to study the Olympia Beer exhibit. A moving picture mounted in plastic, it shows an electric scene of pure mountain water cascading eternally through green pastures, as long as the bar is open.

A stranger, a little tipsy, is calling for a change of T.V. channel; he doesn't know the form. When a customer gets unpleasantly drunk Jonny, tough as her black leathers, can give them a quick bum's rush through the door, no sweat. One night, a setter of crossword puzzles and a friend of mine, was daring enough to sing straight at the bar, 'Oh, Johnnie . . . How You Can Love' – the World War One comedy song – and in a trice Jonny tumbled him out of the door and into the dogs. This was the man who introduced me to Proust. Jonny's husband, Chef Don, would have done the bouncing normally, but at that moment he was busy evicting a tramp from the lavatory. Strolling in from his kitchen next door, Chef Don had discovered the bum in the act of changing his clothes. The idea!

Jonny's wavy bar is divided from the main room by a balustrade of curvy piano-leg posts. Move through one of the openings and out into the main action. . . .

Round the hearty burgundy walls are grim, dim prints in silver frames: inky waves breaking in sickly moonlight, navy-blue oriental mountains of measly size, a green chartreuse junk sludging through a buttery sea, a Mississippi showboat strangled by weeping willows. The rest of the pictures are indescribable because very little light is thrown out by the 1970s Tiffany lamps. But feel, please, the slick surface of the dark brown banquettes beneath the pictures, where sit the members of Sterling's, my friends.

The members drink and they smoke and they talk and they dance. Sometimes they eat a steak – a decent solid well-marbled steak, often smothered in fried onions. No Asian muck here, resembling the bottom of a parrot's cage. No stingy portions of raw fish-lips and sculpted radish arranged round the plate like modern art. No contemporary cuisine! Just hunks of good red meat with plenty of yellow fat, gnarled baked potatoes with craters of liquid butter and gobs of sour cream, and beds of lettuce upon which squats plenty of cold plump macaroni in viscous cheese.

But the chief delight of Sterling's is the music, so now we push our way across the floor and through the fast-jerking dancers and press ourselves against the great grand piano which forms a perfect example of that marvellous American institution – The Piano Bar. An extra-special use has been found for the body of a grand piano: people sit around it as if up at a bar, tipping their glasses, banging their spoons, tapping out cigarettes, thumbing through fat banknote rolls, playing footsie with the person of their choice, blowing all manner of horns, even sometimes squeezing an accordion. Near the keyboard, in place of honour, sits a monster brandy snifter ready for tips, especially notes.

Presiding over the keyboard is Franklyn, a thin and spade-bearded man in his fifties, hunched, lightly dusting the keys, looking in the same direction as the varmints at the bar, preoccupied with something on a lost horizon. Glassily staring, he is also swaying – but not to the Dixie beat, and I am pretty certain he has had a drink too many. Back in the be-bop era, Franklyn was a promising pianist full of weird chords, but sometime in the 1950s he burnt out and now he is reduced to playing Dixie, haunted so effectively by the reprimanding spirits of dead modern jazz greats that sometimes in the middle of a rowdy number he will shout out, 'Bird! Forgive me, please forgive me!' (Other legendary names, such as 'Lester' or 'Thelonius', are substituted weekly.)

Just above the piano, on the platform that acts as a bandstand, is a burly but smiley fellow presiding like a fry-cook over a kitchen collection of drums, cymbals and woodblocks. This is Floyd, and by day he sells used cars. Franklyn and Floyd are the only paid members of Rosy McHargue's Dixieland Band. The other musicians on the bandstand – and it is a crowded place – are playing for the hell of it. Some perform from their piano bar chairs, others from their wheelchairs. And then, scattered around the room, there are men and women with many kinds of horn – flugel, French, contra – as well as plain old trumpet, cornet, tuba and trombone. As to the latter . . . there are too many competing tailgate trombonists, often doing damage with their lunging slides.

Only a select few are allowed to sit slap up next to Rosy McHargue. Tonight pride of place has been given to a skeletal, hollow-cheeked young man with spiky upright hair and granny glasses, wearing a cowboy shirt and cowboy boots, with a clarinet in one hand and a camera in the other. Now he bends, waving his clarinet, to set down his camera and pick up a cassette tape recorder which he fiddles with as he shouts: 'Ho! Sveeng zat ding!!' Oh no! Not another East European

11

pixillated Dixie purist! Behind the foreigner, and almost lost in darkness, is a cadaverous face with a cornet stuck to it. 'Zolo, zolo – pleeeze!' shouts the foreigner to Rosy and Rosy nods. The shadowy man gets up to blow.

The solo, a homage to Bix Beiderbecke, is followed by solos from every player in the room. This is a democratic art form. Rosy, true to tradition, gives the nod to each jazzer. He sits on the far right of the bandstand in a big wooden chair, as if enthroned, his long legs outstretched, his massive head with matching clumps of silvery hair crowned by a yachting cap set at a jolly angle on the spot where Jews wear skull-caps. His curved wide-screen dome reflects a world of simple melodies mattressed by three-note chords, of big-chested women and good cigars, of heart songs with many verses.

Rosy knows the verses to a million songs. He makes me yearn for times past, but he's no foolish old codger. He knows his public, he knows when to stop, he knows lots of up-to-the-minute jokes and the language that goes with them. His piercing blue eyes glint cuttingly, his clothes are crisp and freshly laundered – blue windcheater, white ducks, check shirt – and his footwear is red canvas sailing shoes. He exudes the odour of little green apples. Puffing fluttering, magical notes from an old C melody silver saxophone, he sings and while he sings he gestures, indicating exciting parts of the lyrics. He's always smiling and it's for real. He is an Immortal come down to Earth for a spell. Leaning on either side of his wooden throne are his metal crutches.

Behind the bandstand is a long gilt-edged mirror marbled in gold. The marbling makes the players take on the aspect of a traditional Christmas-card setting. Some nights the picture within the mirror frame can seem Pickwickian. Behind this mirror is the kitchen lair of Jonny's husband, Don Basil (pronounced *Bay-zil*), who is the proprietor of Sterling's and a great slab of a man, with restaurant experience in old Chicago. Let us step back to Don's kitchen for a while and watch him at work – lovingly garnishing with parsley a diamond bone sirloin which is sizzling contentedly in a thick iron skillet. Next he will be turning to a big metal bowl of Iceberg lettuce, and into this he will mix cold macaroni salad. . . .

We have been interrupted by a dreadful racket. This is not jazz. Chef Don drops his parsley. Moving swayingly but quickly he steams out of the kitchen, rolling up his shirt-sleeves even higher, showing more muscle. As he moves through the swing-doors he is greeted by a flurry of dust. We follow.

In the dingy alcove between the kitchen and the lavatory a fight is in progress. Perhaps it is really a brawl. A simian man, with touches of weasel, is now punching, now kicking, now throttling a tottering figure in a blood-stained white tuxedo stuck with a pink carnation. The figure suddenly looks straight at us – a look of utter bewilderment, as if a wrong decision has been made by an umpire – and we see that it is male. He spins and falls and finally rests, slumped in a stygian corner among the mops and pails and cleaning fluids. In a final gesture, his pink carnation falls into the grime-sea floor. His prehensile fingers flicker weakly, sending out some cryptic message.

The simian man is the jazz cornet player. The tuxedo man is me.

*

I admit to throwing the first punch: a straight left to the jaw – nothing vindictive, merely a warning shot I've used before. The cornettist, Ned Gimbel, received the punch full-faced, square on. A very decent punch, taught me in the early 1950s by 'Boomf-Boomf' Baldwin, boxing instructor at Newlands, my prep school in Seaford, Sussex. 'Aim straight for the jaw, avoiding eyes and brain,' said 'Boomf-Boomf' and we paid attention, hoping for examples from his many war exploits. 'Watch your crotch! Who wants to ruin their prospects of marriage?' Throughout the years I had followed his advice and had always had success. The chinless wonder at the Trinity College ball, the old man in the Hollywood bar, the one-legged service-station attendant in Maidenhead, the Mexican leaf-blower in Altadena – all these men had fully deserved my warning punch. And all had accepted their punishment with good grace.

But not Ned Gimbel.

He had leapt from the stage with fists flying, eyes well ahead of body, anthracite eyes flashing lasers into me and my tuxedo. I was standing there below him, standing as erect as any schoolboy hero, and he caught me unprepared and he wouldn't stop punching, then kicking, then throttling. Murder was in those anthracite eyes.

In retrospect, coolly, I realize that bile had been piling up inside all day. Something to do with the frustration of trying to pursue one's dream in this land of other opportunists in the way. On the day of the fight I'd been stuttering badly, and that's always a bad sign. During lunch, in the middle of a pitch to a possible agent, I bit my tongue and blood filled my mouth, preventing talk. But in the cool of the evening, driving a flowing freeway with Regina – my lovely blonde girlfriend – at my side, I felt at peace with the world and really looking

13

forward to a night at the club.

There was no parking space around Sterling's, but Regina went into some chanting (she's a Buddhist, Japanese-style) and we soon found a space not too far away. This form of Buddhism is geared towards instant practical results.

From the trunk of my new Honda Accord LX I removed my musette accordion and banjolele. A group of passing youths laughed at me. Regina took hold of my hand and squeezed. 'Don't be hard on yourself,' she said. We had only a short walk along the front to reach Sterling's, but it meant passing a place I loathe, a hateful *nouvelle cuisine* restaurant that makes me grind my teeth, a trendy joint called The Ivy at the Shore. I know it's trendy because I once went inside, as the dinner guest of Al Jolson's final wife. And I must say I was amazed to find an old friend of the family working there as a parking attendant (valet). Francis was dressed in the same short red waistcoat as the other valets (all Hispanics, as they usually are) and he was rapping away merrily with them as our Jolson party rolled up, so I didn't recognize him at first. But as he hopped into the Mercedes and handed Mrs Jolson a ticket, I saw his face and heard him say, 'Hello, old chap.' I wanted to introduce him to Mrs Al Jolson and I wanted to tell her something about him, but for the moment I couldn't remember where he'd been to school. 'Where? Er. . . .' He grew flustered, combing his fingers through his long Rupert-Brookian hair. But I persisted and finally, with a tremendous gunning of the engine, he admitted: 'Eton. . . . Sorry, *so* sorry. . . .' Nothing to be sorry about – but he was gone.

Francis wasn't parking at the Ivy any more. He'd started a career as a singer of light rock (in the style of the Carpenters) and was making the rounds of the Hollywood clubs. I pushed a way through the motley crew swilling around the Ivy, waiting for their cars to be delivered or for the summons from the all-powerful maître d'. There they were, the fancy people – lawyers, realtors, brokers, movie-makers, stars too I have no doubt – dressed mostly in sexless drape clothes billowing in the breeze, the women with that ratty wet-hair look of salon not sea, all displaying a fearsome carelessness that has no thought for anything that's not their property – not for children, animals or you. I almost barged a bunch out of my way. 'Something's wrong,' said Regina. The restaurant is all wrong: it's not Sterling's. The outer wall is poodle-pink. From the pavement you can see through the clear plastic tent the happening people forking up petit pois and baby vegetables and just-killed baby lamb, seated below posters for campy

South Sea movies like *Moon of Manakoora,* making a racket that almost drowns out the piped Gershwin background music. It's all fake; atmosphere, ambience – real live music, a decent dance band, would be too much of a shock for these people. . . .

Not a good start to the evening. But just a few steps further and we were at the wide-open oaken door of Sterling's. Here they would admire my brand-new white tuxedo, bought at Tropadilly of Piccadilly, just as last year they had admired my wasp-waisted double-breasted brown blazer from Stork of the Strand (on to which I'd had sewn the canary-yellow Bryanston School crest). No, they hadn't cared for the combination of yellow and brown at the Army & Navy Club back in London, in fact they'd asked me to leave. 'And on a blazer!' said the club secretary to the member who had brought me. But at Sterling's they'd accepted the special blazer for what it was: *mine.* They liked me and I, in turn, liked them.

I've already told you I like Los Angeles. But sometimes life there can get you down and then Sterling's is the best tonic. I'd had, as I've said, a rotten day: the bitten tongue, and then people not returning calls, always 'in closed meeting', protected by assistants who cheekily demand to know what your call is 'regarding'. You reply that it's none of their business, which doesn't help your connecting up with the top executive who once was your pal – played tennis with you – but now puts you on excruciating 'hold' while 'easy listening adult contemporary rock' gnaws into your ear and then, when at last he takes your call, he asks, 'And how can we help you?' and you give him the rough end of your tongue and in so doing you get stuck in a stutter and you know that the deal, if there ever was a deal, is off.

It was gala night tonight at Sterling's, with all the booths full to overflowing, plates of meat and potatoes flying about, the dance floor alive with bouncing seniors. I received a few plaudits, took a few bows. How I loved this place and all its people! Regina found us stools at the bar.

'That was Muscat Ramble – Mus*cat*, not Mus*krat*. We get it right at Sterling's,' said Ned Gimbel, leaning into the mike, hunch-stanced as if he was in a horse race. 'and now give a big Southland welcome for tonight's special guest – all the way from Poland: Serge Wallenska!' The cowboy-costumed clarinettist waved his instrument madly. And here was I with an accordion and a banjolele – what price big-hearted ballads, polkas and novelty songs tonight?

The wretched Pole grabbed the mike offered by Gimbel and launched into an impassioned speech about oppression in his home-

15

land and how thrilling it was to be in America watching democracy at work, especially here at Sterling's. He was received with much clapping, whooping and banging of table-tops. Gimbel jutted his face into the mike, sandpapering the Pole's jaw. 'Serge, tell me – what's your favourite jazz number?' The Pole faced his audience and, hands outstretched in the manner of Al Jolson, announced clearly: ' "Back Home Again in Indiana", as played in ze hot style of ze Chicagoans.' 'So be it,' said Gimbel, and stamped his left foot four times.

In the ensuing race the original melody, a good one, was trampled to death and horrid mutants took its place. Every player in the room joined in . . . but that's jazz. I missed old 'Indiana', a decent march carved out on a midnight piano in a cloud-capped Tin Pan Alley cubicle back in the teen years of this century. I said as much to Regina, who eagerly agreed – and that's the kind of girl for me. When I'd run out of steam but the massed band was still taking solos, I suggested that we leave as this wasn't the night for my kind of music. But just as we were rising the hot jam race finished and I heard Rosy McHargue's avuncular voice asking over the speakers: 'Ian – would you oblige with my favourite ballad?'

Now 'Here I Am', a song of the middle 1920s, is a well-crafted number, very melodic and supported by time-tested chords. The situation described in the verse is really quite real: the singer has walked out on his girl but, after consideration, he decides to bury his foolish pride and so he walks back into her life singing, 'I said I'd never come back but HERE I AM, HERE I AM!' I get many requests for this number and have even used it to win back lost girl-friends. But tonight I felt the bandstand atmosphere might poison such a delicate flower.

I was right.

The jazzers, seeking heat, went to work at once: Franklyn hurled some Chinese cracker chords, Gimbel blew out flaming farts and the Pole sat snickering on his clarinet. Only Rosy stayed true to the tune, breathing a flickering life with his honest C melody sax.

I was feeling foolish, standing there emoting in my white tuxedo. I knew everybody was watching, especially Regina.

So I took action: 'For Christ's sake play the right fucking tune and the right fucking chords!'

I think it was the 'fucking' that did it. Gimbel unclamped his cornet, leaned across the enthroned Rosy and growled at me, 'If you don't like our style, then fuck off!'

Automatically I replied, 'How dare you talk to me like that!'

Then I felt sticky liquid running down my face. Gimbel had thrown his beer at me. I was staggered and at a loss as to my next move. A hush had descended on Sterling's.

After a few beats I straightened my jacket, collected my instruments and left the stage with as much dignity as I could muster. I was going to leave the premises and certainly I should have. But . . . a hum of happiness rose once more, and then the band struck up a peppy march. Something clicked inside me. I would NOT be forgotten so easily! Swivelling round I strode back to the bandstand where, fixing an eye on the puffing Gimbel, I levelled a finger at him and said, 'I will deal with you, mark my words!' No, I didn't. I used some four-letter words.

He leapt to his feet, dropped his cornet and seemed to be preparing to pounce on me. It was then that I delivered the prep-school punch. And that should have been that.

He reeled for a moment. He shook his head. Then on he came, down upon me with lancing eyes, leg-of-mutton arms piston-firing, and I soon knew his knuckles, his wedding ring, the piggy bristle on the back of his hand. And then his hands were on my throat and his knee in my groin. It took five men to pull him off me, so they say. They propped me up in the corner and I sat there like a ventriloquist's dummy. I waited, expecting to slide into the old bottomless pit, down and down silently until the sunshine-flooded lane and the cool grey house with many rooms all filled with strangers.

*

Yesterday had been a pleasant time. After my weekly radio show on Santa Monica station KCRW, I met Regina and we headed for the Farmer's Market, just off Ocean Avenue, not far from Sterling's. Once a week, farmers from all over California set up their stalls in the street to offer pure produce. Nothing frozen, nothing canned, nothing chemically treated. No hard-sell barrow salesmen. I wasn't expecting this. 'No expectations, no disappointments,' said Regina. She smiled and so I smiled. There were neat pyramids of multi-coloured apples. I liked the look of them and said so. 'And they like you too,' said the stall-keeper, in clean bib dungarees. His badge advertised 'The Tree People.' We moved along to the nut man, who was busily cracking macadamias. 'Try,' he said. 'Free.' He was a bear of a man and his beard reached his knees. The kernel burst in my mouth like an unexpected orgasm. 'There you go!' he shouted. By his side was the orange man with his cry of 'No wash! No wax! No spray!' The bee man thrust us a lively honeycomb for inspection. He said that beeswax can be used as a depilatory and also as shoe polish, or surf-board wax. And in candles! He paused. Then: 'Next week, folks, I shall not be here – for I go play with my bees back home in Ukiah.' Jim Jones, who had died with his congregation in Jonestown, once lived in Ukiah, didn't he? We were next amongst crinkled parsley, creeping charlie and unknown vegetables, tumors with stringy tails; then we were in a merry jostle of shoppers born in foreign countries and I saw two veiled women in black talking of Yorkshire to a dolled-up woman in golf slacks, and a gold-haired woman in a velvet jogging suit give money to the Bach-playing flute player standing out-side the book store. And meanwhile all around us were shining trucks unloading produce from places with heart-warming names like Hum-ming Bird Ranch and Morning Glory Lane.

After storing our paper bags in the Honda and feeding up the park-ing meter, we crossed Ocean Avenue to take a stroll along Palisades Park. It was such a lovely afternoon, crisp and sharp and not too sunny. I thought of scout games on the Sussex Downs. Near Santa Monica pier I was attracted by a long line of raffish people snaking up to a loaded trestle table. Regina said these were the homeless and the needy. I said we'd take a look.

They were peaceful and orderly, and though it certainly wasn't cold they were bundled up in overcoats and blankets and they all wore headgear – ski-caps, giant tea-cosy or 'bobble' caps, long-peaked macho cheese-cutter caps. An ad hoc group was singing rock songs of the late Sixties. I was thinking of Flanagan & Allen and the Arches, but the image failed. Different tramps. A young black with a Red Indian nose was skipping in and out of the queue to the beat of a cas-sette player attached to his belt. At the trestle table women were loading paper plates with such items as quiche, pizza, pasta, Danish pastries. There was much thanking and doffing of caps by the queuers. I spoke to the woman in charge, Mona of Mona's Travelling Soup Kitchen. The food, she said, is from local restaurants – such as the Ivy at the Shore – and has to be donated clandestinely due to the fastidiousness of L.A. health laws. Leftover food is considered spoiled, no matter how fresh, and must immediately be wrapped and sealed in plastic bags for removal to one of the local landfill sites used for the burial of garbage. Canyons have disappeared, and new mountains are being created by the garbage disposal authorities.

Mona was worried about where some of her regulars were going to sleep tonight: 'They just lost their tent city on Venice beach.' Venice is a couple of miles further down south and yesterday, as we'd read in the papers, there'd been a wicked coastal storm. No one was spared: up in Malibu sand and kelp, condoms and syringes had filled swimming-pools and jacuzzis, while down at Redondo beach in a chic seafront restaurant diners who had been applauding the bumper surf were rewarded by a tidal wave that crashed through the window and drenched lawyer and busboy alike. On Venice beach the tent city of the homeless, fast becoming an institution, was blown away. 'Canvas has been found as far as Beverly Hills,' said Mona. 'We're all in this together.' But mention of a tent city had tugged me back into the past, to the day they had sold Santa Monica. . . .

*

A hot oppressive July day, even at dawning. The sparse grass on the sprawling mesa turning to tough straw and already crackling under the many boots hurrying to the grand auction of choice lots. A new city to be created by hammer at the ocean front above the cliffs – not far from Horace's Stables, which was later to become Hendrick's Garage and finally Sterling's Steak House.

Down on the beach, where summer breezes were blowing, stood many tents of thick, greasy canvas. Some were homes, some were for refreshments, one was a dance hall. There had been a tent city here for several years, but now its days were numbered. Even the smoke seemed to puff with anticipation and expectation. The folks were itching for the auction to begin. In his own special tent auctioneer Fitch, dressed in best frock-coat and smoking a fine cheroot, swore again that he would not bang his gavel till ten of the morning: strict orders from Senator Jones and Colonel Baker, the land-owners. So relax, take a stroll – you might spy a real Don, the guy who originally owned this rancho – they say he rides these golden sands in a terrible foaming fury. Don't worry – we'll blow the starting whistle loud and clear.

The customers have come – and are still coming – by steamer, stagecoach, buggy, on foot. The old rancho crust waits for one and all, longing to be broken into and sliced up for dwelling and workshop. The folks on the mesa, sweltering under layers of city clothes, pass a derelict sheep-herder's cabin and then the white picket fence of old man Wilkinson's farm. His corn, they say, is Brobdingnagian; his wife has cooling, fresh-squeezed orange juice on sale. Don't go near the orange groves – armed guards are on the prowl. Wait by the railroad crossing, for that lonesome moan is approaching. The train, the real drawer, is bringing in the bacon.

'Grand Excursion & Auction', *says the poster. 'Every lot comes with a cement floor.* Build the Dream. *The special train leaves at 9 a.m. on the dot. Seats for all and lunch is free. The sale will conclude after lunch when all hands may repair to the beach and roll in the sand, take a bath, hug their best girl and have a general good time'.*

Senator Jones and Colonel Baker were determined that Santa Monica, founded and registered in 1875, would not be just a town on paper but would develop into a thriving civilization of good people pursuing good living. Senator Jones had expressed at meeting after meeting: 'This is a great enterprise. We are turning Santa Monica Bay to the uses which nature intended but hadn't the time or the money to realize!'

And so, after that momentous summer's day of lot selling, the tent city gave way to beautiful homes, hotels, businesses. Even Senator Jones was shocked at how fast his dream was growing. Soon there were lots of people he didn't know. He gradually spent more time at home. Miramar, off Ocean Avenue, was a very fine solid house with an orchard, a rose arbour and a tennis court. In the library were many treasures of English literature – for the Senator, though raised in Ohio, had been born in England and was increasingly concerned with his background. He enjoyed talking about English culture with his friend and partner Colonel Baker. But the Colonel's lady, Arcadia, an imperious tower who had known wagon-train life, nurtured an older lifestyle. 'Not for nothing did I give myself this name,' she wrote in a realting proposal to her husband and his partner. She went on: 'I see mountains and water and mist. I see, within, a sequestered land of pastoral simplicity where live shepherds and hunters and the great god Pan. Zeus was born here, but there also winds the dreadful turgid sludgy river Styx.'

The year 1887 saw the opening of the magnificent wooden Arcadia Hotel, named for the Colonel's lady. The dining room, fully ventilated, could seat 200 guests; ladies had their own billiard room; there were hot-water baths and upstairs verandahs with shady nooks. Arcadian history, though idyllic, is dull. Nothing much happened, nothing much changed. Happiness hung in the air, torpid. But at the Arcadia in Santa Monica, just as in all of America, pretty soon there was plenty of activity, lots of change. In a few years we see stubby huts with signs advertising 5-cent lager and fried-fish suppers; these huts are attached to the front and sides of the Arcadia, and she herself has grown bulbous with new rooms and fancy cupolas, while around her on the beach gaggles of ordinary people relax with their children. A boy in a slouch cap relieves himself on a small statue of Pan. Mrs Baker is long gone. So is the Colonel. But the Senator lives on, annoyed and bewildered, upset by God's unnatural plan.

In his twilight years the Senator used to negotiate his weary way – avoiding the dogs' messes – to his favourite seat on Ocean Front and watch the sun slip down. 'It disappears at the end all of a sudden, rather rudely,' he was known to observe. Today there is a circular stone bench marking the spot where the old wooden one sat.

*

'Arcadians On Drug Charges' said the headline in the Metro section of the *Los Angeles Times*. Regina had led me from Ocean Front back to Wilshire Boulevard and into an establishment she's quite fond of: Ye Shoppe – A British Center. She was going to have tea just as soon as she caught the hostess's eye. I was killing time with the paper, but the Arcadian story looked intriguing. However, it turned out to concern a couple from the city of Arcadia – a city not far from my Altadena home, up near the foothills of the San Gabriel mountains, thirty miles or so from Santa Monica. The Arcadian couple had been peddling cocaine.

A black hostess with a cockney accent approached us and asked whether she could be of assistance. I stuffed the Metro section back into the body of the *L.A. Times* and picked up *Brit News*, a free weekly. The hostess, a cheerful sort, seated us in the tea-room of the inner shop. We sat on fan-spoked farmhouse chairs under Tudor beams in a corral fenced with a trellis of lace curtains. Just beyond, in the main shop, I could see the shelves of imported goods for which Ye Shoppe is famous: bone-china cups stamped with royal tartans, Toby jugs, Bachelor's processed peas. Regina took her tea with lemon, not very English I said. She did promise to try a sausage roll, and after attracting the waitress soon got into detailed conversation with her.

Meanwhile I examined the *Brit News*. There was plenty of advice on immigration procedures, with lawyers offering their services at attractive prices. Irving Berg, with offices in Tarzana, says that Brits will need a labour certificate before applying for their Resident Alien status. 'Remember – the Department of Labor will present as many obstacles as it can in preventing you from receiving your certificate.' Lawyer Fleischmann, of Studio City, lists the many qualifications necessary for a work permit and as for the pinnacle visa, an H.1, that will only be granted to 'a person outstanding in his or her field, with a degree of skill and recognition substantially above the norm'.

Back in the middle 1960s I had been first granted an H.1 when, as a British Invader (basing myself in Trinity College, Dublin), I had burst into the American Top Ten with a novelty record, an orgasmic panting song called 'You Turn Me On'. In the 1970s, quite faded, I found myself struggling to prove that my skills and national recognition were substantially above the norm: I found myself standing in a long line of babel inside the featureless, no-fooling-about, Immigration building in downtown L.A. *Downtown* – where people reported to real work – work they hated – at regular, never-changing hours, a million miles from Hollywood, scene of my brief success. Fighting for my pop life, I poured 45s, EPs, LPs, press clipping books, fan mail and glossy 8 × 10 photos on to the pristine desks of immigration officials. Startled, they passed me on and up. The day wore on. A new appointment was scheduled for the following week. A month later I was still lugging my suitcase of skills and recognition around Immigration. At night I dreamed of a lanky grey-suited crewcut official finishing my mother's macaroni cheese politely and then getting up to lean on her fireplace and coolly inform me that as a candidate for an H.1 I was negative. 'Who are you? Exactly who are you?' he pronounced with heavy rhetoric.

At last, after months of battle, I was admitted into the sky-high office of a very important immigration official – Mrs Hubbard, a straight-backed woman with frozen hair and an unwavering eye, well-known to British celebrities. From her walls there smiled down upon me Michael York, Michael Caine, Roger Moore, Rod Stewart and many more. All thanked her profusely. 'I have processed them all,' she said, showing me her palms like a magician at the start of his act. Above her Sean Connery eyed me sternly. 'What can we do for *you*?' she asked. After a jerky recitation of my many accomplishments, I handed her a glossy 8 × 10. 'As I say,' she continued, as if I had never spoken, 'I have processed them all – but I have never heard of you.' With that she stuffed my glossy into her desk drawer, got up and showed me the door.

On the advice of a fellow British Invader, I hired a clever and expensive immigration lawyer. Over the next couple of years he managed to persuade the authorities that as a ukulele player and novelty vocalist I was renowned in my chosen field and, more importantly, absolutely no competition to American citizens (Tiny Tim had taken early retirement). Eventually I received the coveted Green Card: a laminated *blue* card identifying me as a Resident Alien with a long number.

*

Regina had left me to my musings. She was somewhere – wandering around the shop, I expect. I summoned the waitress from her radio and ordered a hot meat pie. The pie was a gambit – I loathe them: I really wanted to know whether Ye Shoppe was still owned and managed by Derek Treadle-Smythe. 'No way! He retired to Encino years ago – after he got that M.B.E.' The M.B.E? 'You know – for services to British industry abroad.'

'You put a bit here and a bit there and you grow. Just like any tea-shop grows.' I remember Treadle-Smythe giving me that answer when I asked him the secret of his success, back in the middle Seventies, while I was researching an article on the British in L.A. for *The Listener*. As I recall, the tea-shop builder was a friendly, if blunt, Old Croydonian with a fondness for blue blazers and bright gold buttons. He was, I learned, a leader of the burgeoning new British Colony, a more dynamic group than the cricketing Britishers of old.

My guide into this rather special world was Barry, at present working as manager of a fried chicken franchise. 'But L.A. is my oyster,' he winked, handing me a complimentary bag of fried onion rings. Originally he'd hailed from Ealing, but what with rationing, call-up and the weather he eventually decided to chuck it in. 'At that time the toffee-nosed lot were in charge – no offence, chum – and there weren't any opportunities for guys with git-go like me. So I upped and came, presto. They doled us out Green Cards on the plane, can you believe it!' On a stiflingly hot Sunday he took me on a tour of the British Colony in his open M.G. Down Wilshire Boulevard we whizz-banged, with Barry whistling and grinning because, as he said, there were precious few red lights. 'They're synchronized in favour of the motorist – just one of the many advantages of L.A. life.'

Several motorists gave us the eye. Barry was very proud of the M.G. and the genuine G.B. plates front and back. 'It's a link, isn't it?' I understood – you had to display the links out here, what with the special air and the beating sun and all those palm trees, and mountains behind. 'I'll grant you, though,' he shouted, 'there's also a lot of Yanks in Jags, particularly your Beverly Hills Hebrews.' He switched on the radio by way of an antidote. We were able to catch the end of 'Calling All Cards', the all-British show broadcast weekly and featuring radio comics and the latest news: 'We're told Oxford Street is full of Christmas shoppers – but who'd want that rain?!' said a breezy voice. Barry explained that this was 'air personality' Derek Treadle-Smythe. 'Stand by for the best of Hancock and all the music from Princess Anne's wedding!' Barry nudged me and told me to wait for the plug. Then: 'Purchase these recordings and all your favourite British products at Ye Shoppe – and don't forget to mention Derek!'

I was scribbling away, absorbed in my pad, when Barry shouted, 'Wakey, wakey! What say we drop in on Derek when he signs off?' This sort of impetuousness would have been impossible back home; we'd never have got past those burly ex-Servicemen in peaked caps who guard the doors of Broadcasting House. But in L.A. to visit a communicaster in his studio was a simple matter.

We pulled up on Wilshire at a yellow line, and had trouble negotiating our way through the Sunday sidewalk crowd of elderly church-goers and strutting jolly-boys. Barry took umbrage at a pair of the latter when they refused to move out of his way. After they'd passed he said, 'They're taking their poodles to brunch, you know.'

The radio station was merely a couple of offices on the third floor of a high-rise building mostly occupied by legal firms. We squeezed into a tiny booth where Treadle-Smythe, in blue blazer with gold technical college badge, was slaving and sweating: 'It's Perspiring Sunday,' he said into the mike. 'but now, here he is – the lah-dee-dah gent to take us back to days of yore and mad dogs and Englishmen, the most intriguing Noël Coward!' As I was writing down 'in*tray*-ging' the host swivelled round in his stool and addressed me: 'Hello, sport – I'm Egham '47, what's yours?' I tried telling him about Bryanston in '59, but then he was called back to the mike for his sign-off. 'Sorry, Sir Noël, but we're out of time. Don't forget, you lucky people, that the Thistle Club have a knees-up, in kilts, on Monday, and on Friday there's Major Sewell's lecture on "The Desert War From The Service Corps Angle". So until next week, this is D. Treadle-Smythe telling you that life may be a serious proposition, but deep in our hearts we're all just plain cards!'

Off the air Derek seemed quite deflated. 'You know, it's a shame we can't attract current U.K. entertainers for our show. I mean, does Elton John even know of our existence? And do we care? But seriously – it would be a dead chuff to get, say, Dud and Pete on the prog.' He pulled on a trilby and adjusted it to a rakish angle. 'What's it like back in the old country? Bad as they say? As if I care! Ha!' He'd pulled himself together. 'Well, musn't keep you. I hear Barry's taking you to the brunch-and-jive down at the U.K. Forces Club, and we can't keep the ladies waiting!'

We reached the M.G. to find a Mexican meter maid taking down particulars. Barry became stage cockney: 'Blimey, ducky, we're visitors enjoying your lovely city.' But she refused to succumb. En route Barry perked up after we'd collected a couple of Australian girls from their hotel. Plain-faced but high-spirited, they were keen to get eating and dancing. Barry told them about his parking ticket and they chided him in song: 'Smile, darn ya, smile! Don't bring your umbrella gloom here!' Barry replied: 'Now girls, you must drop that attitude once we're inside the club, because the consul's showing up and we don't want an international incident. He's coming straight from a working breakfast with Rod Stewart.'

By the time we reached Hollywood we were a boisterous group, fired up by jokes from the girls. We blazed a trail down a sidewalk lush with male hustlers and beefy blacks in bush outfits and, at the entrance to the U.K. Forces Club, were rewarded by the sound of bagpipes skirling up from within. 'Après moi le deluge,' said Barry as we descended. We had arrived just in time for the festivities. An elderly gent with a deep tan and a kilt and sporran barked: 'Officers and Ladies, I am Major Chipper Noakes and brunch is up!' I was intrigued by the beach-blond bagpipers, and told Barry I intended to interview one. But he held me by the jacket edge and explained that the pipers were all local lads and that some of them were with the Major. 'And we don't want complications, do we?'

After starters and the loyal toast they got down to the dancing, even as bangers-and-mash was being served. Barry pointed out that this dancing was real English-style strict tempo as opposed to loose American. I said I failed to see the difference. 'But there *is* a *very* real one,' chimed in a woman with a North Country accent and a beehive hair-do. She was introduced to me as the Major's lady. I was in the middle of asking her to expand on dance tempo differences when she suddenly popped a bridge roll into her mouth and pointed to her jaw, which had almost immediately started to revolve.

Moving away as diplomatically as I could to a quiet, shadowy corner, I spied a sofa and on it an old and creased man in a white linen suit and what appeared to be plimsolls. I seated myself at the other end. Then I saw he was wearing a Trinity College Dublin tie. I was wearing mine. Turning slowly towards me, he said, 'Awful nonsense, isn't it? I only come for the steak and kidney pudding, and that's not on today.' His voice was measured and stately; his accent was Anglo-Irish. 'The whole thing is no more than a charade,' he went on quietly. 'It is as if a great battleship, deserted of her officers, is foundering in tumultuous seas and the lower decks have taken over, aping their superiors in dress only. A charade. . . . And now let me sleep. . . .'

Regina shook me. 'I have to leave now, or I'll be late for shakabuku.' Whaaat? 'You know very well. We've been dating for two years now.' What? 'An N.S.A. meeting. . . . Oh well, if you insist – is this for your diary?: Nichiren Shoshu Soka of America.' I see. 'See you tomorrow night at Sterling's.'

*

After my British Colony article was published in *The Listener* a BBC film producer friend of mine, Geoffrey Haydon, was given the green light to make a documentary on the subject, with me as the guide, for 'Omnibus', the culture series. 'L.A. – My Home Town' was shown on BBC 1 early in 1977, relieving a series on Goya. Scenes of the British Consul riding in the Disneyland parade followed scenes of girls with erect nipples and men with long dongs. I was skewered in the papers, and the BBC was sprayed with complaints.

News of the fuss soon reached the L.A. colony and I got a letter from Derek Treadle-Smythe, as leader, stating that I was from now on *persona non grata* and had better lay low. But Los Angeles – that Centrifugal City, that Fragmented Metropolis, that burg where people say hello until they get to know you – is as whopping as the Milky Way and ever-expanding too. It's so easy to disappear when things get too heated. All I had to do was avoid tea-shops, pubs and expatriate clubs. But I wasn't about to exile myself from Santa Monica, my home at the time. The life at the beach had been most interesting – a jaunt, a holiday, an adventure. . . .

A few years before this G.B. Colony project I had come to make a sort of encampment down in Santa Monica. It was all due to the gas crunch of 1973. This acute petrol shortage caused queues and as Angelenos were not acculterated to such disturbances there were punch-ups and one or two murders. At the time I was not a resident alien but I *was* on one of my extended forays from the family home on Putney Heath to the world of Hollywood show-biz. I had been putting up in the San Fernando Valley at the Studio City apartment of my old friend 'Jumping' George Sherlock. In 1965, as head of West Coast Promotion for Tower Records, he had seen the hit potential of my 'You Turn Me On', persuaded the company to release the disc and taken it upon himself to groom me as a teen idol. He pulled up my collar, mussed up my hair, picked girls for me and presented me with personal deodorants. ('You British!') He informed the show-biz trade papers that I was 'The Next Peter Sellers'. But the guardians of the gates of Hollywood were indifferent. However, the Rolling Stones immortalized him on the flip side of 'Satisfaction', ('The Under-Assistant West Coast Promotion Man') and whenever I arrived in L.A. he always provided me with floor space. 'We'll show the world one day, just you see.' He had such touching faith.

Anyway, here I was on yet another trip to stardom and staying on a couch in George's apartment. One afternoon, cruising about on some errand, at the height of this '73 gas crunch, and the air thick with tension, I found myself with an empty tank in Santa Monica, a city I did not yet know. I had conked out on a broad, palmed boulevard and when I got out to stretch and curse, I suddenly went all ardent. Abandoning the car – it was only a rental – I went adventuring. It was thrilling enough just to be on foot. I walked into Santa Monica proper and bought a bicycle – a five-speed Raleigh with matching saddlebags – and soon I was peddling away, heart full of chimera, along the ocean prom and then down along the special concrete bike path that waved through the beach sand.

At sunset I started looking around for somewhere to rest. It was wonderful, this feeling of being a wanderer, a vagabond. As luck would have it there loomed up slowly to the left of the bike path, almost on the sand, a massive stone building with strong square shoulders and a pointed coolee hat, towering and romantic, rapidly getting swallowed by the gathering fog. All around the high, azure-painted skirting, and on the concrete strip separating building from beach, bohemian types were circling, many cloaked in capes or blankets, as if at some Old California rancho meeting between Don and Indian. On the mauve front wall, in bold yellow letters, was painted: 'SEACASTLE'. I liked the idea.

The front door, of sliding glass, was locked. Adhesively taped to the pane was a visiting card telling me, in classic italic, that P. McDonelty, Esq, had an address in Greek St, Soho, W.1. and, in ballpoint pen, that he was Seacastle's manager and lived in Number 1. To the left of the front door was a speaker phone and I used this to announce myself and my intention. A Midlands accent, shabby genteel, agreed to buzz me in. But just as I was sliding the glass door a caped shape materialized out of the dusk and tried to squeeze past me and into Seacastle. The next moment there raced slopingly into the inner lobby a lofty man with long, pony-tailed white hair who rushed up to the door and shooed away the caped invader. The latter, after much cursing and spitting, slunk off the premises.

The lofty man pulled me inside, leaned back against the door and by wiggling his thin shoulders and bony bottom, slid it closed. Wiping his brow theatrically with a red handkerchief, he said in a fairly educated voice, 'Phew! It's all go in these parts, isn't it?'

He was a chatty sort and seemed a gentle soul. As he led me up the grand staircase of this desiccated and peeling palace I learned that he was Philip McDonelty, English, and that he was a writer. 'As yet unpublished. But isn't this an excellent ambience for an artist? There are many of us living – and partly living, as the poet said – at Seacastle.' He stopped on a landing, coughed up some phlegm, apologized, put two fingers to his lips and whispered loudly, 'Just listen to those waves, eh!'

By the sixth floor I was quite worn out, but here he showed me a small square room with a bathroom and an ocean view. He peered out of the window musingly and I noticed that his long white hair was ponytailed by an elastic band. The sound of the waves I found mutinous, but I didn't tell McDonelty because I was coming to rather like him. And the room, though bare, smelled of fresh paint and disinfectant, and was cold and spotlessly clean. Reminded of school dormitories at the beginning of the term, I felt a surge of blood whoosh through me from top to toe. I agreed to take on this Seacastle room.

Philip invited me down to tea in his apartment. He lived, among books and surfboards, with a bounding floppy dog as big as a pony. During tea a bare-chested teenage boy burst in and started riding around us on a skateboard, pursued by the happy dog. He seemed very much at home, and after a while disappeared into a bedroom. McDonelty continued telling me the history of Seacastle, how in the Twenties it had been the elegant, exclusive Breakers Club, and how in the Fifties gangster interests had turned the place into a shady hotel. 'Times do change, don't they?' he said. When I mentioned that I was in show business – sort of – he exclaimed, 'I know the name,' and straight away became excited, describing in detail a musical he was writing, based on *The Pilgrim's Progress*. I was telling him that I'd never read the book when he announced, 'I have Andy Stewart in mind for the lead.' But he suddenly grew despondent and lay down on the shag carpet. 'My work, I'm afraid, is Christian-angled – but there it is,' and he shook his head violently, making the ponytail swing to and fro.

I excused myself and went to an A.M./P.M. Market to call up George Sherlock. He said 'No problem' and drove over that evening from Studio City in his brand-new Audi, bringing with him his lovely new Kansas bride. Both agreed that the room showed potential and both volunteered to help me decorate and furnish, right away. I couldn't have agreed more, because it was a peculiar, if convenient, arrangement we had at the Studio City apartment, Laurelwood. There I shared their bathroom and slept on a couch only a few feet from their bridal suite. Walls at Laurelwood were wafer-thin (several nights in a row I had been woken by squeaking and moaning from the room above me, where lived a randy airline hostess; I had even made a tape-recording of these stop-go-stop-go sex sessions); yet George and his bride were quiet as church mice. We were a peaceful trio, sharing healthful dinners.

But Dame Fortune had plans for my immediate disencampment. As my new digs were still bare I returned with the couple to Laurel-wood, where George, although strong on Seacastle as a weekend home, urged me to consider carefully before quitting the safety of the San Fernando Valley. But at 3 a.m., when all was quiet, Mrs George received a phone call. The voice introduced itself as 'Ian Whitcomb' and then said: 'I'm horny as hell – come ball me in the hall!' George came to me on my couch in his underwear to tell me the news. 'It's weird,' he added.

So we were all agreed about the move. That weekend George wangled some cans of gas and we drove to a Sears superstore to see about furnishings. He tried to persuade me into buying a fancy bar stool in rather overwrought iron with a stem of ornate scrolls. To conciliate him I agreed to take two gold cushions with jet-black tassles. For myself, unaided, I bought a folding aluminium beach chair with a seat of green plastic strips, and a bookshelf stand of metal printed with an oak grain pattern. This had come from Taiwan in pieces and the instructions were in pidgin English. Thus George had his day mapped out.

Back at the Seacastle there was much traffic around the front door and in the lobby. People were coming and going like railway customers and, apart from suitcases, I saw tea-chests, upholstered sofas, love-seats, motor-bikes. On the fine staircase were many loiterers. Were they residents? A girl in flared jeans with no pockets brushed past us giggling at some private joke. A piratical man glared at us and George wished him a happy day. Philip popped his head out of his apartment and shouted up, 'I know you used to be a personality – but I must confess I can't place you, sorry!' George offered to educate him later. 'Certainly – and he must sing us his song with joy to the world!'

Up in my room we knuckled down to producing an instant home.

George pulled out his Black & Decker power tool and started assembling the bookshelf structure; I tossed the gold cushions about until I liked the pattern, and also set up the beach chair. While in the bathroom I found a quarter-full bottle of body-lice killer, a greenish liquid. I showed it to George who cried 'Crabs and lobsters!' and hurled it out of the window. I looked out and saw the exploding bottle scatter a knot of Seacastle lurkers.

With no more home-making to do, I left George to his work and wandered my floor. A smocked girl skipped by me singing the blues, carrying a sack of groceries up to her chin, a carrot behind her ear. She pursed a smile. After she'd gone I peeped through an open door from which spacey cool jazz was exuding. In the middle of a bare floor was a big black stereo system and sitting on top of the high pile was a frighteningly thin black man staring out of the window and nodding his head. But his nods were to a different beat from the jazz below him; his nods were frantic jerks. There was no furniture in his room, not even a mattress; only the stereo system – and an oblong brown box on which was written: 'KEEP OUT! *MY ART*'.

George finished my bookcase by early evening, just as the fog was rolling in. 'Man, I'm bushed,' he said. As I let him out of the front door a grubby man in rags tried to ease in. I told him 'No' unless he was a resident. 'Gimme a break, please,' he said. George took over, talking to him in his own patois. When the man had slunk away and we were walking to George's Audi he said, 'If you ask me, there's a high percentage of flakes round here.'

I returned to find the flake back at the front door. As I operated my key I apologized as best I could. He said softly, 'I understand, believe me I do.'

When I had shut my door, turned the lock and slipped in the security chain, I realized that for the first time in ages I was alone. I longed for the bustle, the violence, of dormitories. Before long I was feeling lonely. The horrible silence was soon filled by a distant pounding – rock and soul, no doubt – from within the building but, much worse, coming from the beach below, was a dreary and silly smashing and splattering as the Pacific up-chucked at me with its chant of oblivion for all and sundry.

So, making myself comfortable in the beach chair, I pulled out a 1940s *Film Fun Annual*. In the last picture panel Frank Randle, famous stage and film comedian, is sitting pretty at a swell feast: a mountain of mashed potatoes studded with red bangers, a bucket of bubbly leaning in – his reward for beating some seaside spivs. What price the Pacific when you could look at the *Film Fun* sea with its enormous red-rubber-ball sun radiating smiles over still and friendly waters, and in these exceptionally cool waters are curly girls with large water-wings near bobbing men in cheeky hats who are ready to pull out the water-wing stoppers – yes, and to the left are the sweet chalk cliffs of old, and to the right a bouncing pier with onion domes; and on the sands are striped tents and shady groynes and stop-me-and-buy-one ice-cream carts, and there should be bathing machines, bathing machines where madam must be careful lest the pony gets excited and, running amok, drags you over the sand so that you'll go home and give your old man the gravel when you're both abed and bobbing up and down like this, like this!

*

To solve the problem of loneliness, coupled with a touch of boredom, I tried taking runs along the seashore from Santa Monica, past Ocean Park, and finally to Venice. Running was definitely therapeutic, and there were many runners to keep me company. They called themselves 'joggers' and they wore special jogging costumes of differing designs, some in velvet and velour.

At Ocean Park I passed a run-down, dilapidating amusement park which appeared to me like a fun-fair after a Nazi bombing raid. I liked the Swiss Chalet Café with its ice-cream-cone windows and gingerbread roof, all boarded up. I thought of Brighton Pier in the early Fifties on a rainy Sunday, with the chocolate-bar slot-machines empty and the pig-iron rusty and the Al Jolson marionette – 'the blubbering masquerader' – broken down. These things caused dreams and the learning of the old songs for themselves.

I ran along the boardwalk of Venice and was wondering 'Why Venice?' until I rounded a corner and found myself in a square called St Mark's, where there were porticos and columns and balustrades and Renaissance carvings. There were also criss-crossing crowds of blacks and Mexicans and hippies and push-bikes and motor-bikes. Further down the boardwalk were trestle tables where old men were sunk in chess games; in the mouth of the plain Cadillac Hotel old folk spoke Yiddish and cursed the sun; seaside entertainment included a 'friend' of Lenny Bruce's, a well-dressed man playing the classics with spoons on glasses of water, several bongo-drum bands, two young Negroes discussing philosophy, and a gnarled varmint with a Basset hound taunting a wiry negress with a monkey on her back.

After Venice the path wound out on to the beach and here, I

noticed, the sand was like dirt. I tripped up on a wine jug, but quickly pulled myself together. Nearby was a bronzed male in a skimpy bikini sunning himself with a silver foil reflector. He seemed tightly content. Shifting a thigh, he said melodically, 'Welcome to the Venice of the West, where the debris meets the sea.' There had been nothing like this hospitality in England. Around him were other bronzers in bikinis, while threading his way through the group was an older man wearing battle fatigues and a baseball cap, vacuuming the dirt with a metal detector. 'Don't be so puzzled,' said the bronzer. 'Sit down and join us.' I did – his voice was so pleasant. 'The guy's a sand surgeon and he's searching for bounty. Cold water contracts the body; that's how the surfer boys lose their gold rings, and that's when the sand surgeons suck 'em up.' In the distance, across a sea wall, I saw a forest of masts and clumps of shining towers. 'That's ritzy water – the flush boating marina for the upwardly mobile,' he said. 'And when the cataclysm comes and Venice meets the Marina – BAM!' and he punched the sand with passion. 'Unless the earthquake gets there first – WHUUUMP!' I thought I'd made a friend, but you never know.

Late in the afternoon I actually located a canal. It had smelly, dark water but a picturesque bridge and I lingered awhile to drink in a view which was romantic when I framed it with my hands. On the other side of the canal was a charming doll's-house Tudor cottage, thatched and with ivy climbing up the walls. Geese and ducks were waddling around, chattering happily about this and that. I got a good feeling of the past. At sundown I plodded home to my Seacastle room and wrote a novelty song, 'Wurzel Fudge in London'. Then I ate a health supper of crunchy granola and raisins flooded with Mocha Mix, a non-dairy creamer. I felt very improved.

Eating well, running on the beach, writing songs and polishing my act. But not enough to keep out the panic that arrived at weekends when my date book was empty. Many a time I'd decide to get married – but where were the subjects? Calls were made on the pay-phone in the hall of Seacastle. Friends from inner Los Angeles were persuaded to come out and have dinner and see my new situation. McDonelty would take care of the front door.

*

'Altogether a most interesting ensemble,' said Dr Ronald Bund in the measured tones of a classical music radio host. He had been gracious about my room, but then he was invariably gracious. Elegant and cool in his white tropical suit, he sat at attention in my beach chair as I

32

fussed about him with sherry and nuts. His pressed brown hair, brutally short at the sides, and his Hitler moustache and green-tinted glasses were in marked contrast to the normal residents and visitors one found around Seacastle.

I had been introduced to Dr Ronald Bund by a long-time friend (dating back to my days as a British Invader), Simon Witham. An Old Marlburian who had fled England to become a Malibu surfer and then a rock publicist, he had survived the Sixties so skilfully that he was currently head of the Country and Western division of R.C.A. Victor, with a special interest in the Japanese market. Simon had been the very first invited guest at my new home, but he had never arrived – having been put off at the entrance to Seacastle by what he described as 'a floating scum of grunge and fungus folk'. There's nothing like the ire of an ex-hippie. He was speaking to me by phone from the confines of his air fortress in West Hollywood, a 1920s Beaux Arts apartment building where, every weekend, he'd play card cricket with ideal international teams including many long-dead players. 'Do not ever again subject me to such people – I am no longer in rock. It's bad enough here in West Hollywood – in a swill of back-passage boys, most of whom seem to make their livings by painting roses on bath-tubs.'

Witham knew Dr Ronald through classical music. The doctor, a writer of technical manuals for oil companies, lectured on Wagner and his Ring Cycle as a hobby. Witham's friendship was based on that – and that alone. 'I never prise open my friends like you do,' said Witham to me. Minutes after first meeting Dr Ronald he and I were discussing all manner of things. He seemed particularly interested in the world of rock. 'It gives me an entrée into present-day youth,' he told me, long after Witham had left us and returned to his card cricket. We went on to an all-night coffee shop in Hollywood where he told me he was a practising pederast with a particular interest in teenage Marines.

On the evening of his visit to my new home he brought with him an example of his specialty, a hunky lad with a football head, a washboard stomach and a form-fitting T-shirt which more than adumbrated his sculpted pectorals. Though Dr Ronald spoke soft and level to me, he would bark out loudly to the Marine: 'Confirm our reservations at Scott's at the double!' 'Marshall, the transportation!', etc. Then, turning gracefully in the beach chair, he would return to his chosen topic (generally prearranged), which tonight was 'The Development of the Arcadian Ideal and the Hellenic Body in the beach cities of Southern California'.

Dr Ronald (he had bought his rank from a mail order diploma mill, but was well-versed in matters cultural) explained to me that a combination of Anglo-Saxon genes and California sun, sea and air had produced the blond beauties one might see in the beach cities. But, he warned, the darker uncivilized races are presently penting up these boys against the Pacific Ocean. 'In a simile which you will immediately grasp, these boys are Tommies at Dunkirk with their backs to the Channel.' I didn't pursue the simile because this would mean discussing Japan, and I was anxious to get to dinner as my stomach was rumbling and the Marine was swivelling his eyes around my room with an inventory gleam.

At Scott's Seafood, a nice local restaurant well protected by wrought-iron grilles, Dr Ronald continued his theme through the Caesar salad and into the abalone (another endangered species), pointing out the various muscles being flexed by his hungry companion. The waiter – who had earlier told Dr Ronald that he was really a modern jazz dancer – interrupted us to ask whether we'd care for a liqueur. I asked what could be offered in the way of puddings. 'Any desserts, Randy?' said Dr Ronald, interpreting. 'Oh, no way!' replied the waiter, with a shiver-quiver from head to toe. 'Summer's coming!' 'Ah, bikini time,' said Dr Ron, nodding wisely. While I was settling the bill with my Access card I noticed Dr Ronald slipping his calling card to Randy. I had seen these cards before: 'Ronald Bund & Associates – Casting Directors for Motion Pictures, Commercials, Print Ads. Call Any Time of Day or Night'.

We returned to Seacastle around midnight and found Philip McDonelty pacing about outside the front door. Both he and his floppy dog were looking very forlorn. Dr Ronald suggested we all repair somewhere amusing for a nightcap, and McDonelty led us to a bar next door called Joe's Landing, nothing to speak of outside but full of coats of arms and Spanish spears inside. The dog seemed quite at home, bellying up to the bar on hind legs. 'Not funny,' said McDonelty rather too shrilly. Dr Ronald bought us all brandies and then, in his special way, got the poor Englishman to open up. 'I've had two successful suicides and one murder in the last month. This isn't what I came here for. My playwriting is affected.' 'That is to be expected,' chirped Dr Ronald, quoting some clever poet. I expressed surprise at my ignorance of so much death around me. 'You're an artist,' said Dr Ronald soothingly. Then he clapped his hands and ordered the Marine to lighten things up by demonstrating some of the latest military strangleholds. The barman, a Vietnam veteran, leapt over the bar to assist the Marine. The dog barked merrily and his master smiled.

*

I needed cuddlesome company, so I consulted my black book and eventually got through to a girl who had been president of the Torrance chapter of my fan club back in 1965. Rita Garcia, a plump Mexican-American, was now the legal age and once in a while she turned up at my shows and afterwards we'd go off together. Tonight she invited me over to her apartment in Hollywood. Come and see my seaside place, I countered.

(The only time I'd been in her apartment, a couple of years ago, we'd had the complication of the snakes. The evening had begun O.K.: I sat on her couch and she stood in front telling me about her new job, her belly-dancing, and how the steps dated back thousands of years to religious ceremonies of the African Empire, and she demonstrated a few of these steps, getting closer and closer until her belly touched my nose and knocked from my lap the scrapbook she'd kept, so carefully, of my rock period.

Next we were on her water-bed, beside a table crowded with massage oils and unguents. She promised to give me the massage of my life, but first I must see her snakes. They were soon out of their black box and thoroughly enjoying being handled by her. They showed their affection by twining around her lovely squidgy naked body. She bounced up and down on the water-bed and then she had the slimy beasts embrace me, and I had to say that enough was enough.

However, next Valentine's Day she sent me a heart-shaped carrot cake with a note offering me a free back massage at my own convenience. So I kept her phone number.)

'Come on, please,' I insisted, promising her dinner at the restaurant of her choice. Later, up in my Seacastle room to the crashing of waves, she came through with an excellent back massage and so I turned over. I congratulated her on the fullness of her bosom and she returned the compliment by praising my thighs and balls. We had greedy, athletic sex. But next morning she started prattling on about E.S.P. and conversations with the dead, so I excused myself and went out to buy coffee and Mocha Mix. When I returned she was sitting on the grey carpet with my journal on her lap, weeping and sobbing. She lifted the journal with a finger and thumb and said sadly, 'You hate me. Why? What have I done?' I was very angry and told her she was

35

violating private property and it was her own fault. She was being a Pandora, I said. But I felt pretty bad myself.

On the first page of this W.H. Smith 1973 journal, I'd written some New Year's resolutions: 'To pay more attention to other people. To speak slower and marshal my thoughts and stop stammering. To pin the world down by writing, writing, writing. To perfect a comic song delivery style.'

In October I got a chance to concentrate on the last resolution. Right here, in Santa Monica. Two Americans – lovers of England to the extent of wearing Scotch tweeds even in summer, and buying up London pubs and suburban maisonettes and shipping them across to L.A. – were, I learned, opening an authentic British music hall on Santa Monica Boulevard and naming it The Mayfair. The two Anglophiles knew me by reputation and when I applied for a spot on the bill they agreed, provided I performed no rock and roll. The idea!

We opened on a suitably foggy night. Bagpipers skirled and mime artists jerked about under the flashing marquee. A child star of the Forties was our V.I.P. guest. Our star, Beatrice Kay, an American cabaret singer of the same period, wanted to open her act with 'Pistol-Packin' Mama' because her fans expected it. But, after much persuasion by the Anglophile owners, she agreed to substitute 'Maybe It's Because I'm a Londoner' so long as she could enter from the back stalls twirling her signature parasol. I sang 'I'm Shy, Mary Ellen, I'm Shy' and the number written in my Seacastle room, 'Wurzel Fudge in London'. I also told a long joke about proctology and the musical director, a jaded veteran of Big Bands, hissed up from the pit, 'Kid, you need a soap-box.' The applause was generous, though.

But the reviews called me a '*double entendre* act, dragging Music Hall by the hair into the 1970s' and 'a singer of uninspired ballads who fails to amuse'. Still, the Mayfair was paid work and only a short walk from the Seacastle. Also, I got to perform with a host of real British acts who somehow turned up on our bills: Jimmy Edwards, Jessie Matthews and various people from the pages of *Film Fun* and *Radio Fun*. It was a dream come true. One night Frankie Howerd was in the audience and afterwards he said to me, 'Very good, very classy accent – but you'll never go down in Britain because you're a wee bit too posh, you know. They prefer someone common, like me.'

Here, though, in the mists of Santa Monica, I was safe. The early reviews were forgotten, the audiences came to love my act, somehow I was different from what they saw in 'Upstairs, Downstairs' and 'Monty Python'. All day, in and around Seacastle, I relished the delicious thought that in the early evening I would be strolling the pier, catching the briny, then savouring a light supper amidst the red plush of the theatre 'grub pub' before stepping out on stage, resplendent in top hat and tails, to sing of the tricks of Edwardian couples out 'In the Twi-twi-twilight'.

I invited Mae West to come down. In the late Sixties I'd produced her on an M.G.M. album called 'Great Balls of Fire' and we'd stayed in touch. Now, I told Miss West, I needed her support because I was having trouble with Beatrice Kay: she was complaining about me hogging the stage and doing too much comedy and sticking in ragtime numbers too close to her own style. 'Come up to the apartment,' said Miss West. She was being fitted for a flared pant suit when I arrived. 'Gimme more bust!' she said to the designer. After the fitting she addressed my problem: 'This Kay person sounds like a coon-shouter. I used to do that kinda stuff in vaudeville. But this person ain't no star!' Encouraged, I said that Miss Kay had also objected to my using 'goddam' in the act. Miss West had an answer to that: 'She must be a devil-worshipper and hearing the God word spooks her, see?'

The night Mae West came to the Mayfair she was mobbed in the lavatory; even Beatrice Kay was seen peering under the cubicle door. It was a splendid occasion. My act went down well and friends told me that Mae West laughed especially loud at my proctology joke. Afterwards, when her escort – a male model called Bartlett – was seeing her into the limousine, we heard hoarse cries from across the street. The habitués of a tavern, lovers of fortified wines, were shouting out things like 'Come in here, sweetie!' and 'We'll show you a good time!' Miss West, throwing off Bartlett's arm, turned to the winos and gave them a magnanimous wave. And how the winos cheered and clapped!

Mae West's visit was the high point of my career at the Mayfair. The dream now started turning sour. Details piled up: like the pit band pianist playing jazzy cocktail-bar chords to my version of that stout old number, 'Bobbing Up and Down Like This'; like the Chairman, a genuine Englishman, refusing to join me on stage for 'The Seventh Royal Fusiliers' ('You can die the death on your own, old boy!'); like the agent who saw my act and said I could be O.K. but right now I was 'swimming around and floundering'; like sharing a dressing room with Freeman Love, the Jewish comic, who never stopped talking – more like shouting – about such matters as the balancing act, an Austrian who had been in the Hitler Youth and had designed the forged pound notes that Hitler planned to flood Britain with – didn't I know? – and how this same man was continuing to counterfeit right here in Santa Monica – and how he, Freeman Love, used to drink to excess, even pouring gin on his cornflakes, but now keeps sane by blowing glass and selling crystal fish at flea markets and if reception for his jokes gets any colder then he'll have to commit suicide again. . . .

All this stuff affected me so badly that one night I went on stage and sang my composition, 'Charlie's a Cripple, You Know', got roundly booed and offered to fight any member of the audience who cared to step up.

But there were compensations at the Mayfair. The barmaids and hostesses wore wench costumes – tight bodices which squashed up their breasts, and very short skirts that showed bits of bottom, plus high and wide and slinky black kinky boots – and I'd always got a thrill from girls in costume, *frauleins* in uniform. I worked up a friendship with hostess Katerina, a sensuous Jewish girl, and soon I was invited back to her communal 'crash pad' in Venice. She made me start the session by getting me to take a swim in the lukewarm, soupy and smelly sea. There was never any moonlight over Venice, California.

After the swim I was allowed into her pad – a shack she called 'Biltmore-by-the-Sea' – where we literally crashed on to an oily mattress. Above me were strips of coloured paper hanging from the ceiling, and on the walls were stuck cotton-wool clouds. We got into a yoga session which ended with full-blown sex. During the act she demanded, 'I have to know the name of your cock.' I told her 'Jack' and she let out a loud sigh of relief. 'You're lucky it's not Moses or Jacob.' Afterwards I asked if she ever made any moaning and such. She replied, 'Only when using a hose filled with strong, hot, running water.'

This was not a good life. It lacked pity. But in her bathroom I was touched by the neatly folded clean towels – three kinds: one for body, one for face, one for hands – and the bar of peppermint soap on a rope. And then there were her shoes – so very small, so petite. Shoes have a tremendous pathos for me. But this was not a good life and though I saw a lot of Katerina over the next few weeks, always afterwards I'd make some excuse about having to be dashing.

'Biltmore-by-the-Sea' was used as a clubhouse by hordes of drifters and ne'er-do-wells who called themselves painters or poets or performance artists. I loathed all of them. Their voices had built-in danger sounds like fire-alarm sirens. They knew nothing of old songs or ragtime. They'd never heard of W.H. Davies or Jerome K. Jerome. They had come to hang out, to talk rubbish and to buy from the supermarket of drugs which Katerina dispensed from off her floor. One afternoon she gave me some speedball and I shot up and sprinted back to the Seacastle at 100 m.p.h.

At the front door an ancient and tiny woman was being carried out on a stretcher by breezy young paramedics. I watched as she lovingly fingered through the contents of her handbag, chanting psalm-like the name of each item: 'Keys, talcum, photos, pills, a lock of Harry's hair.'

There are signs which are given to us and we must heed them. I had been given warning signs. My days at the Mayfair were numbered. While I was singing 'I Live in Trafalgar Square' on stage one night, mutiny was brewing in the stalls and foyer: one of Katerina's Venice pals was a gross and ebullient cockney woman calling herself Skylark. She was employed as a rabble-rouser by the management; her job was to encourage the audience to sing along to 'Boiled Beef and Carrots', etc. But her ebullience was turning against her employers – the tweeded Anglophiles. At the end of 'Trafalgar Square' I became aware of the rumpus. Skylark was throwing sausage rolls at the owners; Katerina had joined her with pies. The tough bartender threw them both out as they shouted 'Heads in sand!' and 'Cunt power!' I felt a prep-school surge of sweet righteousness – *I* was not the troublemaker.

The mutiny became a strike. Next evening saw Skylark and Katerina plus a lot of Venice 'artists' parading up and down outside the theatre with placards reading 'Skylark Scandalized', 'Cunt Power v. Cock Power' and 'Truth is Power', while old folk in leisure suits and blue rinses tried to peacefully proceed inside for an evening of the good old days. Skylark saw me sliding by and grabbed me: 'These old music-hall songs are irrelevant bullshit, *bullshit*! Join us or betray us!' Katerina nodded vigorously and pressed a book into my hand. It was a Herman Hesse paperback. 'Look inside,' she said. She'd inscribed: 'We come into this world alone and we leave alone, so let's get together while we can, Love Kathy.' Touched, I gave her a hug.

Just then the manager and the barman came outside and approached us with furious faces. When the barman started man-handling Kathy I tried to hit him. And that was the end of my stint at the Mayfair. I never got through the Herman Hesse book.

*

I gave up the Seacastle and slunk back to the safety of the Laurelwood and George. He welcomed me like I was the Prodigal Son and we worked out a sensible living arrangement.

My stint in Santa Monica Bay had stimulated an urge to dig up its history. When life goes awry I usually retreat into the past. I had read a little about the glory that was once Venice, California, and, of course, I had been visiting among her ruins. It seemed that around the turn of the century Abbot Kinney, a cigarette magnate-cum philanthropist and Indian-lover, had spent a tidy sum building his Venice of the West out of the marshes near Santa Monica. His dream was to bring culture to the Southlanders and he planned concerts of fine, uplifting music, improving lectures, grand opera, classical plays – all that was best in Old Europe. In under a year 16 miles of canals were dug, later there arrived real Venetian gondoliers to ply the waters. But folks didn't want high culture and the canals started silting up, too. Pretty soon Kinney sold out to the fairground people and Venice became the Playground of the West, with rollercoasters, dance halls, pleasure piers, tarts and drunken sailors. In the Fifties the Beats settled in; in the Sixties there were hippies; in the Seventies I met Katerina of Venice.

The turbulent past brings me serenity and a sense of roots. Perhaps there had been Englishmen in these parts. I learned that a fine repository of materials relating to Venice, California (as well as to Chaucer, Shakespeare and poet-peers) was situated over the hills from Studio City in San Marino, near Pasadena. The Huntington Library, one of the nation's great cultural and educational centres, I read, was founded in 1919 by Henry E. Huntington, an exceptional businessman who built a financial empire which included railroad companies and real estate holdings in Southern California. But, continued the pamphlet, Huntington was more than a businessman; he was a man of vision – interested in books, art and gardens. And during his lifetime he had amassed one of the finest libraries in the world, established a splendid collection of British art and created lovely botanical gardens. This was the spot for me to rest, recuperate and study.

I showed the Huntington authorities a list of my books and records and a kindly lady processed me a reader's card. Once inside I dived into the basement book-stacks in search of Venice and old L.A. But as I rambled the lanes I was soon diverted, stopping to sniff into leather-bound histories of Wigan (home of George Formby) and of Wimbledon Common (near my home). So tranquil and dark down there away from the perpetual sun outside, so pleasant to find a nook and sit with a cool breeze blowing from the state-of-the-art air-conditioning, perhaps to snooze and dream and wake and read and fart and snooze again! And then up, up for more rambling through the stacks. Sometimes I'd stumble on a fellow reader: Professor Jim hunched over his graph paper, adding more numbers in his search to find how many times Shakespeare had used certain words like, for example, 'leg'; and old Professor Leroy revising his history of the African-American cowboy, currently spending most days scratching out 'Negro' and substituting 'black' in conformity with the sensibilities of the Seventies.

Upstairs was more normal. Here one found grim po-faced professionals padding about – the men so often in elbow-patched, dogs' mess jackets and bow-ties, the women so often in shapeless reformatory frocks – all flush with grant money and rolling with self-confidence, talking of 'tenure' and the latest 'chair vacancy plum in Eng. Lit.'. I avoided them and they avoided me. The worst were the English.

During coffee breaks in The Footnote (a basement room full of vending machines), I would munch crème-filled sandwich cookies as I read the news on the notice-board. A New York Ph.D. is requesting local housing for his summer research at the Huntington: 'I will be at the library for three months and am desirous of accommodation with pool and/or hot tub.' The word 'will' had been crossed out in a shaky hand, and above it had been written: 'SHALL!' But 'SHALL!' had in turn been crossed out and above, in a clear firm hand, was the final: 'WILL! WILL! WILL!!'

Early in my time at the library I was befriended by Edwin Brackenhurst, custodian of the Americana department. Learning that I had been at an English boarding school, he asked whether I had ever witnessed a de-bagging. Actually, I had – it was at my Seaford prep school, 1953. 'Ah, that would be the year of the Coronation!' he exclaimed. 'And were the trousers, as you call them, removed with or without violence?' I told him how the boy had been roughly handled by a gang of six or seven, and how he'd taken the de-bagging stoically, hardly flinching as he stood there. 'Like the Spartan lad with the fox under his cloak, gnawing his vitals,' said Brackenhurst with enthusiasm. Actually, at the time of the incident I had been reminded of Jack Hawkins' jaw. 'I must show you my thesis on the use of the word "shit" by GIs in World War Two' he said, but he never produced it.

On days when it wasn't too hot I would eat a sandwich lunch behind a privet hedge in the famous Shakespeare garden. Here were all manner of flowers and shrubs, mentioned by the Bard and now printed on

41

planted signs: 'Then heigh-ho, the holly!/This life is so jolly' (*As You Like It*). Here too was a huge spreading tree with sign attached: 'English Oak – same as found in Sherwood Forest, haunt of Robin Hood'. Near this nostalgia was a fierce-looking, malformed monster whose sign said: 'California Live Oak – same as found in Westerns'. The thing was alive with ants and bugs and insects with no name; invariably they made a line for me and my sandwiches.

But sometimes, through an enchantment, Nature would declare peace and I was able to relax into a lotus land of tranquillity. I'd stretch out on the thick juicy grass and, up on my elbows, would gaze at one of the classical statues lining the hedge opposite: a Greek youth, nude and posing with one hand akimbo while the other held aloft a goblet. Could he be cruising? And was this youth the Southern California ideal personified, the perfect racial specimen that Southland developers had encouraged to be bred along the beach towns and inland plains of Los Angeles? I had been strenuously researching at the Huntington. . . .

From my magpie files I devised a story set in 1917, concerning one Hollis Hungerford, Southland realting magnate, and his ambition to create in L.A. an Arcadian society rivalling the 'demi-paradise' England of Shakespeare's day. England, then, was a Garden of Eden, soft and gentle with all nature lying at rest, bravely walled from the barbaric races to the North and to the West: the Scots, the Welsh, and the Irish.

Hungerford, an Anglophile (and sucker to unscrupulous English art and book dealers), managed to fool his long-time pal Horace Lummox (lover of native Americans and their lore, culture and dishes), into believing that the original inhabitants of the Southland were not Indians at all but blond, beautiful Anglo-Saxons, a lost tribe which had established a brilliant civilization in the L.A. basin centuries before the arrival of the nomadic, illiterate tinted peoples.

This grand hoax – effected by a careful planting of artifacts – had been engineered by a Hungerford henchman called Arthur French, an English-born hack whose father had been cook at Roverdown, a Sussex prep school. But French, a decent fellow at heart, suffered an attack of conscience and sent out clues revealing the trickery. A couple of Old Roverdonians, visiting L.A. at this time on a public-speaking engagement, recognized one of French's distress signals: a pair of white gloves dug up by Horace Lummox in his search for ancient artifacts. The two Old Boys knew at once the significance of 'White Gloves', a hallowed Roverdown Sunday ritual: when the school had accumulated no bad conduct marks during the previous week the vice-headmaster would march into the Big Schoolroom proudly sporting a pair of white gloves on his left shoulder, and the school would respond with hearty applause.

At the finale the two Old Boys confronted French with his crime and he confessed, but he followed quickly with a defence of his hoax: 'This excuse for a community, this modern L.A., has become a mecca for quarter-breeds without the law. Don't you see that the ideals that I'm trying to save are exactly those embedded in the ivied walls of Roverdown? I mean good manners, honour, decency, accent and bearing. I mean a sense of duty, of grand purpose, of connecting a civilized past to a civilized future and cutting down the coarseness along the way!'

One of the Old Boys chipped in, 'But we never took any of that Sunday guff seriously!'

'Ah, but you seeped it in through the very sheets and blankets, and the aroma of laburnum on the tennis court wall. Your kind will survive anywhere, because you have been prepared. And in my own lower-class, half-made-up way, I too have burned with the school flame even here in this vile desert! Roverdonians Ho!'[*]

So stirred was I at times by my writing that I would have to leave the rare books reading room to go gulp in some fresh air in the Shakespeare Garden. Over the hills and far away, I could see through the yellow mist the slow rivers of freeway life.

One summer evening, fired by this tamed nature, and perhaps by overwork, I hid behind my privet hedge after closing time. On sweet-tasting grass I spent a dreamless night. Early in the morning I was gently tapped awake by Warner G. Arnold, curator of the Huntington. 'I hate to disturb you, but our gardeners are here to lay the sods for the annual replacement of the lawn. And so I must therefore ask you to vacate this area.'

Eventually my work and therapy at the library and gardens were finished and I was ready to have another go at breaking back into mainline show business. And when the outside world went wrong I would lie down, close my eyes and call up my favourite Huntington painting, 'The Golden Hour'. . .

Set in a gold-encrusted frame, built from strokes of protuberant oil paint good enough to eat, is a darkening glade in deep apple countryside somewhere in England, the quick-setting sun throwing a last

---

[*] My story was eventually published as *Lotus Land – A Story of Southern California* by Wildwood House, London, in 1979.

spotlight on a dumpling cottage and fellow pond. Nobody is outside, twilight time is near, drinks are being prepared, appetizers too. For some lucky people twilight is the time for painless childbirth. . . .

All over the Southland I searched and searched for a pleasant spot that never changes, a carapaced club with a piano bar where I could meet friends and make them as well. A place where the old songs and dances were everlastingly celebrated. There was nowhere in Holly-wood. In the San Fernando Valley, near Universal Studios, I almost found the right spot, but the music became too cocktail and I lost the woman I found there to a married Silesian. Further afield, in Palm Springs, I was taken to Banducci's Italian restaurant and there I wit-nessed George Momb, the amazing entertainer at the piano, and there I thought I'd found the answer to my prayer. But soon, too soon, the dream went sour. . . .

In a setting of red and white George sat behind his piano bar, wear-ing only a powder-blue cashmere sweater, segueing from a 100 m.p.h. 'Rhapsody in Blue' into 'I've Got a Luverly Bunch of Coconuts', never missing a note, greeting customers as they entered his Carnegie Hall, throwing the mike to Herbie, a distant relative of Frank Sinatra, or Marge, a distant relative of Jeanette McDonald, urging her to 'Go for it – sing from the diaphragm, and I sure hope you're wearing one,' winking at me, crossing himself as she wobbled on the notes, swallow-ing a Scotch as the other hand soldiered on, commenting on her technique with the mike cable – 'I can see you're happily married' – applying some more lip-gloss, winking at me again, leaning across to tell me that 'I've reached a point of insanity where every note's a trea-sure,' never leaving his piano-bar pilot seat, not even when the two veterans got into a brawl about Vietnam battles while the loser with the swivelling left eye sang, 'Start spreading the news, I'm leaving today, I'll make a brand new start of it, New York, New York!' The marbling in the mirror behind George looked like brown spit; I could see his bald spot, while from the front his hair was full and well-groomed; I hated this song; nobody asked me to sing; Palm Springs was a long way from real life. I needed a haven in the middle of real life.

And so, at last, I came to Sterling's.

I was led there one night by Tom Middleton, the literary crossword puzzle setter and a listener to my radio show, and I was also accompa-nied by Charles Sprawson, the art dealer swimming writer, a fellow graduate of Trinity College, Dublin, in town on an art sales attack. And so, once again I was back in Santa Monica – but now I was safe

44

from the doom toll of the waves, safe in the womb of songs spun by the enthroned captain, Rosy McHargue, born 1902.

With eagle eyes set in a beautiful big shiny baby head, and a pointing panoramic finger, he ruled over all his domain, a fine blue-marbled mirror behind him, crutches leaning against his throne, with two full snifters of brandy in front of him and an empty one atop the piano, for tips. Woe be to those who dared to speak when Rosy sang the song, with all the verses! I saw even wheelchair people told to 'Shut up, goddammit' for talking during 'America, I Love You'. I saw Rosy lead a singalong of evergreens (with many doctors and lawyers joining in), which stimulated some real old touch dancing and climaxed with Doc Brown, the noted cardiologist, piloting a long Conga snake-line round the premises and in and out of the kitchen. Only my friend Charles Sprawson refused to make room for the spectacle, but he's always been that way.

During breaks Rosy received his fans, the young women being bounced on his knees, and so forth. I lined up to pay my respects and was so pleased that he remembered my recording of 'Where did Robinson Crusoe Go with Friday on Saturday Night?' We were interrupted briefly as Doc Brown led a ritual party into the men's room to the tune of 'Going to the Lavatory Blues'. Then Rosy turned to me and said, 'Won't you give us a number?'

As I sang 'Here I Am', announcing the chords between the lines, I became aware of a simian cornet player beside me, enjoying the tune, standing proud with back arched like a banana, feet splayed firmly, neck swelling, subsiding, swelling, subsiding. Afterwards he gripped my hand and shook it fiercely, telling me I had a good number and his name was Ned Gimbel. Encouraged, I went on that evening to perform more of my repertoire, from saloon ballad to novelty point number. There was much applause and the owner Don came out of his kitchen, wiped his hands on his apron and, on the strength of a handgrip, told me I could sing here for my supper any time, and if I ever asked for a bill he'd kill me.

By this time I was living in Altadena, near the foothills of the San Gabriel mountains, and the journey to Sterling's-by-the-sea was a good 30 miles. But, religiously, every weekend I appeared there to sing and eat and drink. Now I was armed with my ukuleles and musette accordion and I sat in with the band, even to the extent of taking jazz solos. 'Play an accordion – go to jail,' said a horn player, but Ned put his arm around me and told me the man was only joking. I could see that out there in the dark room the old-timers were won over by the plunk of the uke and the plangency of the musette. 'Keep 'em close to the ground!' shouted a retired judge. At 2 a.m., closing time, we'd all play 'Show Me the Way to Go Home', and then off we'd go, a little slowly, to Zucky's, the 24-hour-a-day delicatessen on Wilshire. Rosy would have a grilled cheese sandwich, Ned would have fried onion rings, and I'd have deep-dish apple pie *à la mode*. Sometimes we'd strike up a barber-shop close harmony arrangement of evergreens like 'Down by the Old Mill Stream' or 'Shine On, Harvest Moon', and at the end the Zucky customers would applaud – I mean punks and pimps and minorities and young stockbrokers, everyone. We were all one at dawning and it was bliss to be part of a team, the team I'd never gotten into at school! Song was the great cement, the great healer, and I told Rosy and he winked.

*

When I regained consciousness I saw blood all down the front of my white tuxedo. Then I saw Regina, smiling with tears in her eyes. I didn't dare look any further; there was an awful hush in Sterling's. Then I realized I'd done it again – I'd gone and wrecked a treasure trove, I'd smashed up a happiness room, like in the late Forties at the flat on Putney Heath when I'd stamped on my favourite toy soldiers and snapped all my best 78s.

But Gimbel had behaved worse than me; he'd tried to murder me. Maybe he'd had a bad childhood. I looked around for him. There he was, in a corner booth, nursing his cornet while his girl-friend stroked his hair. I got up and walked over to him, kind of like a Western film hero. Everybody was watching, I felt. I told him I was very, very sorry and I held out my hand. He wasn't sure what to do. But then he gripped it. *Hard*, much too hard. He said, 'O.K. – but don't ever try that stuff on me again!' That rather spoiled my scene and my exit was none too graceful, but Regina was there to steady me at the door. I never looked back . . . I was never going in there ever again.

The glory of the righteous passion! Regina said she'd drive and I sat with my uke on my lap, nursing it. The glory! But soon I became aware of a stinging pain on my face, on my neck, on my bottom, all over the place. And I knew I deserved every bit of it. Ned Gimbel was God's schoolmaster sent down to punish me . . . .

Always the descent into bathos, never concern for the world.

'Have you ever thought of taking up chanting?' asked Regina unshovingly. We were diving into the Santa Monica freeway, on our way to my home in Altadena. Chanting? No, the old songs were my cure. I found a cassette in the glove compartment and fed it into the tape-deck slot. It gobbled it greedily, and then there came the sound of ragtime. After a minute or so I pressed the eject button and the cassette clicked out noisily.

The time had come for me to set out in a different direction, away from Bill Bailey and Alexander. In their day they had been dancing on the cutting edge, but now they were tired old warhorses of the treeless plain, whipped on by mouldy figges. Where were the lovers of yesterday who had danced to the kid Bill Bailey? Shades, all of them, hardly remembered, and I had better be careful lest I became excess baggage not required on the journey, soon to lie on the freeway shoulder with the tyre treads and squashed animals.

We reached the comfortable plateau of 65 m.p.h. and Regina pressed the cruise control, eased back in her seat and started massaging the back of my neck with her spare hand. Slowly there started to well up in me a tremendous affection for Ned Gimbel. I began to love his bandy legs, the wild scrub of his hair, the piggy hairs on the back of his fists and sprouting out of the V in his golf shirt. But more than anything I loved his split upper lip, juicy and red rare. I should have hugged him in Sterling's, the way Americans do! I almost produced tears, but not quite.

Now there came a great drumming on the roof and I looked out and saw rain, hurtling down straight as arrows. Earlier in the day there had been talk of rain on the radio, the weathermen saying excitedly that this would be the very first June rain since 1878. A 70 per cent chance. I push-buttoned to KFWB, a 24-hour news and information station: the storm was dumping humungous amounts of dirty water steadily and evenly all over Los Angeles County. Not soft refreshing rain as in the school hymn but vicious, Godless rain.

Below our concrete channel, under the roofs of L.A., was a dreaming world of ever-grasping hope, immune to the hard rain. I knew this to be as true now as it had been since the days of the first settlers. Now, as we descended into Altadena, I felt a resolve coming on, akin to those spirits under the roofs. There'd be some changes made and order would enter my house, even as the weather raged pointlessly outside.

When we reached my front gate the sky was quiet, but I swore my sea-change resolve to Regina just the same. I told her the hot tub would soon look as fresh as the pond. 'I've got an early start tomorrow, so I'll let you go,' she said. I saw her to her car and then moved slowly towards the dark and dripping house.

Part Two

Home In Altadena

Why can't the world be like stories,
        Where the lanes all wend to a happy end?
Nowadays people find they've blood on their mind –
Freeway fighters, nasty blighters trying to unwind.
So I escape into territory unknown:
Come fly with me to my heavenly home!
One more day and I'm going back,
To my cute little country shack
        In Altadena Lane. . . .
I know that every hate that I had will die,
'Cos out there 'neath the western sky
I'll be myself again!
Imagine me beside my little peaceful pond
Just thinking thoughts of here and now and not beyond.
I'll have my old dog too and he'll lead the dance,
I'll give life just one more chance
        In Altadena Lane. . . .
Imagine me beside my cool and placid pond
Back with the girly-girl of whom I'm awfully fond.
I'll have my parents too, life will be worthwhile,
I'll end up with a sunny smile
        In Altadena Lane.

                              (An old song revised by I.W.)

Sometimes when I'm half-asleep I dream of Altadena. The morning
after the fight I was down the well of dreams again and deeper than
ever, unconcerned by the whizzing cars outside and the gospel thump
from the house next door. Over my bedspread was a mess of local
history books, pamphlets and real estate maps; down in the well I was
sloshing in the ooze of Altadena, before the land was named and im-
provement made. . . .

*A long line of Indians, horsed and loinclothed, making a slow progress
along the shimmering mountain ridge. 'Let's get us a brace before sup-*

48

per,' said Jed to Zack, and they popped them off like tin targets at a fairground. Canyon injuns, Shoshonees – nobody would miss them – miserable, benighted creatures, almost naked, always painted – living in huts made of earth and branches, living off acorns, berries and roots, with grasshoppers as a real delicacy.

The Spaniards had relieved the Indians of their homelands during the settlement of Alta California. Then they put their new wards to work in the walled missions; the trauma killed off a goodly number. After the break-up of the mission system the wandering tribesmen were attacked by disease, whiskey and the likes of Jed and Zack. But by that time, the second half of the nineteenth century, you could read all about the more interesting, more noble red man in pulp magazines, and pretty soon there would be hardbacked novels telling of evening bells pealing from the ivied old mission and Father in his clean brown habit beckoning ever so kindly.

Meanwhile bold Hugo Reid, from Scotland, had ranged the arid scrublands of the entire Los Angeles basin, studying the local tribes and their customs. Twenty-six different Indian villages, he'd noted. Twenty-six. He loved his Indians, sharing roasted grasshopper with Chief Hahamovic, ruler over several tribes in the Arroyo Seco (future site of Pasadena and Altadena). Hugo went partly native, taking out Mexican citizenship and marrying a local squaw. Gringo land squatters and homesteaders, tough varmints staked out on Mexican rancho land, told tales of the ex-Scotchman's strange breakfast ritual: his bagpiping at dawn on the highlands slope – standing kilted at the foot of the Sierra mountains as his Indian bride, below him, prepared their meal of porridge sprinkled with the sweetest crushed acorns.

'Never forget where you came from, and leave things as they are' was Hugo Reid's advice. But American progress could not be blocked, conservation was not in fashion, thrusting forward to destiny was the whole point of the new nation. Why, in President Jefferson's time the map of the West had been thoroughly gridded, even up and down the mountains, and now that plan must be carried out until every inch up to the Pacific had been platted ready for cities and civilization! Alta California sprawled hirsute like a wild and voluptuous woman waiting to be taken. Hugo Reid was amusing, but the Spaniards were in the way. American businessmen moved in. Manifest Destiny.

*

'Rancho-ho!' shouted Don Garfias, tall in the saddle. All very well for the new owner of the mission lands, but the ledgers showed he was low

49

in funds. Cattle simply didn't pay. Already he was borrowing heavily from clever gringos just in from the East. In shuttered offices their lawyers patted sheaves of figured papers. Don Garfias would rather have been charging his best stallion through the surf at Malibu. 'Rancho ho!' bounced off the boxy suits of the grim businessmen and their wily lawyers. Soon, though, the Don was able to spend as much time as he liked riding the wild surf: he defaulted on his loan and lost his huge Rancho San Pasqual, and so were we nearer to the establishment of Pasadena, Altadena and the site of my future home.

The new owners of the rancho were Dr Griffin and his partner Ben Wilson. Both were no-nonsense Southerners, tough as British bacon. The doc had sawed bones at many a battle in the recent war between the states; Ben had been a trapper and trader. Now they were getting smarter and more civilized, sticking on wing collars and wide ties, speculating on the scrublands. Make a killing in the West and move on. Where to? Ben Wilson liked the place so much he went a touch native, calling himself 'Don Benito'. Even the doc agreed there was something special about the air. But all that crumbly rock and choking dust and noisy, hungry insects!

The suckers from Indiana saved the day. Lured by booster literature promising them health and wealth, these mid-Western immigrants came in search of the ideal community, a new Arcady founded on sound Christian lines. They were middle class and middle-aged. Some were on borrowed time, coughing up blood, tossing back all kinds of nostrums, bent double as they scanned the land and missed the sky. Glinty-eyed colonists from a beastly climate, full of big dreams for a ranch of plenty, exploding with healthful foods. The San Gabriel Orange Grove Association, they called themselves, and Doc Griffin quickly sold them a hunk of the rancho.

Their leader believed in farming as therapy, a salvation in a New Arcady brought about by hard labour. The sweat of the brow would nourish the soul, he said. There would arise a great fruit culture and bee ranches and heaven knew what else. At the end of the day one could rock on the verandah watching the foodstuffs grow.

The leader grew excited as he spoke and had to wipe away the foamy phlegm collecting round his mouth. Doc Griffin averted his gaze – and looked at a jack-rabbit racing a tumbleweed over the foothills sand. He wrote to a friend in Virginia: 'Have sold 4,000 acres to fool ranchers and the whole 4,000 will not support one family.'

That was in 1873. Two years later the village of Pasadena had emerged from the dust. The health-seekers had exchanged tents for houses and yet claimed that, such was the intoxicating purity of the mountain air, they slept just as soundly, deeply and dreamlessly as they had when under canvas. Also intoxicating was the water (but that was where liquid intoxication stopped, for the colonists were strictly teetotal). This water was their life-giver, nature simply sprang up around them, you couldn't stop the growth. Water – the answer to the major block in bringing paradise to the Southern California demi-desert. Water – flashing in from elsewhere like God the Dancer to help bring about that land of milk and honey described in the Bible. Water – had been piped in courtesy of a cunning judge-businessman called Eaton. Soon the colonists were busy in agriculture and the planting of fruit-tree groves and the removal of squatters. Word spread to the East Coast and Raymond & Whitcomb Tours responded, shipping in loads of invalids and semi-invalids, and setting them down at the company hotel high on a hill from where the sprouting new paradise could be viewed and envied. Many settled in to build their nests.

Splendid gingerbread mansions rose up from the dust and, of a morning, their owners could be heard greeting each other in shout and song across the otherwise empty, treeless valley. 'Weoquan-Pa-sa-de-na' sang colonist Elliott one dawning, and his neighbours were enchanted. 'It's a Chippewa name meaning "Crown of the Valley"' he explained later at a meeting of the Orange Grove Association. 'A college pal, a missionary to Indians, suggested it as a name for our new community.'

Pasadena thrived, especially in the coming land boom, and the health-seeking ranchers were joined by some very rich folks from the East. The latter had lavish winter homes built for them so that, sitting in their heavy furniture, they could look out at an ever-reliable sun. Up in the foothills above Pasadena they also found some delightful sites, far from the nosy crowd. This was to be Altadena, my future home.

How did Altadena come to be? At the time of the original land deal between Griffin, Wilson and the Indianans, 1,400 acres up in the Sierra foothills were thrown in as a token of goodwill. It was considered worthless land – bone-dry, and full of earthquake-style gullies and choked with chaparral, worse than the land the colonists had purchased. But the taxes had been paid, there were no strings attached, and the colonists accepted the gift. For years they left the god-forsaken region alone to the shades of forgotten Indians and an eccentric Scotchman.

Then in 1881 the new Pasadenans sold their wasteland tip dirt-cheap to another bunch of adventurers, headed by the Woodbury brothers of

Iowa. As with the Indianans, the idea was to develop ranching and light farming but, as with Pasadena, it soon became apparent that the real money was to be had in subdividing: the slicing up of the land into parcels, and the selling of the parcels as sites for charming blue heaven homes of the future. First came the Eastern rich, then came the littler people, and gradually the land got sliced into smaller and smaller dream pieces.

The Woodburys, like so many Western town-starters, proposed their land deal as a Utopia. Taking the name from a nearby nursery, Altadena (meaning higher Pasadena) was sold as an ideal on paper at a time when the whole L.A. basin was up to the same game: crawling with realtors, criss-crossing each other in their beetle buggies, ready to pounce on strangers and wrap them in a well-platted map of the future township. Here's the church, here's the hotel, here's a street called Euclid, and here's one called Carol – that's my wife. All this will come to pass. . . .

The Woodbury's richly-coloured, sweet-smelling lithographed sales pamphlet read 'ALTA DENA – Lying on a sunny slope 500 feet higher, and three miles north of Pasadena, with the grand panorama of the San Gabriel Valley at her feet stretching southward to the sea, and eastward to the beautiful Jacintos; sheltered from frost on the north by the Sierra Madre range with its ever-changing shadows, and with hill and vale on the west – ALTA DENA affords the choicest spot for the artist, invalid or businessman to make his home.'

The first of the settler-businessmen were big men in their field: Joseph Medill, one-time Chicago mayor and newspaper proprietor, built a large foothill estate and was fond of drinking snow water from his mountain reservoir in order to wash the lime out of his body; Henry Ford had a house on Santa Rosa street where he was said to have invented vital motor parts; Andrew McNally of Rand-McNally, the map publishing company, lived in a high Victorian house with a well-stocked pond, but his neighbour Colonel Green, the patent medicine king famous for his German Syrup, objected to being bitten by mosquitoes from McNally's pond, and to his neighbour's planting of taller and taller fir trees so that his view of the mountains was vanishing. Still the two men remained on civil terms because both were bound by the common bond of having lots of money; the list of Altadena's top businessmen must also include Stetson, the baked bean millionaire, and Smith and Armstrong, the railroad officials.

Leading the artists was Zane Grey, who lived in a sprawling mansion designed in the Spanish renaissance style; and there was his friend

Jackson Gregory, another Western author, living close by in an 'air-plane' bungalow with a rooftop 'cockpit' sleeping porch so that the cool night air could blast away any tuberculosis. Altadena attracted more than its share of invalids because there were many sanitaria established up at the tip of the mountains and along Fair Oaks; the air was supposed to be sweeter nearer the mountains, but the man who started the big Mountain View Cemetery did a roaring trade.

Businessmen, artists, invalids – and there were soon to be eccentric religious groups and cultists joining them, and yet isolated, because in Altadena it was possible to own a lot of land and wall yourself or your group in and never be bothered by public or police. Altadena remained steadfastly unincorporated as a city, and by the 1920s it had become more desirable as a bedroom community of the foothills where, at sundown, tired clerks could be seen wending their way back up the lane to heaven and a welcoming wife. A brochure published by L.A. realtors Rigali and Veslicu in the later 1920s paints an enticing picture of the suburban subdivision beautiful, Southern California-style:

'On any given morning hikers are already stalking the hills of Altadena by 6 a.m. They are marvelling at the roseate hue of the velvet-draped mountains and, turning, they see below them the vista of Los Angeles, twinkling excitingly with all the promise of a succulent future – the stars being actually below them, for a change, in a heaven that is man-made electric. Immediately beneath our hikers, on gentle slopes, is the work of Mother Nature tamed and trimmed for a home-owner's delight: wide-spreading oaks whose gnarled branches record the flight of centuries; rustling groves, pumping the air with the perfume of orange, lemon, lime and kumquat; here too dwell in friendly contiguity the banana and the avocado; indeed all the world is, or can be, present from the modest violet of Minnesota to the sensuous tuberose of sunny Italy. What a pity that for so long this splendid land was the preserve of the few! But recently, through the enterprise of a powerful syndicate of capitalists, choice tracts have been cut and cut again so that, in the true spirit of democracy, this paradise can be placed within the reach of your pocket. All requisites are embodied. Please note our protective restrictions: each home must cost no less than $5,000 and can never be owned or occupied by any race other than Caucasian.'

When there came war clouds over Europe, Altadena remained above it all. There was no unpleasantness in any form around the town. The world knew Altadena for her 'Mile of Christmas Trees' – the old Woodbury driveway electrically lit-up every Christmas week, courtesy of the Kiwanis. More locally, the charming little burg was known for her gardens and vistas. In 1939 Fred Walters of the Rose Society lectured on 'Gardens – the Answer to Our Quest for Happiness'. As far as crime was concerned Altadena was a 'white spot'. Citizens were encouraged to report to the sheriff the presence of any suspicious-looking strangers. When apprehended, those strangers had better give a logical explanation for their presence in this quiet residential community. Recently it was discovered that a Negro, a prize pugilist, was living in Altadena. An overhaul on the restriction rules was immediately undertaken by leading local realtors.

And so, like a fairy tale, Altadena slept. Film stars and writers and cult groups and ordinary law-abiding people were tucked up and away from the hurly-burly below, and worse over the hills. In winding lanes that bent the rigid grid could be found, if you sought hard, higgledy-piggledy and often rickety cottages, bungalows and shacks. Many seemed to have been claimed by nature – strangled by ivy and nameless vines, defended by barricades of shrubs and tall hedges. No one quite knew who, back in the teens and twenties, had smacked together these light-hearted structures of wood, lath and nail, but you felt they had whistled as they worked, producing ramshackle pleasure homes that would see a soul through all kinds of weather and would rock with sweet equanimity in an earthquake.

There were mansions too, of course, rising above the carefree homes of the poets, quilters, gardeners and the like. Mansions testifying to the success of captains of industry, and often very classical with many a Doric pillar. But when the Santa Ana winds blew through the canyons they spared nobody, not even the mansion owners. Watch the old woman in the boulder cottage on Maiden Lane as she tries to protect her fat candles blazing on her long-premature Christmas tree, and then fly down Lake Street, make a right on Calaveras (Skull Street) and stop at the hedge just before Christmas Tree Lane. This is a Deep South type estate owned, says the record, by Archie Andrews, the weighing machine mogul who's always away on business or pleasure. Hop over the high hedge and see the waves lashing the sides of his long straight swimming-pool. Now a big wave rolls right up and over the Dixie-Greek columns of the temple house itself, very weird and wonderful. Round we swoosh to the back garden, but this is very grand – a long sward of waving grass, with groaning orange trees on either side, stretching all the way to the next parallel street, Alameda (Shady Lane). The end of the grand sward is marked by a large ornate stone fountain, spitting everywhere in the Santa Ana storm. The fir tree nearby takes both storm and fountain in its stride. The fir tree will be there when I move in.

But after World War Two the orange groves started to disappear and the names of the home owners in Altadena grew more colourful. On Alameda St where once there had been – for ages it seemed – a Carlson, Everett, Scott, Wadsworth and Mrs Friendly Rogers, were now the mail-boxes of Alonzo, Psomoas, Ituarte and Ong. Still, the front gardens were tended and bloomed as of old, and the lawns were manicured to perfection. You could examine these front yards from the street because, in this age of real neighbourliness, real Americanism, there were no fences and hedges, no stuffy elitism. Whatever your name or colour, you bought your tract and you built what you liked, but it usually turned out to be an O.K. regular.

In 1947 Mr and Mrs Shea built their dream house on a site at the end of Archie Andrews' green sward, near the ornate fountain. Similar dream homes were being erected all up and down the street. In 1951 Mr Charles Hutchins, a salesman for Kaiser Steel, took over the house and moved in with his wife Gertie and the kids. He soon found that on either side of him were coloured families and they were real nice folks, proper and quiet, neighbourly and churchgoing. It was quite a job keeping up with their lawn-mowing.

And there the Hutchins lived as an honest-to-God American family till the late Seventies when, with the children grown and gone, Mr Hutchins decided to move to a smaller place, a condominium perhaps, in nearby Temple City. In 1979, on an impulse in the rain, I bought the house, hoping for a home. After living there a little while I had a hot tub installed. Many years later, when the hot tub had silted up, I had a pond dug. I was very fond of peering into my pond, not to see a reflection of myself but to watch the fishes gliding and dashing and coasting all in their own special world. I was a god examining and envying them.

*

My dog Beefy woke me from this reverie, lifting up my chin with his wet mouth. He was staring straight through me, knocking the untruths; a clever dog, a wilful dog, the love of my life and the still centre. He does run around a lot, but it's only twisting and turning and circling, returning always. He circles in panting glee when I come home – say from forays into Hollywood. I'll be tired and down-hearted from the old struggle to establish a niche in mainline show business, but Beefy revives me because he believes in me, ever my fan. He is like those groupies I had during my brief rock-star life in the

55

summer of '65, only he's much more beautiful.

I'd better describe him since he's a hero of this story of my house. Beefy Whitcomb is part German Shepherd and part Husky (or maybe Malamute – nobody's clear about his ethnic origins). His head is awfully large for a dog, as large as mine. He used to have two enormous ears like dusky, furry angel wings that sprang erect at the slightest excuse, even the approach of my most boring friends. Nowadays only the right ear springs up because the mechanism inside the left ear was irremediably destroyed through the negligence of one of my boarders.

Beefy has a sturdy compact face, unlike the long, pointed, almost dainty faces of the pure-bred German Shepherds. His snout is too big, and so are his paws; his tongue is too long, and is always hanging out, bouncing; he pants constantly, he's a chronic hyperventilator. He'd never win any prizes at dog shows, but he'd make plenty of new friends there.

His coat is so huggable, kissable – much plusher than any woman's fur. Overall this coat is jet-black, but it's as if his maker primed him in snow-white and then – with a master's brushstrokes – painted on the lustrous black with finishes on legs and face that move to a cusp, leaving little islands of the original white. His maker then stood back to view his work – and decided to add some finishing touches: two big blob eyebrows and, under the U-shaped mouth and thick bacon tongue, a fluffy ruff. These accessories are all in white. I don't know how Nature really works, but there has to be some master designer because Beefy is so beautiful and is definitely one-of-a-kind, I don't care what they say.

Now I tried staring into the turquoise eyes, but they lanced at my conscience. I let the wet black snout wipe across my face. I must get up, I *will* get up. I did get up and went about the early morning chores.

First I tugged the bedspread over the bed, creating a cloud of dust and dog hairs, leaving lumps underneath. To make the bed properly requires a helper for I own an enormous bed, a 'Kalifornian King,' the biggest made. I bought it several years ago to facilitate my after-sex life. I don't know what the normal drill is, but I prefer to separate sex from sleep and after the action is over I like to retire to my part of the bed and not be disturbed by cuddling, kissing, toe-touching and such. The 'Kal King' is perfect for this, almost like living in another country from your partner, but it's a hell of a bed to make on your own.

56

The master bedroom is a cheerful spot and I have a lot of time for it. Painted a powder blue (the choice of lady house painters I once hired), the appointments are all my own: curtains run up from a South Seas shirt pattern depicting palmy desert islands with sailboats tilting gaily by, in cheerful colours. A friend of mine, the film director Curlew Worthington, very sensitive and steeped in Art Nouveau ('Not Deco!' he will scream) can't stand these South Sea curtains. When he toured the bedroom he covered his face as if in the presence of Satan, and he brings up the subject whenever we're dining out.

On the walls are pictures for setting me in the mood for re-membrance of times past: stark winter fields and muddy lanes in Dor-set – rugger's over and there'll be sausage rolls in the tuck-shop and Danny & The Juniors in the study; a 1940s poster of an English fun-fair, gilt and gold in a blue light, fathers in trilbies, sons in grey shorts; a Victorian Narcissus loving his reflection in a Home Counties rock pool (I bought this print in an Oxford Street tourist shop)[*].

In the left-hand corner of my side of the enormous bed is tacked a gallery of framed photos: school and house groups of Bryanston, Dorset, Summer 1959; my mother, father, sister, brother and our various dogs, snapped over the years and blown up by a Hollywood film fan photo company; best of all, my mother and father sloped in deckchairs in the tiny garden of our seaside boarding-house during the Summer of 1949, when every wave was a thrilling battle and comic books had tough men riddled with dripping holes. Below this ex-hibition, almost touching the bed, is a big steamer trunk given to me by Vik, once butler to Bette Davis (more about Vik later). The trunk acts as a table for the stacks of books I'm dipping into: improving stuff, classics by Joyce and Proust and Dickens. Years ago I set myself a chapter each morning before bathroom duties, but I soon dropped out of the course. Inside, the trunk holds a supply of provisions for when the big earthquake comes. The food and drink is elderly and because much was bought fresh, as opposed to canned or dried, I have left well alone under the heavy steamer lid and the stack of books. If the big one comes . . . then *kismet*!

After bed-making I exited and, closely followed by Beefy, took a left down my corridor (longer than you'd think) lined with genuine World War One posters and Ian Whitcomb album covers ('The rare ones are the unsigned,' quipped Dr Ronald, on several occasions, to

* Curlew Worthington has this same print hung up in his 'Art Nouveau' Hollywood home – only his is gold-framed and with a shaded light. And he has the nerve to criticize my curtains! Still, he's a good friend and I need good friends.

visiting servicemen). There are bathrooms at both ends of my corridor, so I can take my choice as to where I go to the lavatory. The first door past my bedroom contains Troy and Cassandra, a husband and wife team; next door are younger brother Max and girl-friend Kimberlee. I like the idea of running a boarding-house because you're never alone and yet never too emotionally involved, besides the rent helps offset the mortgage. Sometimes I pretend we're a boarding-school with Cassandra as matron, Troy as head boy and Max as the bad egg. Of course, I'm the headmaster. The boarders don't understand the conceit but they humour me. After all, they've no place else to go until they strike it rich.

Sometimes I've stopped at their doors to eavesdrop on arguments and once or twice, when really lucky, I've caught some love-making noises on my pocket tape recorder – all for research, of course.

But this morning I about-turned after the briefest inspection – everything seemed sepulchral and I wanted it to stay that way. I wanted my whole world to stand still – and, after bumping into faithful Beefy, I walked back. But now, instead of turning right for the master bedroom, I turned left for the drawing room, crossing the front door hallway (with a niche for bell chimes and a floor strewn with affordable Persian rugs made in Belgium), a hallway narrow enough to allow me, years ago, to punch one of my boarders out of the master bedroom, across the hallway, and on to the hardwood floor of the drawing room.

The drawing room walls are a dirty white, but the sofa and reclining lounger are brown and so are the 1924 upright player piano and the high bookshelves on either side and the very fine hardwood floor. Mrs Chas Sprawson, the wife of a best friend, examining polaroids of my drawing room in the comfort of her picturesque Cotswold kitchen, summed up the decor as, 'Very, very bachelor, almost Somerset Maugham, lonely colonial.' London Transport posters adorn the walls; a many-paned window stretching the whole of the garden side of the room affords a patio view of great possibilities and personal memories: weed-choked planters, dying desert vegetation, a rusty barbecue, and a redwood hot tub whose long-closed lid conceals a horrible slime I cannot face. Fred's rubber frog feet lie nearby as they have done since he left long ago.

*

I hear the sound of the boarders rising and so we must hide.

Out of the front door, under the wood-pillared porch, down the stone steps and into the garden where sits an artificially confined body of water – my newly dug pond, my pride and joy and solace. Here I will lie on the grass and peer over the boulders into the pond where at this hour the fishes are doing their mating dance, chasing each other madly and occasionally leaping high out of the water like fishy ballet boys.

The waterboatmen scull across the plain while the dragonflies whirr overhead and, down in the clear clean below, little fishes dart to and fro, always knowing their place in the cosmos, unlike us above. I can hear from inside the house the noise of showers thundering and lavatories flushing and New Wave music. Beyond the front fence a car armed with a rap-filled jukebox passes by, and the great sonic boom ruffles the pond surface and now, instead of seeing vivacious fish, I'm faced with a fun-fair crazy mirror picture of my face. What a mess! Have I anything in common with this ordered nether world of contented fishes on their diurnal round?

The boarders have left, so I can proceed to my study at the end of the corridor, with Beefy in the lead. I'll pull out my big W.H.Smith journals and select some entries so that you can learn a little about how I came to buy this house, the place I hoped would eventually become the kind of contentment home in the West I had heard so much about in old songs.

*

Since the middle 1960s I had been an Englishman abroad, but unlike those decent Empire outposters of the past I had constantly let the side down. The trouble was there were so few public school men around to invigilate, and the two I knew as best friends delighted in my misadventures. Their lives seemed smooth sailing, whereas I thrashed around in rough waters, even after I'd bought the bungalow in Alameda St.

Whenever things got too stormy I'd fly home to England, to Putney Heath and Wildcroft Manor – luxury flats of the 1930s designed to look like a country house, with clipped hedges and Tudor beams, but none of this comic architecture meant a bean to me because Wildcroft Manor meant No.18 and the unchanging rooms of my childhood since 1947. The same rippled wallpaper, like icing on a birthday cake, the same spongy wing-backed chairs, the same green and white bathroom with the pyramid step tiles, and also the radiant sunburst door-handles promising a super future, the merrily gurgling cast-iron radiators, the scratch marks of long-dead dogs on the back door and

59

the bowler hat and umbrella of my late father hanging in my mother's wardrobe. There are bell buttons everywhere that can be pressed and pressed in vain to summon servants to lounge, dining room, bedroom, bathroom. How I loved to laze in our long green bath with a good book and constant hot water! And then my mother's cry of 'Sup's up!' But I was pushing forty, and I still felt my destiny lay in the Los Angeles basin.

In January 1979 I returned once more to the last frontier, little knowing that this was the year I was to become a householder, if not a home-owner.

Freezing fog at Heathrow, but worse was saying goodbye again. I was always saying goodbye to family and friends but, on the happy side, I was always saying hello. Keeping on the move and thus welcomed at many a home because I never, hardly ever, outstayed that welcome. The lesson had been learnt way back at prep school: on a visiting weekend, I was travelling with a best friend and his family in their Bentley; for hours I regaled them with jokes and they roared and howled and the father slapped the wheel with his gloved hand; just as I was embarking on an Indian army tale the father turned round and barked 'Oh, do SHUT UP!' I'd overdone it. Timing is all.

At the passport control barrier I said goodbye to my mother. Then she turned away, as she always does, to hide her tears. The ancient family labrador gave me his usual recriminatory look. 'I'll be back soon,' I said and marched ahead. Every time I turned I saw my mother still standing at the barrier, forlorn. Sitting in the crowded departure lounge, out of her sight, out of her world, I had a vision of her fallen down in the flat in the night with nobody to help her except the old dog licking her face, and she apologizing profusely. In my mind I started singing, 'If I Had My Way'.

The departure lounge, a shed of tubular hard-edged gleaming metal, soon threw me into the slough of the present: a sleep-walk voice announced my flight and the rush was on. Now to be jostled about in a carnival of nations, where only I was the unidentified subject, assaulted by so many veils and habits and swarthies who might be terrorists, my Trinity College Dublin tie unrecognized. . . . How excruciating and embarrassing to crash to death with such a circus! To be whirled to oblivion washing-machine-style, limb against limb, sari on blazer, the odour of strange herbs and aftershaves, far away from a Wildcroft bedroom death to the tune of my mother's anodyne voice.

Safely aboard the jumbo and strapped in, I pulled out the big blue W.H.Smith journal and wrote up the start of the new year, a traditional list headed 'Goals'. This year it read: 'To try to be less selfish. To give as much friendship and pleasure as possible to my ever-widening circle. First and foremost comes family, then friends, and after that the world, or some of it.' After bar service I added: 'Their world will be my world and vice versa.' By this time I had been enjoying the California wines offered, Chardonnay from Sonoma county and Governor's Cuvée champagne, and I was feeling pretty all right with the world, very laid back. On my Walkman tape I heard Al Jolson heading for the 'Golden Gate' where, he cried, he'd live in the sun and love in the moon; on the screen in front was Jackie Gleason, a fat pop-eyed comedian, plus his goofy sidekick and his wifey, silently overwrought in an airless T.V. film-set room; on my lap was a glossy menu in language more satisfying than Dickens and Proust: 'Your flight includes regional specialities culled from our country's rich bounty. During winter the harvest continues, moving to our southerly boundaries. As spring approaches we especially enjoy the abundance for which our land is famed. . . .'

Strapped in like a baby (I always keep my seat-belt tightly fastened), my selection is glad-handed to me by the wholesome stewardess with the chromium cart. Spread in front of me is a splendid feed, sensibly divided in pools of plastic, and I read on as I fork into the tray: 'Enjoy our marinated garden salad, our tidbits of beef tenderloin lightly sautéed in a sauce of beef stock, herbs and cream, with a touch of Dijon mustard, garnished with fresh-buttered fettucine and petits pois, all presented in a garland of wild rice.' To complete my dining pleasure there are liqueurs and also Bailey's Irish Cream, and the print shoots me back, like Proust's plump little cakes, to Trinity College Dublin days and the visit to the Guinness brewery where we failed to locate the legendary sides of aged beef dripping their liquor into anxious vats, but we did sample the extra-strong stout that is exported to certain rowdy African countries where it is used by administrators as a pacifier when the weather is ultra-oppressive and passions run too high. . . . What an annoying keening coming from the man next to me, an Asian in Harris tweed, reading his wine-bottle label, picking his teeth with his own steel toothpick and responding to something on his Walkman! I'm angry, but I won't make a fuss, I won't! Because I remember a flight from Nashville to Los Angeles when, encouraged by my travelling companion Simon Witham (the record executive and Old Marlburian), I complained to the chief steward about a drunk two seats forward similarly headphoned and screaming disco lyrics. I remember how the brute, on learning of my complaint, had confronted me with his great belly and, upon being ignored, had pulled back his elbow in order to slug me but instead had hit the steward who was passing behind him laden with brandies. A federal offence had been committed and so the pilot made an emergency landing in Phoenix, Arizona, in order to deliver the drunk into the arms of the law. At the exit door the brute was in the middle of a threat to fix me when the F.B.I. guys, in rugby shirts, grabbed him and hauled him off to jail. I'd downed a jumbo jet, hadn't I? My deed-crowing was halted when Witham sketched a future scenario: the drunk is an executive, a top one (we were flying first class) and he's fired, his wife divorces him, he ends up flaked-out in a flop-house in downtown L.A. One night he's watching the Johnny Carson show and I come bursting on to the screen with my ukulele and some silly song like 'Frankfurter Sandwiches'. The guy goes berserk, hunts me down and blows off my head with a semi-automatic assault weapon. . . . I wish I'd taken a Valium with my Bailey's Irish Cream.

*

'We will shortly be landing at Los Angeles International Airport. On behalf of the captain and crew, I hope you will have a happy day and that you will fly with us again real soon.'

Below me I saw a wasteland of volcanic crust scored with snaky black lines, a vile place to crash, but shortly we were over brown flatlands squared up like an expectant puzzle, Man's mathematics, safe at last. Now there were friendly green mountains gracefully creased, as if some giant was sleeping under a great billiard table cloth. Into the L.A. basin and more math grid lines, and now rigid, grim, serious industrial buildings that clashed with the map names – San Fernando, Sun Valley, Eagle Rock, Cypress. Ah! But there *was* the City of Industry and the City of Commerce. Were we near them? We were over carefully laid-out houses, many with turquoise swimming blobs, and winding, flowing freeways, frequently meshing cleverly, their silent freight moving inexorably someplace for some reason. What reason had I in L.A.? What purpose? To be a star again? Over Watts all seemed shimmering quiet in the late afternoon haze. Were they really murdering each other for drug turf like the papers say? My *Daily Telegraph* told of No-Go estates in Peckham, not so far from Wildcroft Manor, where milk floats are now armoured with metal grilles and steel sheets to protect milkmen from missiles hurled from tower blocks, and from customers with meat cleavers. I was trying to feel less homesick.

'We have a message for passenger Whitcomb.' (My mother has died, the dog has died. What is it?) The steward handed me a note as I exited: 'Tommy Conway will greet you with French champagne and salutations.' Oh, no! He was sitting on the baggage carousel, legs akimbo, travelling around merrily, toasting me noisily. He was wearing the waistcoat and trousers of my best suit. I stood there, scriptless, aware of my fellow passengers. As he passed me for the second or third time on the carousel, he thrust a plastic champagne glass at me and cackled hideously. I took a sip, but it was all very embarrassing.

He drove me 'home' in my silver Ford Granada and there were more toasts en route; I noticed new tears in the upholstery and odd smells. When we arrived at my rented Spanish-style bungalow in West Hollywood, I also noticed new dents in the car. The *Daily Telegraph* was another country, and I threw it into the trash can. Already I was sticky with jet-lag and drenched in depression.

Outside the house I determined to shut my eyes to the unkemptness I knew lay behind the stucco. Inside I swallowed another Valium, washed down with cold champagne ('Not cold, duck, but real champagne, just for you,' said Tommy) and I fell into bed, which was a queen-size mattress on the floor. I just about heard Tommy say something about going 'tom-catting' before I reached the Land of Nod.

*

Tommy was 21 and I was pushing 40. How had I acquired him? No . . . how had he become my friend? Dr Ronald Bund enters the story again: in late 1970s Hollywood, while continuing the struggle to recapture my stardom, Dr Ronald had presented me with young Tommy on my thirty-fifth birthday, at a restaurant on Santa Monica Boulevard and La Brea. 'Not a gift, as it were, more like a potential companion who might be fashioned into an ideal friend in the great tradition of modern English literature,' explained Dr Ronald over the eggs benedict.

The lad had recently blown into town from a remote farmstead in Minnesota, so I was told, and had no place to stay. He told me he wanted to be a star, like me. We were both wearing T-shirts and jeans. 'He'll be a good specimen for your studies of Southern California life,' said the suited Dr Ronald. Well, that *was* possible – I *had* started contributing the occasional article to *The Listener* and *Radio Times*.

Tommy was a hunky blond of the Nordic type when we first met, and he had spent some time in the U.S. Marine Corps. But after a few months of the sybaritic side of Hollywood life he developed into a rather stocky blond with a Prussian aspect. I hadn't been seeing that much of him as he'd been tremendously busy with parties and things. He showed me his appointment book to prove it. Now he was moving with a rolling strut and dressing in a variety of three-piece suits which were usually several sizes too small. His head was shaved crew-cut, his red face glared angrily (and I knew it meant that the world owed him a living), and altogether he cut such a formidable figure that passers-by would frequently jump out of his path when we were out in public, even in Hollywood.

Indoors one had to be careful too, watching out for and removing, if possible, any fragile object that might be in or near his path. Objects – I had noted wine-glasses, eye-glasses, plates, watches, jewellery – tended to break in his grasp, although he didn't mean to destroy them. He took great care of his own many pairs of glasses, wearing a special tinted pair for our theatre outings. But as a rule he wore contacts since these gave him what he called 'animal magnetism'; he gave me examples of this magnetism as he faithfully followed me around to my meetings, auditions, gigs etc: he would immediately stick out his hand to any person I was talking to (or only contemplating talking to) with, 'Hi, Tommy Conway's my name. I'm an actor.' But no work commensurate to his ambition came up and, after being a victim of a car crash which he was promised would pay him a handsome sum if only he'd be patient, he returned to his Minnesota home to await his fortune.

During the floods of '78 my Hollywood Hills apartment house collapsed under the weight of a sliding hillside, so I moved temporarily to digs in the once-illustrious Montecito Hotel down below, near Hollywood Boulevard. But the place was decaying and drug dealers and other dubious characters were holed up there. The Seacastle all over again . . . I was lonely and suddenly I got a call from Tommy. 'Congratulate me! The lawyer says the accident money's almost through so I'll be *riiiich*!' I told him he could come out and join me at the Montecito and perhaps deal with these drug wretches. 'Yippee!' he said. 'I'm coming!'

He arrived right on the day when I'd just had some worry lines removed by an ace dermatologist; I assured him the scars were not the work of the druggies. He seemed anxious for action. We celebrated with champagne and he pulled out his high school year book and a collection of unstrung tennis rackets he'd somehow acquired en route. As we talked into the night he grew more animated, outlining his driving ambition to make it big in Hollywood. He wasn't strong on game plan details but he had tons of energy, jogging up and down the floor and sometimes pummelling the walls. For my part I questioned him (for possible future articles) as to his family background, but his story kept changing – his father was rich one moment, poor the next, now dead, now alive. A few days later I did discover one hard fact (through an examination of his suitcase): his real name was unpronounceable Italian.

Gradually I introduced Tommy to my friends and for the most part they were tolerant because I have some very loyal friends. Curlew Worthington, the film director and expert on Art Nouveau, gave him a private audience and called me to say he foresaw a career for Tommy if only he could stick to his guns. 'He's trying so hard – and very handy with the motorbike.' Simon Witham, the public school man, answering my query, replied that the living arrangements were perfectly acceptable so long as I didn't mind being considered as queer as a coot. I assured him there'd be none of that in our world. 'Well, you're living right in the middle of the fudge-pounding fraternity,' he said. 'But carry on – it's all good stuff.' Our fellow countryman Basil Jenkins, an Oxford-educated screenwriter with no credits as yet, called round one evening for some Valium and was politely surprised to meet Tommy. I explained, and I think he understood, but then Tommy spoiled things by trying to sell Basil one of his unstrung tennis rackets, with too much energy. Basil, sleek and sallow and quite portly, is not a games player and he beat a hasty retreat, forgetting his Valium. Later, on the phone, he told me that my life was always 'dangerously interesting and interestingly dangerous'. I laughed and then he followed quickly with one of his usual requests for a loan: the deal is 'closing', Jack (Nicholson) will star and Warren (Beatty) will direct, Tri-Star are 'extremely excited', and 'seed money' is coming through any day, but in the meantime, in-between time, can I loan him $500 because he has appearances to keep up, working lunches, breakfasts and teas, not forgetting the cigars.

I lent Basil the money, as was our ritual, and he took a brunch with me at Musso & Frank's, the entertainment industry funky power restaurant on Hollywood Boulevard. Over flannel cakes and bacon he told me that the Montecito was bad for my image and that I should re-locate in a healthier neighbourhood. Beverly Hills was outside my pocket range, I told him. He looked surprised. 'Then it'll have to be West Hollywood,' he said sighingly. 'I know an actor-writer who's a part-time realtor and he happens to have a bijou twenties bungalow for rent. He's a queen, but he's a nice queen and the price is right.'

Scott Brackett was a nice fellow, gentle too, so I pacted with him and moved into the boxy stucco bungalow on La Jolla, near Melrose, in a neighbourhood of basic stucco boxes. But I noticed that the fronts of many of them had been tarted up with tack-on Doric columns and outsize Greek-classical front doors. The owners of these houses seemed, to a man, neat and tidy, even clipped. All wore well-tended moustaches, hardly any walked poodles, some brandished bulldogs and drove high-sprung jeeps and dune buggies. These, I learned, were newly-liberated gays – and their enemies lived on the same street in unimproved boxes: Italian families with lots of children and macho sons-in-law. I told Tommy we were going to try to fit in.

*

After a couple of hours the Valium wore off and I woke up in a muck sweat. Pitch-black, not a chink of light. I panicked . . . where was I? Disorientation on a mattress, but the very fact of the bedless mattress told me I wasn't in the old childhood bedroom on Putney Heath. Then I heard the sirens wailing, felt the unseasonal closeness, smelled the acridity of the room and fell back against the wall in utter depression. Miles from home, miles from my people, miles from success. And my friends, college chums, tucked up in their snug, brick-solid Cotswold cottages and East Sheen maisonettes, all Sir Garnet, lucky devils – while I'm still abroad, still at sea, trying to make that sudden fortune so that when I come back the sheep that was black will be the whitest of them all, like in the music-hall song. But too late, because wife-less, to enjoy twilight years in England when the children build a grandfather house over the garage and there's a nurse to clear up the incontinence and, at the end, dutiful beautiful grandchildren gathered round the bed.

Sod this for a lark! I fished out my black book and called up my friends and even acquaintances, and soon the next week was filled with dinner dates. I felt much better. I told them I was finished with the junky days of my last trip (trips, they're only trips, just here on a visit, back in England soon as April's here), and that I had turned over a brand new leaf – new goals, getting up earlier, going to the gym, making commercial product. Ready for a New World beginning from tonight!

But I couldn't get back to sleep in that fetid hut. Then Tommy appeared from nowhere, breathless, and handed me a sherry. 'British

– I bought it myself – for you.' I soon learned he'd laced the drink with a wicked hash. People, friends even, have been playing this trick on me since the Sixties. They will not accept that I am on a natural high. The result of the tainted sherry was that I became as hyperactive as Tommy, we were like over-candied kids, and we proceeded to dash around the hut for what seemed like days. Tommy was yelling curses on the major studios and agents, prophesying that he would become 'the star to whip all other stars', while I was flashing to soft, wet summer evenings amidst the silver birches of Putney Heath, and my mother in the kitchen preparing a supper of macaroni cheese with grilled tomatoes and best back bacon . . . and she looks out of the window for me, but sees only butterflies flirting in the rain.

The scene changed and I found myself in a hellish corner surrounded by friends who were turning into enemies. So Tommy tried to bring me back to the world I knew and loved by playing an Al Jolson record. But tonight I hated the blubbering masquerader and I shouted, 'Turn off this false prophet who takes Mammy in vain!'

And we commenced racing round the house again, with the stucco falling steadily from the shuddering walls.

*

Next morning Tommy phoned from work to apologize. He was always excellent at apologizing. His current work was in what he called 'tele-marketing' and he'd only been in the business a few weeks (this was the general length of his jobs), but already he knew all the tricks and first names. As a tele-marketeer he sat in a windowless block in the City of Commerce and phoned 'leads' (members of the public), badgering them to buy whatever it was he was selling: stationery, I believe, at that moment. He was making tons of money on paper, on forms, but very little of it seemed to reach his pocket due to 'follow-through failure' and 'deductions'. The boss drove a Mercedes and lived in Newport Beach. Tommy had told him to 'watch out behind', that very morning. This job wasn't going to last long.

Still . . . what was I doing to earn a living? Witham would say that I was 'scrimshanking as usual' – avoiding real work by enjoying myself in self-indulgent hobbies such as singing novelty songs and writing books about them. But, I always protested, such activity is real hard work for me. 'Real work is having to do what one thoroughly dislikes,' he replied. 'And you take a touching delight in your diversions. Don't get me wrong: I envy you, I really do.'

At this time I was preparing to start research on a book commissioned by Doubleday Inc., titled *Rock Odyssey – A Chronicle of the Sixties*. Doubleday, a real major New York publishing house, had given me a large advance and so, relaxing on their cushion, I knew I had my usual three years to spin out the research. Only in the couple of months before promised delivery date would I have to get down to some heavy pounding on the Remington. And I knew I would at some time have to face the horror of dealing with Bob Dylan.

So while Tommy pitched at the telephone down in the City of Commerce, I got ready for a day's book research. A coffee-shop breakfast, though, always came first. Today was the turn of the International House of Pancakes on Sunset Boulevard. A good hour spent slowly masticating bacon and eggs or a tuna melt sandwich, slowly reading the news. Especially the Hollywood news. I could see the steam snorting from these lucky show-biz workers as they focused lenses, inked pacts, wrapped up pictures, took meetings, fixed power breakfasts at the Polo Lounge of the Beverly Hills Hotel. In all this feverish activity, couldn't there be found a place for me? How I hankered to be up there in lights again! The great merry-go-round whirls and I must jump on again and catch a Kleig light, for then all that has been dark in me will be illumined and life's true purpose will be revealed and realized: to be loved by all and to acknowledge that love, pulsing up from the gloom below, with a smile and a wave and the signing of autographs later.

This morning *The Hollywood Reporter* announced that one Jeremy Padgett had opened Crown Management on Sunset Boulevard – why the office must be only a few blocks away from this House of Pancakes! Among the list of clients was Joe Baker, comedian. Now, I knew old Joe because we'd shared variety bills at the Mayfair Music Hall in Santa Monica. Joe had been a star of British T.V. in the Fifties; he played a decent ukulele. I liked old Joe – so I dashed to the nearest pay phone and called him up. Oh yes, said Joe, Padgett was a good 'un, bit of a public school accent but tough as nails. Which school? Joe didn't know. But Padgett was fixing T.V. guest shots, movies, commercials, you name it.

I immediately called Crown Management, spoke to a pert young woman and arranged an appointment. This afternoon, sixish. A quaint weathered shingle hung over their front door. Interior decorators were at work on the staircase. I saw a London Palladium poster from the Forties – Issy Bonn and Jimmy Wheeler, with full chorus. If they'll take old Joe, they'll certainly take me on because I'm more contemporary.

Jeremy Padgett was many years my junior but he had a certain languorous authority, conveyed by his upper-class accent and the way he stuck to his chair. I hadn't the nerve to ask where he'd been to school; I just stood there with my box of records and books. He said, 'And what can we do for you today?' My sales speech was at full throttle (and he was a bit startled by the attack) when there was a buzz on his intercom. Gratefully he took the call. A dinner date. 'Not to worry – I'll be at the café in a jiffy. Order me a ramon fizz and some of those nachos, I love 'em.' I resumed the attack, but he cut in softly with an apology and then, 'But what can *we* do for *you*?' I told him that the movies was the only field I hadn't yet made progress into. . . .

He handed me a long piece of paper. 'Run your eyes down our list. We're very proud. Benny Hill, John Inman, Lance Percival. . . .' I wanted to tell him that Lance was a dear friend of the family, but I didn't dare. 'We're talking with John Cleese at this very moment. If Hollywood needs a star Brit, they call me and I call London and . . .' He clicked his fingers and put on his jacket. 'The British colony here isn't serious about show business. They're part-timers – an Elks Lodge here, a benefit there. A commercial if they're lucky. But they make their livings managing a Burger King or running a foreign auto-repair shop. Gosh! I'm going to be late. . . .' On my way out I left the box of books and records for his future perusal and consideration.

Two weeks later I called up Crown Management. An American girl said, 'Mr Padgett is in a meeting. But he told me to tell you that you may pick up your material at your convenience.' As I was going down the staircase with my box I saw Padgett coming up with a pink-faced man who might have been a 'Yes, Minister' regular. I greeted Padgett and forced him to accept one of my books. He seemed perplexed, casting his eyes around at great speed. When I got home I rang Witham to moan about the experience, ending with the statement that I was retiring from show business. He uttered a long 'phewwwwww' of relief.

Meanwhile I had not neglected quality time devoted to relaxation. The flurry of phone calls I'd made upon arrival was starting to pay off – many dinner dates, too many perhaps, because these were affairs where one went dutch in a public eating place and bills tended to inevitably top the $20 mark (after tax and tip). So I was relieved to be invited to a proper 'at home' dinner by Jack Wontner, a detective-turned best-selling *True Crime* writer. Somehow we had become fast friends (perhaps because of his interest in 'closed institutions', in my case my prep and public schools) but all my friends said it was an odd relationship and Witham pronounced it 'downright unhealthy'. Wontner and his voluptuous blonde wife Wanda were constantly inviting me to join them in 'dining experiences', and when these were to take place in expensive restaurants Wanda would place a special call assuring me that I was *their* guest. Of course, it was understood that I would have my ukulele in the car. The Wontners had lived on the wrong side of town before Jack's success in the literary world, but nowadays they were safe behind a multi-million-dollar walled estate in San Marino, next door to Pasadena, and culturally far removed from Hollywood or Beverly Hills. They were surrounded by old money and non-Jews, and show-biz was a dirty word in these parts. Mrs Wontner's great task was to find ways for Jack to kill time between best-sellers. He would knock off his docu-thrillers in a few weeks of frenzied typing and then return to brooding on the futility of life. At our dinners he'd interrogate me on how exactly I killed my time between dawn and bedtime (and even after bedtime). He believed he might get some 'pointers' from someone as 'fancy-free' as me. Of course, I'd presented him with signed copies of all my works.

Their dinner turned out to be a surprise birthday party for Jack, his dreaded fiftieth year. Wanda had arranged for a helicopter to touch down on their lawn during cocktails and pick up Jack and a Green Beret colonel and then, from a reasonable height, to drop them in a free-fall parachute display for the amusement of the guests. 'Old farts can get it up and bring it down,' she told us through a bullhorn. The stunt came off efficiently and effectively, with Jack spreadeagled against a blood-orange sky and the colonel lashed on top of him. Somehow the couple parted and made a safe landing on the spongy crab grass where they proceeded to wrestle around with much whooping. We were then trooped indoors to watch an instant replay of the adventure on a 45-inch projection T.V. while poker-faced black servants in white tuxedos started serving us Japanese delicacies. After dinner I sang a few dirty music hall songs, followed by Wanda and a woman friend performing a hula dance within the cavernous Spanish-grandee fireplace. They'd squashed their breasts together with masking tape so that the effect was as if they were aiming fleshy assault weapons at us. After Jack's thank-you speech Wanda presented him with a loaf of bread baked in the shape of a phallus. We all laughed and some cheered. Later Jack confided to me, 'The problem in life is being a lapsed Catholic.'

*

70

I had had a letter from Dr Ronald Bund welcoming me back to 'this cultural wasteland' and inviting me to 'partake of a brunch'. He never was much of a dinner man. Evenings he reserved for working on his 'escape projects', the latest being a speculative book to be titled *Great Cities of the Century*. He was anxious to pick my brains about life in London and Dublin during the Sixties, but I was interested in hearing him tell me about the weird side of Los Angeles. We brunched in a dark, dank place off Wilshire Boulevard, a faceless building except for a wavy neon sign that blinked, even in the glare of noon, 'The Shamrock Citadel'. I tackled boiled beef and cabbage while Dr Ron fiddled with a chef salad. 'Summer is i-cumin in again,' he said, patting his grey waistcoat. Before he could wade into the *Great Cities* project I asked after his lads. He replied wistfully that a recent promising discovery, Fred, another ex-Marine, had proved a bitter disappointment. After a period of butlering and maiding at the Bund apartment, the lad had committed a major social faux-pas: in the middle of a Ring Cycle lecture-concert given by Dr Ronald to a circle of local music lovers, Fred had rudely burst in and marched around shaking hands and announcing his name and number. 'I showed him the door in no uncertain terms.' Fred was at present rooming with a transsexual above an animal hospital off Hollywood Boulevard. Yes, that was weird enough for brunch. 'How's young Tommy shaping up?' countered Dr Ronald.

Tommy was between jobs, I said, and then we talked about music.

In fact, Tommy was becoming rather too bossy, one of his less attractive roles. He'd been fired from the telemarketing job, but had immediately been hired as a security guard at Kaiser Memorial Hospital in Hollywood. They gave him a book called *Principles of Security* with a coat of arms embossed on the plastic cover, and a blue uniform covered in bright badges, accessoried with Sam Browne belt and truncheon, completed by a peaked cap smothered in filigree. When dressed up in this rig he had a distinctly fascist appearance; my friends were reluctant to stay long at the house when Tommy was in costume and in the truculent mood that went with it. For a week now I'd had to put up with him barking orders at me to fix him a vodka martini or tie up my gym-shoe, etc. I humoured him, of course. I can see him now leaning back on the sofa, peaked cap smashed in at the back, truncheon swinging from one hand while the other holds one of my show-biz trade papers, sneering at the success of young film actors. 'I'm gonna star in James Clavell's *Tai Pan* if I have to kill! Fuck! I *AM* TAI PAN!!'

Near Kaiser hospital was a Thrifty drugstore, and Tommy had started dating a teenage girl who worked behind the counter. At our house there soon appeared all kinds of goods from toilet requisites to bulky boxes of candy, sunglasses and chewing gum. Then there were cameras and cassette tape recorders. Something fishy was going on and I plucked up the courage to tell him my fears. In a surly voice he replied, 'She just likes to gift me. Why don't you go and get yourself a gift horse, too?'

He had a point; I certainly was in need of some kind of release from the problems heaping up around me. Some easy girl, like the playful ponies I used to get in my rock-star days. Here I was, fresh back in L.A. and brimming over with goals, yet already I was needing Valium to calm me and Lo-Pressor tablets to stop heart palpitations. I must get down to the rock book! But my research was interrrupted by an ultimatum from my landlord, Scott Brackett: he dropped round to tell me he was selling the house, and that the lowest bid he'd accept would be $150,000. I was flabbergasted. 'See here,' he said gently, 'you can join us in my Santa Monica condominium. We're setting up a gay community – we have to stick together – and you're welcome. But no Tommy, absolutely no-no.' I asked him why not. Apparently Tommy had 'no class' and there was also the 'culture gap'. But there was more . . . and sinister: Tommy had been exercising his security guard authority on Scott and his visitors. Scott kept a garden shed in our backyard where he'd entertain his casual boy-friends; Tommy took a dim view of such goings on, and I must admit that the racket was sometimes irritating. Anyway, it seemed that last week Tommy had sneaked up on the lovers and, at the height of their passion, banged on the window with his truncheon and yelled out football plays in a mock-female voice. 'Tommy is a no-no – I'd go further and say that there's dynamite inside that boy which could explode any time.' I thanked Scott for his information and told him I'd let him know about the house. But I had no intention of joining any community, gay or otherwise. All I wanted was peace of mind on a sunny day in a cool house of many rooms, and 'let the rest of the world go by'. I was playing this ballad on my rented piano when Tommy came home in tears.

The hospital had fired him. For taking a short cut through an active operating theatre and 'stuff'. What next? 'Get drunk and get laid.' And off he went.

All this sex talk had fired me up for action and I was determined to get some. I consulted my address book and rang some possibilities, but no go. So I went to an older book and eventually made contact with a flame I hadn't been with in over a year: Beverly Golden. She owed me money and was embarrassed, that's why she hadn't been calling. 'Seems like old times – hope you still wear your tight clothes,' she said cooingly. 'I'm working in cosmetic sales, car work, and you should see the weight I've lost.' I said I'd love to see; she went on to tell me her nose had been fixed better, and that the Jewish Princess face was disappearing; she was excited and we made a date for that very evening.

She wore the same gold lamé sausage-skin jeans she'd worn the first time we met – at the Mayfair Music Hall in the Seventies, chaperoned by her mother. I congratulated her on the weight loss and the new pert nose with the ski-jump finish. 'Yeah – but we still got the overbite to deal with.' Those buck teeth had certainly proved a hazard during oral sex, I remembered. I also remembered that very little of interest ever came out of her mouth, but a lot of expensive food went in. I think she used to starve herself all day in order to gorge at my expense. Of course tonight I'd caught her unprepared, so I was hoping the bill would be reasonable. Although the restaurant was Mexican and usually inexpensive she ordered a special 'Gringo Mignon' steak, the highest-priced item on the menu. Then she had to ask for a doggie bag because she couldn't polish off the chocolate 'suicide' cake. 'You'll get your reward later,' she whispered, wrapping her leg round mine. Thank God for an Access card!

Finally we arrived back at the house and the place was empty. I was trembling with anticipation and ready for my dinner – but was she about to play the card where she complains of food poisoning and asks for a 'rain check'? Luckily I only had to wait while she gobbled up the 'suicide' cake. 'I'm ready for you, lover boy. I'm through with Irv, you know.' Irv, a jeweller, was her on-off fiancé, and the cause of their latest estrangement was his continuing demand for what she termed 'butt fucking'. California heterosexuals, I gathered, were fond of this rearguard action and I told her that I had to agree with Witham that, regardless of the unnaturalness of such a set-up, wasn't there always the chance of an intruding dong colliding with a turd doing its duty? She said, 'You know what? You're worse than Holly-weird.'

At last she was naked and lying on the mattress with hands cupped behind head. 'Tell me when you're through,' she said. I told her the bill total from the Mexican restaurant and that she was being unfair. 'Only kidding,' she said. Then: 'Try this one – *fuck me all night with*

73

your big hard cock!' Not very sincere but it did the trick and I got relief even while wondering whether the action was worth the price of the steak and cake.

While we were cleaning up Tommy poked his head round the corner and said he'd like a 'private audience'. Somehow I felt he'd been spying on us – he'd confessed to voyeurism in the past. Beverly didn't greet him, she hid in the closet and later, after she'd dolled herself up, I let her out of the back door. Then I faced Tommy.

He was the worse for drink – and for lack of sex. He was maudlin, too. 'I heard you talking about the house to that fag Scott. Please don't abandon me in this city of sin.' He started striding around the front room (in one of my Harris tweed jackets, I noted), cloud-bursting his heart. This was the gist: without me as his 'mentor', he might slip into 'degenerate ways', losing sight of his goals. 'You see, I'm like you.' Then he sat me down to see his spiral reporter's notebook and the list of resolutions inside. Next he pulled out from under his sofa-bed a card-file box with words on one side of the card and the *Webster's Dictionary* definition on the other. I was touched.

'C'mon – let's have a study session.' I pointed out the lateness of the hour. 'The night is young, the night is your friend,' he said solemnly. What film was that line from? I agreed to write up my diary on the sofa and he lay on the shag carpet, kicking his legs a lot as he circled job offers in the classified ad section of the *Los Angeles Times*. After a few minutes he said he was going out to remove his contact lenses 'for better study'. He reappeared with a heavy pair of horn-rimmed spectacles perched professorially on the tip of his nose. I laughed with him and felt a little happy.

Now he completed his study environment: switching on the portable T.V. picture only, pulling up my beach chair close to the screen, sitting in it with his newspaper and his dictionary. Every so often he'd jump up and go to the bookshelf to consult one of my books. His favourite was *Our Island Story*. He'd fire questions at me: 'Did good Queen Victoria come before or after the merry monarch?' and so on. Once he got up and pressed his fist against the T.V. screen: 'Remember when we were watching the Grammy Awards and they spelled both Beethoven and Brahms wrong? Boy, was I mad! I could've punched those guys in the mouth.' Eventually we fell asleep.

*

Scott Brackett called to say that he'd had a firm offer for the house: $175,000, half down in cash; the client wanted to move in directly 'escrow closed.' I understood the nub after he gently explained. D-Day was coming . . . and I panicked. Was the Santa Monica community-condominium still available? 'We have real problems establishing our gay paradise. My renters aren't paying their rent, blacks are fighting latinos, there's mess everywhere, and I'm prohibited from evicting a soul because those bleeding heart, knee-jerk liberals on the Santa Monica City Council won't let me raise the rent. I tell you – it's unconscionable!'

After Brackett's bombshell I sat in my poky front-room 'study', head in hands, trying to work out options, desperate for stability. A car horn started blaring long notes – *blaaaaaagh*. . . . A pause. . . . Another *blaaaaaagh*. . . . A pause. The pauses were worse than the blaaaaaaghs because they provided a false peace. I strode outside to deal with the situation, and immediately wished I was wearing long trousers and a jacket instead of the khaki shorts and T-shirt. The noise was the work of the Italian family next door: a fat oily old slug plonked in a stretch Cadillac blasting the horn to move momma out of the house. The lazy bugger had bothered me several times before with this habit but I'd never taken action. Today, on this unnaturally hot afternoon, an explosion filled my skull – I know I heard the *poooooosh* – and I was determined to get this loathsome spaghetti-eater's hide.

I told him he was a blot on Western civilization and more, but he countered with a stream of Italian invective. As language was no use I had no choice but to use force. I swiped the cigar from his mouth, then spun on my heel and strode home, giving him a chance to shoot me in the back. He shouted, 'You know what you are? You're plumb loco!' Such decent American idiom surprised me.

Time to leave the Hollywood life before it got the better of me! That Sunday the March heat-wave was broken by the fall of heavy rains, dumping remorselessly and excessively. I opened the windows and welcomed the rains with outstretched arms. They danced on the greasy sidewalk, creating a running oil which might, by some alchemy, turn into a balsam to soothe the seething anger of this unhappy area – once, long ago, a real neighbourhood. But when at last the sun came out and the street steamed there were the gays same as before thundering around in jeeps and desert vehicles, tight-lipped, I felt sure, behind the regulation moustache and driving without care, of hitting old folk, children or me. On the sidewalk the Italians continued to scream at each other with what I had been told was native natural affection. On the corner of my street Book Circus was once again offering a wide selection of male physique magazines on its out-door racks, and I knew that inside the glossy pages the perfect pecs, baskets and buns were ready to attract business as usual.

My anti-social mood evaporated as we drove out of West Holly-wood, over Laurel Canyon and down into the steaming San Fernando Valley. Tommy and I were to have brunch with my friend Cherie Nussbaum, a fortyish classical cellist who had an enormous bosom, and an earth-motherly effect on me. Two years ago she'd been ex-posed to Scott Joplin and become a born-again ragtimer; of course, in due time, she had been introduced to ragtime's chief disciple, yours truly. After a short talk with me she formed a ragtime orchestra from her symphony colleagues, bought ragtime costumes, named her cat Elite Syncopations and appointed me spiritual leader.

This morning, at her hilltop home in Sherman Oaks, she was ready for us with a 'Ragtime Brunch'. Thank God she hadn't gone the whole hog, with ham hocks and bull's beads and chicken necks. The pork'n'beans (named after the classic rag) was delicious, especially when washed down with champagne.

Cherie was her usual overwrought self, breathlessly telling of new old rags she'd dug up and ragtime buffs she'd befriended (most of whom I'd met during my conversion and was now avoiding). Tommy had wolfed down his brunch only moments after sighting the Aztec tureen; next he sprawled on the chaise-longue with a champagne bottle and glass, ogling Cherie's outstanding breasts as they rose and fell, the waves of her ocean of constant excitement. 'I am truly so *ex-cited*,' she was saying. 'Don't we live in exciting times!' I said I was at present *excitable* rather than *excited*. 'Oh, you intellectuals!' she brayed, throwing back her wide hips and fixing me with a piercing stare. 'Why do you have to be spanners in the windmills of my mind!' I told her I was jittery, worried silly about my need for a new resting place, a base upon which to build a home. She came up close to me and said, 'Why not re-locate where I'm going to re-locate? I'm joining the Ishi people of Altadena!'

Now, I knew of Pasadena from the songs 'Home in Pasadena' and 'The Little Old Lady from Pasadena', and because I had had to drive through that stately city on my way to the Huntington Library. But I knew nothing of *Altadena* except as the name of a vile-tasting raw milk consumed by tree-huggers, sandal-wearers, bitter old hippies and the like. She dismissed this drivel with a wave of her hand. 'Alta-dena is a place of much mystery and enchantment, of hidden man-sions behind stone walls where one can practise one's own belief system. It's also most affordable – Let's trip there now. . . .'

Cherie had always exercised a maternal hold over me and today, with so much insecurity washing about inside of me, her hold became a grip. We three were soon speeding up the Ventura freeway towards off-beat Altadena, and as we passed the Pasadena signs the mountains, sheer and massive, loomed and the rains started again, but now they were soft and bouncy. We turned off at Fair Oaks – what a pleasant, Arcadian name – and our road was lined with fine old trees, stately palms and historic-looking wooden homes, everything glistening as the sun came out to shine on the rain.

But I grew queasy when I realized that the inhabitants, man, woman and child, were shot through with negritude. 'You need to be reconstructed racially – and fast!' said Cherie, waving to a fat woman in a bandana with curlers sticking out. 'You – who like ragtime and jazz and boogie.' I corrected her by adding the 'woogie', trying to lighten my dark remark. Tommy loudly cleared his throat. 'This is nigger town, isn't it?' he said. Cherie replied sternly, 'This is an integrated neighbourhood, probably the most successfully integrated society in the United States. I got that from a U.S.C. professor.'

From Fair Oaks we turned right on Woodbury – the mountains were very close now, I felt I could almost touch them – and at a sign that said 'Christmas Tree Lane' we turned left. 'Cute, isn't it?' she said. Mighty fir trees, like those in my childhood *Wonder Book of Nature*, stooped guardian over us on either side of the convex lane, which was lined with deep storm ditches made from boulders. Still I had seen no white folks; I longed for Fifties families, brushed and upright, walking their dogs and children, but the houses between the firs appeared kempt and their shorn lawns shone a brilliant green. 'Where, prithee, is your so-called estate?' taunted Tommy. Cherie was ever calm and collected. 'Up further, on Santa Anita – but Ian's future comes first. . . . Ah, here's a sales post. . . .' She turned right on a street called East Alameda and there, almost on the corner and sitting on a grassy knoll, was a long, one-storey white house with a green trim and green shutters, and a little red brick chimney on a dark green hipped roof. There were roses round the porch and a tilted wooden post that said: 'Sunnyvale Properties – Affordable Housing – Open House – Step Right In'.

The rains had gone, the sun had triumphed and everything was in 3D, farm-fresh and edible. An old poem from prep school sprang to mind, 'The House of Dreams':

I will make you a little house with a roof of thatch
And a window as clear as crystal dew, and a door
With a knocker of pearl, and a silver dream for a latch
And a carpet of little blue feathers to lay on your floor.

'Come on, sleepy!' said Cherie. 'Maybe Fate has played us the right card.' She parked the Mercedes on the broad driveway in front of the spacious garage.

The front door was wide open. She pressed the door-bell and chimes rang out. 'C'mon in, y'all' cried a high-pitched voice from deep inside.

The front hall led straight into a big airy room with a window stetching down an entire side, and spread all over a couch in front of this window was a bean-pole fellow in stetson and pointed cowboy boots, sucking a pen. Gangling up to greet us, he said, 'Hi, there – my name's Herb Gate, and I'm here to do you a service.' Cherie immediately took charge, asking for an inspection; her voice was hard. Herb blinked, but then beckoned us and we followed his lope around the house. It was much bigger than it appeared from the outside. There was a whole wing attached, complete with what Herb termed a 'half bathroom' (shower, basin and lavatory). The doors of the bedrooms had family names in curly lettering, pink on custard cream: 'Dad & Mom, The Bosses', 'Belinda's Room – Keep Out!', 'Baby's Lair', and 'Ada's – Full O'Secrets.' I started to hum 'Little Man, You've Had A Busy Day' and I thought of Shirley Temple. What the hell game was I playing at? In 'Baby's Lair' a hamster in a cage was working hard on his treadmill; knick-knacks decorated the walls and cot. 'Dad & Mom, The Bosses' was dominated by a huge oxygen tank on a trolley; a canary sang in a corner by the window and there were more knick-knacks. Cherie grimaced. The living room had no books but plenty of blue landscapes and sad Asian women in profile; the carpet was of thick green shag. No doors kept us from dining room or kitchen; the latter was real down-home country – knotty pine cupboards, scalloped wood, two big sinks, a wallpaper design of repeated fruit clusters. Herb wiped his brow and sat down on the bench in the breakfast nook. 'Phew! What y'all make o' this weather?'

I quizzed him on the history of the house. Cherie sighed. 'Bit of a buff, are you?' said Herb. Mr Shea had built the place in, oh, around, 1947 or 8; he was a builder and she was a homemaker, but she didn't care for the house even though he added the wing for her delight; anyway he passed away and she didn't care to live there alone, so she sold

78

up in the early Fifties to the Hutchins, nice friendly folks. Yes, yes – they're white, white as can be. Where are they? Well, see, they're sentimental about having raised a family here and can't bear to see strangers here. (*Interlopers* was more like it, I thought.) 'No offence, people, Gertie's a great ole gal and you should sample her peach pie. . . .'

Cherie was a sharp modern Valley person and she cut into Herb with, 'Let's talk. This is definitely a property for my colleague. Let's talk deeds and escrow.' So while they did that I wandered about the back garden while Tommy swung ape-like on a swing hanging from a sick-looking tall old fir tree. Then I repaired to the front porch and sat and stared at the roses. Was this a world I should intrude upon? I was no family man but a bachelor, possibly confirmed. When Witham and I, exploring L.A. on one of our weekend trips, had happened upon a cheery restaurant and were bent on entering Witham had pointed out the sign saying 'Family Restaurant' and held me back. 'We can't go in there because we're not family.' I was coming in on a family nest and about to despoil. Yes, I might well find the money to put down on this property but that didn't buy me a home . . . for that takes a heap of living in it with babies born and little shoes and death-watch round a loved one's bed while all the while the honeysuckle you planted grows and grows and grows. . . .

Cherie called me inside. 'Put your first payment down and fast.' I said how nice it would be living so close to her and the Ishi people. 'All in good time,' she said. That night, in West Hollywood, I gave Herb a deposit for the house on Alameda St, Altadena. Now all I had to do was wait till escrow was completed and a loan approved. Family accountants were consulted; forms filled out. In the West Hollywood hut I held on, creating a dream home of domestic stability hard by the foothills of the San Gabriels. I envisioned black and white check tablecloths, sizzling roasts, a crackling log fire, a bouncing dog.

Cherie took care of the dog. She had the very animal for me waiting in the Valley, near Studio City. A violinist of her acquaintance had a German Shepherd mixed breed and no time for him. Take him on loan, don't commit, do it now, the dog is you.

We drove out to see Karen Stewart the following Sunday, a day of breezes. Her bungalow on Rosalita Avenue had been taken over by her dogs, mainly African miniatures – she was breeding them everywhere and over everything they were making their mark. Her own tiny living quarter was a sunken room in a corner of this tract shack, covered in dust like everywhere else, but free from dog messes

79

because cordoned off with fencing. She looked harried and grimy, but she grinned when I told her I would like a great big friendly dog like the ones I grew up with in England. A story-book dog.

She led us past the nasty yappers out into a bleak and scalding concrete backyard – and there, racing around crazily everywhichwhere, was Beefy. He was broad of beam in those days and both ears were sticking up. He had only a few scars.

Karen put him through his paces; he had a small but impressive repertoire: he could sit and lie down and put out his paw in supplication; he could race for the ball, especially one with a bell; and he had a party trick which was to slink off with tail between legs when the magic word 'pooh!' was spoken. Above all, he was very, very affectionate. He seemed to take to us immediately. 'He takes to everyone,' said Karen. Then, hastily, 'But yes – he certainly takes to *you* . . . and er, you.' Tommy ignored her and I said I'd take Beefy for a walkie. 'He's all yours,' she replied, waving us out and jerking her head round in response to a howling. I told her that Beefy was actually still *hers*, but maybe we could give him a nice home.

We tested him in Griffith Park. On the way he straddled front seat and back seat, stretched out over the gear lever; he drooled with excited anticipation, he barked deep and long, too. Immediately we arrived and opened the door he was out in a flash, rushing up to people and licking them. At the public lavatory near the Observatory he scared away a gaggle of men. 'That's where they caught Sal Mineo with Rock Hudson,' said Tommy. I congratulated him on his history. 'There's lots I know – just watch me,' he replied. Beefy rushed us through the park, but eventually I got him back in the car – no thanks to Tommy, who had been encouraging his wild racing by yelping out 'Yippeeeee!' and competing in the race.

We took him back to tea in West Hollywood – I wanted to parade him and watch the reaction. With the dog and the boy flanking me the neighbours at last displayed some respect – they jumped off the sidewalk fast. And at tea, when the Italians started in on another operatic screaming match, I merely took Beefy outside and past their front window. A terrible silence fell.

In the evening we returned him to Karen until the day of the move. All I needed was a wife to complete the picture.

*

While escrow and loan were pending I made many trips up to the new house, showing off to friends, wanting their approval. Witham came first and approved of the house. ('Neat but not gaudy') but was fearful of the setting, stating baldly that this was a ghetto, and insisting on parking his Jaguar in my garage lest natives steal his gem. The Jack Wontners agreed to inspect the property but they concentrated on land value and appreciation – 'Fix up and then sell up' was their advice. Had I seen 'comparables?' Had I haggled over the price? When Jack was on an advice kick you didn't butt in, you simply nodded and answered, 'Yes, sir.' He had my best interests at heart, believe him. He took an instant dislike to Herb Gate. With his lazy way of talking, his slouch, his dopey face, his Colt-45 belt-buckle, Herb maybe reminded Jack too much of his own proletarian background. Anyway, under Jack's piercing blue-eyed stare Herb went to pieces, staggering into furniture and dropping his Gs. He'd seen some T.V. movies of Jack's best-sellers and kept saying so.

But Jack was a good friend and he sent up a detective colleague to check out the neighbourhood and report back to me. 'You got boarded-up store-fronts and abandoned supermarkets – always a sign of a deteriorating area. Let's face it: when ethnics move in, property values go down and will never rise again. That's a fact of life, and life is what we deal with.' I called Jack for his final comment and he said that I had better start facing up to real life. 'But we love you just the same,' said his wife on an extension phone.

Dr Ronald was not enthusiastic. He blanched at the oxygen tent and tripped over a turtle in the back garden. Then he took me out front to see his car, a rented Rolls Royce. In the midday glare I noticed that he was wearing full make-up, but he quickly explained that this was his weekend for entertaining new recruits from the Camp Pendleton Marine Corps base, and therefore car, powder and paint were necessary for impressionable lads. 'Give them some culture and good victuals and you'll get some ladslove in return. Fair exchange, no robbery.' He ordered his Marine of the day out of the Rolls: 'Meet THE Ian Whitcomb – singer, writer, actor, personality and general all-rounder.' I asked the boy what *his* speciality might be. 'Same as you,' he said. By this time Herb had ambled out to join the party (Was he camping there? He was always around) and Dr Ronald, pleased to have more audience, said to the boy, 'And I suppose, like Mr Whitcomb, you're English, too.' 'I am, sir – from England-land through and through.' Whereabouts? 'From the border between Britain and England-land.' Even Herb had a cackle – he was in much better form than on the Wontner day – and then he waggled his hips, put a finger to his mouth, and led us on exaggerated tiptoes into the kitchen.

There, hunched at the breakfast nook table, was a craggy old man with upstanding tufts of grey hair, puffing on a cigarette. His face seemed full of the sadness of ages. 'Meet THE Mr Hutchins, the old owner himself,' announced Herb, in the style of Dr Ron. I felt Herb was getting a bit above himself. The craggy old man staggered to his feet and stretched out a hand. 'He ain't talkin' today 'cos he ain't so good,' said Herb, waving Mr Hutchins back into his nook. 'House holds a lotta memories and he don't like to vacate. His soul is sorta wrapped round everything, even the 21-inch console. Still, I moved 'em to a real desirable apartment in Temple City. . . . Life rolls on.'

I told the old man I'd take care of his home, keep the traditions going. But I wondered if he believed me and what he thought of this weird group – the painted Dr Ronald in his too-tight ice-cream suit, the bullet-headed Marine, and the foppish, stuttering foreigner. Dr Ronald stepped into the awkward pause: 'Never fear, Mr Hutchins – my friend may be an ex-rock star, but I can assure you he's fully house-trained. Ha, ha!'

The day was bright and clear – and there was no Tommy around to complicate matters (he was in Hollywood, seeking work, he'd said). Herb offered to take us on a tour of the area in his Jeep. We saw the site of the railway terminal where, in the Gay Nineties, tourists used to take the trip up to Mount Lowe and stay in fine resort hotels. All gone, long ago. We saw the Zane Grey house, a Spanish affair where he wrote many of his Western novels – now the building was deserted and derelict. 'Looky over yonder – that's the house where Henry Ford invented his auto engine, and here's where a movie star lived.' We also learned that the broad avenue, Lake, which neatly divided Altadena into two, also divided us economically and sociologically: to the West (my side) the householders grew blacker and poorer, to the East they grew whiter and richer. Herb confessed that he lived on the East side. 'But don't be frightened, you're safe where you are. Mind you, if you go further down you'll find recklessness – they don't honour no red lights or stop signs over there.'

By this time in the afternoon the Marine was growing restless, singing loudly and kicking the back of Herb's seat. He'd also taken to hurling racial taunts at bystanders. Said Dr Ronald, 'High time we took our leave – Hollywood ho! – for us.' I was rather relieved to see them go. Herb said he could safely introduce me to some of the local folks who might be of use. We dropped in on the post office, where the postmaster arranged for a P.O. Box. At Security Pacific Bank, an

82

example of Fifties blockhouse, I shared a joke with the manager, a magnificent bejewelled black woman in a Pan-African shift. While there I noticed Mr Hutchins huddled with a teller, both figuring furiously. 'He's withdrawing every penny,' said Herb. 'Pulling up stakes. End of an era. *Psssssssht!*' He spat some phlegm into a trash basket.

Finally he showed me the charming, tree-shaded library and the 1920s country club – and I pictured myself swotting up for my rock book and then, in the late afternoon on a sunny day, dropping in to the club for a cold beer and perhaps a few games of tennis. Who knows? I might even take up golf.

The grandest visitor to my new property was my friend Vik Goodleaf, the ex-butler. An extremely practical man, full of ex-pedience ('Well, I did graduate from the School of Hard Knocks') and always well-supplied with material from his previous employees (silverware, sofas, chests of drawers etc), he was not particularly well liked by my other friends. Witham said he was 'common as muck and queer as a coot'; Dr Ronald found him lacking in true culture ('A "piss-elegant queen" describes him – if I ever used such language'); and as for Jack Wontner – he was ever alert when Vik came visiting with me, suspicious of his intentions regarding their precious antique collections, especially his wife's silver snuff-boxes: 'If I caught him I'd blow him away with a Magnum.'

But Vik had been very kind to me in the past, tidying up my Hollywood digs and apartment, providing me with useful equipment like corkscrews or couches, sometimes from the homes of famous movie stars. He'd had access to a lot of expensive houses because his main background experience was gained from many years as Bette Davis' butler. Since leaving her employ under a dark cloud, he'd taken on much of her personality – the firing out of words, the hip stance, the circling of the cigarette, the general waspishness. He was always a good show, but a bit trying after a whole day's performance.

The day Vik came up to the house he was at his Bette Davis bitch-iest and old man Hutchins happened to be hanging around, and at his saddest. I was letting Vik rip because he'd kindly agreed to supervise the big move. Hutchins wandered in from the back garden, wearing denim overalls smeared with dirt. Today he was talking and he immediately went close to Vik and confided with much melancholy, 'I been out with the turtles, tryin' to corral 'em, but they don't come easy.' Vik said, 'Let me at them and they'll soon be soup, the *real* not the *mock*, as dear Cole Porter used to say.' But old man Hutchins didn't seem to hear, just headed for his breakfast nook and pulled out a cigarette. I sat down with him, and thought I saw a tear in his eye as he talked and talked about leaving his home. 'Like a heaven she's been, this ole house,' as he puffed and polished the buttons on his overalls. 'Raised five children, all daughters, raised 'em with my own hands – hand-raised, you might say.' Luckily Vik was with his measuring tape in the living room, so we were spared any joke about 'hand-jobs.' 'Gertie – that's my other half – she won't come near the house – too many fond memories. . . .' I asked delicately about the tint of the neighbours on either side and across the way and in fact down the street. 'Oh, they're coloured all right – but they're good people, quiet and law-abiding, and they take especial care of their lawns. Very church-going, very – I'll say.'

He got up and said he was going to have a final 'mooch of the house', and when he was mooching past the living room he *must* have heard Vik state loudly and shrilly, 'These *drapes* will *have* to go!And *lots* more besides in this house of low kitsch!' Vik fixed his eye on me, rotated his wrist speedily and announced, 'Hold on to your hat, ducky – you're in for a bumpy move!'

*

The Move, on a clear, clean April day, didn't go so badly, all in all, and taking everybody into consideration. I let Vik be commander-in-chief with Tommy as his aide-de-camp and general dogsbody. For me the day started pleasingly as one of the moving men turned out to be a fan from my rock days. 'Did you make any more records after that crazy one?' Immediately I informed him of my dozen or so albums and singles. 'Get on with it!' ordered Vik.

Tommy jerked a picture nail out of the wall and a heap of rubble fell to the floor. Through the new hole I peered, past the chicken wire and thin wood struts and into the street. What a jerry-built shack! Thank God I hadn't the money to buy such chintz-trash! Vik commanded the moving van to stop off at a 'friend's' house en route to Altadena. We never met the friend – there was nobody there – but Vik had a way with a window and he soon had us loading furniture into the van – a studio couch/bed, a Greek statue and a futon. He also insisted on my accepting an enormous and hideous oil painting of bad-tempered waves breaking in yellow moonlight. He said I needed a touch of class in my new house. 'Maybe even a touch of mink.'

When at last we arrived at Alameda St it was late afternoon. The house was empty and stripped of every sign of the Hutchins family.

Well, almost every sign: Vik wanted to rip all the curtains down at once, but I prevailed. I liked the homey curtains. 'Then get a wife,' he said. Tommy chose the bedroom next to mine (which of course was the master bedroom, now minus the oxygen equipment), and set to work chipping off the notice that said 'Belinda's Room – Keep Out.' He chipped with a vengeance. I said that 'Baby's Lair' should become the T.V. room, but nobody was listening.

Out in front I found Vik shrieking at a Japanese gardener (another inheritance from the Hutchins) about whether or not a holly tree should be cut down. I was amused to hear Vik describe himself as 'Mr Whitcomb's manager.' The little Japanese shrugged and continued hacking at the holly tree.

After a while, realizing there was little I could contribute, I retreated to the room at the back of the house, at the end of the wing – 'Ada's Room – Full O'Secrets' – a room sunk below the back lawn so that looking out I felt like a worm. The fir tree towered and even the blades of grass bossed me; I was getting a worm's-eye view when what I wanted in life was an eagle's-eye view, all very symbolic. A squirrel popped round the window pane to examine me rather imperiously, looking down at me as I kneeled there. I decided this room would become my study.

For a long time I stayed in that room – long after Vik and Tommy had carried in my typewriter and my ukuleles and left. I gave these favourite things a heartfelt welcome because they were old friends, very reliable, and had travelled two continents with me. I talked to them about the new and ordered life that was to commence in this house of fresh-painted cream walls and shag carpet smelling of country-pine aerosol. From my rustic perch on the hill above the great Los Angeles plain I would survey the bustle of the Angelenos, and I would record and comment and not be drawn into the battle – unless called upon professionally. Perhaps I would get to know myself.

Herb interrupted my reveries; he entered the study noisily and stood at a crooked angle, hitching up his jeans. 'Jest dropped round to make sure everything's fine and dandy.' Before I had a chance to thank him Vik appeared and said apropos of nothing, 'I'd like to know about your *wife*, Herbert.' Herb knocked back his cowboy hat, leaned against the wall and said, 'Hell, I ain't got one of those!' 'I didn't think so.' Hastily I made an introduction. 'My dear Ian,' said Vik, 'we've been acquainting ourselves while his majesty was dreaming. Some of us *work*, you know.'

I suggested we all go out for a celebratory dinner. 'Who's in the chair?' demanded Vik. I told them I would credit-card the do and everybody was happy. Herb suggested Monahan's, an 'Oirish' pub-restaurant run by a genuine ex-Dubliner called Monahan. During dinner Tommy and Vik got a bit drunk and Vik, in particular, got silly – taunting some Irish-Americans at the next table who'd been discussing tartans. Fortunately the bill arrived as the situation was growing tricky, and I created a diversion by making a fuss with the waiter about the price of the wine.

Afterwards Tommy and Herb helped me bundle Vik into his Ford Pinto and we waved him on his way back to Sherman Oaks where he was currently butlering for a T.V. soap-opera-star actress. He'd been jolly helpful, though, and a good friend at heart.

In celebration of our first night in the new house I offered Tommy a brandy. 'We have no brandy glasses. You have to have that special glass,' said Tommy. I said we'd have to make do with coffee cups. I put on a record of the old cowboy song 'There's a New World Beginning from Tonight', an inspirational number. Tommy listened for a while, swilling his brandy around in both cup and mouth. When I began to read aloud from *Boys' Own Annual of 1919* he said 'Goodnight' and staggered off to his own private dorm while I was left contemplating my new world alone.

As I had yet to buy a proper bed I chose to sleep on the living-room couch, one of Vik's many gifts. I tried to make it resemble a proper bed by wrapping it in sheets and blankets and crowning it with an eiderdown. Once inside, and wearing my pyjamas again, I read the deed to my new property: 'Home-owner: Ian Whitcomb, a Single Man.' *A Single Man* – what a sad, hollow ring! I tossed about to this thought. The deed wasn't doing the trick of sending me off to sleep, so I fished out the *Old Bryanstonian Yearbook (1978)* and turned to the *'News of Old Bryanstonians'*:

I. WHITCOMB (Salisbury House, 1959). I am now a permanent resident alien in America, living in Hollywood, which is full of crime and vice and excitement and I love it here like one loves danger. I exist as an entertainer, but my main and most serious work is as a writer. I return to England from time to time, and sometimes sneak down to Bryanston to watch the cricket. And as a civilized touch to my Hollywood house I have hanging a framed Bryanston School group of 1958.

My eye roamed to the next entry:

J. WILLINGTON (Dorset House, 1945). Still happily farming near Sandringham, Norfolk. Captain of village cricket team, lay preacher in local church. 'Cast your bread upon the waters' – we have been blessed greatly by our children, our youngest Timmy being now at Oxford reading Theology. We have three grandchildren and more on the way. 'By their fruits ye shall know them!' Thank you, Bryanston, for preparing me for a satisfying life.

How awful I felt! But then I consoled myself by thinking of Beefy . . . for tomorrow he would be joining us, coming to stay here for ever and ever, amen.

*

I awoke with an aching back and a sense of impending panic. There was an aroma coming from the kitchen which should have been bacon and eggs but wasn't; it was burning cigarette. On inspection I found a smouldering Marlboro' cliff-hanging on the knotty-pine breadboard; in the sink was a wet butt; in the bath was another dead one. Cupboards were open, crumbs were about, and so were pieces of clothing. Tommy was gone someplace; I must have overslept, I must start laying down the law as head of this house.

So I pinned a note to the bulletin board in the kitchen: a numbered list of house rules. Then I went down to Pasadena to join the Y.M.C.A. When I returned, Tommy's sports car was parked on the front lawn but he wasn't in or around the house. I searched and searched but all I found was a scrawled addition to my house rules: '*Who do you think you are?* GOD?!?'

But I cheered myself by looking forward to the day's important job. Adding Beefy to the household would be a major step towards transforming this house into a home. I drove to Studio City via some high-numbered freeway which hugged the side of crumbly hills and afforded me a fine panorama of L.A., to my left, complete with downtown skyscrapers and Griffith Park. The Ford Granada was rolling smoothly, the steady movement elated me, and I had a heart-lifting cassette of George Formby, the Ukulele Man, playing. Yes, in the far horizon there was a rusty strip stretched across the whole view and I knew this was smog – but in all my many years here in L.A. I have never been aware of the harmful effects of smog. In fact, the soupy brown haze gives a romantic, even mysterious air to L.A. and I'm in favour. This merry morning, with Formby's hen-cluck plucking, the friendly competition of the cars beside me and the splendid view, I felt in rattling good form. At peace with the world, safe in my musical car.

Beefy was all over me, recognizing me at once. Karen gave me his stone drinking bowl and some complimentary cans of Kal Kan, the meat of her choice. She spent some time hugging him, the great cuddly beast with a head as big as mine. After releasing him from the hug she didn't speak another word, to him or to me. As we drove off I waved but she didn't acknowledge either of us. She just stood motionless in her doorway on Rosalita Avenue, watching us go. She was still standing and staring as we rounded the corner on to Roscoe Boulevard.

Back at the house Beefy spent the first few hours sniffing his way towards a knowledge of every nook and cranny, though he didn't seem very taken by the trees. Meanwhile I busied myself by removing the controversial house rules and composing a more positive and constructive notice titled 'Getting Our House Together Days'. Around tea-time Tommy returned from wherever he'd been and was in an expansive mood, slapping me on the back a lot and trotting along behind me when I moved around the house. Beefy came too – an odd but touching trio. The boy and the dog watched me as I hung pictures – a Constable reproduction, a school group, the family at Sandringham – and hung blankets on the bedroom windows to act as curtains. Vik had promised to run up some real curtains when he had the time; he'd also promised me a tie-rack, which I didn't need in these parts. Our first evening together was celebrated with a Tommy Conway Special Blue Plate Dinner: a skillet fry-up of the various odd-bod foods we'd brought from the West Hollywood house – Chinese sub-gum soup, spare ribs, hot dogs and macaroni cheese from a packet. We washed down the concoction with Mountain Rhine wine from a Gallo jug (only $3.50 from the supermarket). By the end of the evening we were friends again for life. I offered to read some R.L.Stevenson, but Tommy said he'd rather watch T.V. – 'The educational channel'.

I had bought Beefy a collar and lead and I decided to harness him up and show him the neighbourhood – a quiet walk round the block, so I assumed. But almost immediately after we hit the street a massed barking and howling began. What had my dog done to deserve such a noise? Lights came on and doors opened but I marched on regardless. I was taking my dog for his evening walk and that was that. If certain Americans kept dogs as vicious guards and never exercised them on the street, then it was their problem if a racket resulted from my perfectly legitimate activity. When I told Tommy my feelings he said I was a 'fool asking for trouble' and that I risked being 'gunned down by one of these coons.' As we hadn't met our neighbours yet, I suggested we reserve judgement.

Beefy was very restless during the night, wandering from room to room, his nails making much noise, then his tail would thump the floor when he scratched himself. I lay on the sofa in the living room and made a mental tally of what was right and what was wrong with my life at this point. I really wanted to call this 'living room' a 'sun lounge', like you have in Eastbourne or Seaford. Beefy jumped on top of me and licked me and cheered me up no end.

'Getting Our House Together Days' involved work for me, and me alone. Tommy stayed in his room till past noon – sleeping on my old mattress – and after that he snoozed on the sofa till I'd finished supervising the arrival of the new furniture (which included a real bed). Selecting a brown vinyl reclining chair – a Barcalounger – he stretched out and spent the rest of the day lounging. Even when the 7-foot brown bookcase (the tallest made, said the company) had difficulty getting though the front door, Tommy remained in his chair, leaving me and the Mexicans to negotiate the journey to the far wall, next to the brown upright piano. Everything in the lounge was a shade of brown, and the World War One posters had a tawny overall colour. This brownness made for a nice masculine smoky club atmosphere; no feminine frills here.

Herb dropped round and pronounced the house 'different' and generally 'neat'. He reminded me that I'd asked for metal gates and wire mesh on all the side-door windows. 'To keep the critter in or out or whatever – *you're* paying.' He had the materials with him and he ordered Tommy to assist him in his work, kicking the lazy boy with his pointed cowboy boot. Amazingly, Tommy obeyed him – something in the voice, perhaps – but I felt Herb was taking a chance because Tommy could turn mean, especially when drunk. Yet here was Tommy dutifully following Herb out into the garden. And Beefy followed in turn. So far, all was well.

*

At the weekend life started going awry again. Little things, but they added up. First off, I came back from the Y.M.C.A. on Saturday morning to find that Beefy had clawed through the new wire-mesh screen door in the corridor. Herb's tone of authority had persuaded me to keep the dog outside. Herb had said, 'Outside is where a hound dog should naturally live – guarding and living like an animal. Inside is for human folk.' There simply wasn't time to get the screen door fixed because there was food and drink to be bought at the local supermarket.

For I had decided to throw a little dinner party, a sort of house-warming. Vik arrived early to run the affair. He started by ordering around the Japanese gardener (whose name, I learned, was Benjamin Watson), and I had to quietly take the bewildered Benjamin aside and tell him to ignore Vik's instructions but to keep smiling. Vik was determined to have my rambling, unkempt garden 'landscaped', but I wanted a natural 'English' look. 'English, my foot!' he said. 'You want chaos – and I bring you a new order!' I tried to humour him, because he was cooking dinner and he'd also brought more furniture; this time, he said, from a 'famous film star who shall be nameless!' One piece was a fine 1930s steamer trunk, another was a Louis XIV/M.G.M. chaise-longue. Both went into my bedroom before Tommy could seize them.

When it came to food Tommy shaped up. He eagerly accompanied Vik, me and Beefy to the Market Basket supermarket a few blocks away on Lake Avenue. It was at this point that I became aware of the large number of blacks in our neighbourhood. In fact, I had yet to see any local whites, apart from Herb. Of course, in theory, and in class-room, and on the media, this situation would have been nothing to complain about. Here was a decent, peaceful, clean, leafy, manicure-lawned town – testimony to the fact that blacks could live as bour-geois as whites.

And yet, tonight in the gathering gloom, I felt uneasy living in an inkiness relieved by white moons. Minstrel shows and the blues were one thing, but this new reality was quite another. Still, I could pre-tend to be the district commissioner in an African outpost. I thought of Conrad. Or, at least, of what Whitham and Dr Ronald had told me of Conrad's Africa.

Once inside the Market Basket the world was bright and vivid and bursting with all kinds of wonderful foods. Vik selected some sirloin steaks and a clutch of fresh corn ears; I selected some more Gallo wine – such a reasonable price. 'And anyway, none of your friends have any taste,' said Vik. I gave him a hurt glance. He was wearing sandals with no socks, and a bright mauve tennis shirt. But he had been most helpful to me all through the Seventies.

Beefy, tied up at the Market Basket entrance, was greeting shop-pers with tail-wags and panting. I was dismayed to see that most of the shoppers jumped away from his hospitality. Again and again they would ask, 'Do he bite?' Finally, in exasperation, I replied to a dear old black man, 'Of course he bites – he bites his food and those who attack him or his friends!' 'Oh, do shut up!' said Vik.

At the crossing on Lake Avenue a group of young black kids shrieked and roared when they saw Beefy. I lost my temper yet again. 'Don't be so stupid! How can you react so to such a beautiful creation? You who are so misbegotten!' Luckily they didn't hear me, or they didn't understand what I was talking about, because they moved away and started singing exuberantly. But I instantly regretted this outburst and Vik said I was lucky to be an incomprehensible alien. 'I'm in charge now,' he ordered in a World War Two pilot voice.

During the dinner party I kept quiet, ruminating and regretting; so I don't remember much about the occasion. The guests appeared to be enjoying themselves; at least they were eating and drinking. Tommy made an entrance during the main course, carrying aloft a tray of beer, nuts and potato chips as he announced, 'Can-apays and ors de vore!' I hadn't the heart to tick him off for parking his car on the front lawn. Dr Ronald arrived late but almost immediately tapped his glass and called for a toast: 'May your ships come in at last, and may your new house become a still centre of tranquillity.' 'That's a bit piss elegant,' said Vik. 'I don't think you're from the class of old England that I so love and admire,' said Dr Ronald. 'No, mate – I'm from the Academy of Hard Knocks,' said Vik. The other guests talked among themselves. Tommy said, 'You guys!' and bear-hugged them both. Dr Ronald, ever the perfect gentleman, turned to me and asked, 'At what place do you develop your admirable pectorals?' I told him about the Pasadena Y.M.C.A., but Vik chipped in, 'Aren't we there under false pretences, ducky? You're neither a young man nor a Christian!' I made a mental note about not mixing my wide circle of friends in future.

Around 10 p.m. when we were at the coffee stage and Tommy was wishing we had some brandy, the phone rang. I answered it and a gruff voice said, 'We don't like faggots moving into our town. Get out now or we'll kill you!' This scared me tremendously, but nobody else seemed worried when I told them. After the guests had gone and Tommy was flat out on the floor of his room I called the local Sheriff's Department. Three hours later the police arrived – two bluff, burly officers, ranging around the house and garden, sniffing suspiciously, swaying like cypresses in the wind. No, they wouldn't sit down, no coffee, no drinks. They wanted to know my age compared with Tommy's. They rattled some doors, banged on some walls and told me I was a 'burglar's dream'. They recommended new locks all round. I went to bed lonely and frightened.

*

Now when the morn was newly arisen, and long after roseate-fingered dawn had been and gone, I rose from my bed feeling much better (a dose of Homer, by way of *Classics Illustrated*). At breakfast time we were visited by a sweet old lady bearing gifts from local merchants. 'I'm the Welcome Wagon,' she chirped merrily, and I told Tommy to put some trousers on. Examining her gifts later, over All-Bran, I saw that most were discount tokens. The Welcome Wagon lady had strongly recommended a local eatery, Applegate's Landing, as a 'real family house with home-cooked farmhouse-style meals.'

That evening I entertained both Tommy and my girl-friend Beverly at Applegate's Landing because both had recently been fired from whatever jobs they were doing, and because I hoped Beverly might be persuaded into some sex later. We ate baked meat loaf with mashed potatoes and jelly, followed by apple turnovers and ice-cream; we drank lemonade or iced tea. In order to get Beverly in the right mood I stopped us off on the way home at a liquor store and bought cans of ready-mixed margaritas, a Mexican tequila cocktail which is quite potent.

Tommy and Beverly had a laugh when we arrived back at the house: Beefy had smashed his way through the big plate-glass window and into the living room; waste-baskets were upturned, cupboards were open, the dog was so very pleased to see us. I rang Herb for advice. He said the dog was lonely and bored and needed proper training. 'Call the German Shepherd Association.' I said that was all very well, but I was a busy man. 'Then get rid of the critter.'

Meanwhile, in the living room, Tommy and Beverly had broached the margaritas and were sprawled on the floor, deeply engaged in a game of backgammon. Beefy was lying with them too. They were oblivious to me, so I fiddled about at the piano on an old saloon ballad. And later, much later, Beverly was persuaded to my room where, eventually, I persuaded her to give me a back rub. But just as I was at the point of turning over to ask for a front rub the doorbell chimed. I only had a towel covering me, but the two policemen registered no disapproval. Refusing margaritas and seats, they handed me a long list of anti-burglar devices involving dead-bolts, chains and

92

talking alarms. 'Example number one will say "You are trespassing on private property – the police have been called – please leave quietly and at once". Highly recommended.' I thanked them profusely and ushered them out. But Beverly was up and dressed and applying her make-up when I returned to the bedroom so the evening was a washout as far as sex was concerned. I saw her off into the night and then went to bed with *Sorrel and Son* by Warwick Deeping, who knew all about the lore of the true gentleman.

*

Over the next few weeks I attempted to settle down to research for the Doubleday rock book. I bought yellow legal pads and a box of Japanese 'rolling-writer' pens; I bought a tin of Dutch cheroots because I had found that, in the past, the act of lighting up could ease me into starting work; I bought a ton of books about the rocking Sixties. Tommy was always off somewhere in his sports car, but he never told me where – except on one day when I caught him inviting Beefy into his car, to join a giggling teenage girl. 'We're all going to the beach,' he said. I told him he was NOT taking *my* dog Beefy to the beach. He turned on his heel, let out the dog and screeched off, flinging out the lead. But after all, Beefy was my dog and my responsibility. . . .

Tommy was gone for days and I was alone, except for my dog, and he didn't want anything to do with me. He even went to bed in Tommy's room and all day long he lay around near his bedroom door. One night I was woken up by bloodcurdling howls and found him sitting on the front lawn, long lean head pointed to the sky, eyes closed and howling like a wolf. I guessed he was pining for Tommy and dragged him in lest the neighbours complained.

I needn't have worried about the neighbours; they turned out to be a peace-loving, almost complaisant people. I had my opportunity to meet them when Herb and his men came to put up a wire fence so as to keep Beefy inside the property. The neighbours were all very interested, explained Herb, because they were not used to domestic fences. 'T'aint considered *democratic* round these parts.' Strolling over to the lawn on my left, I was able to catch a mixed-marriage couple bringing their child home from school. They were Franklin, black, and his blonde wife Gloria, and they wished me a happy day but had to tend to the child. On the other side of my house I saw a stocky, moustached black man in a pin-striped suit directing the mowing of his lawn and the polishing of his car by two young boys. As casually as I could, I strolled over and introduced myself, but I couldn't help a few stutters, I was so nervous.

He wiped his hands on a large handkerchief and gave me a hearty handshake. In a deep, melodious and secure voice he said, 'Good afternoon. My name is Norton Goldsmith.' We chatted a while and I learned he was vice-president of a savings and loan company as well as being a Baptist minister. I asked if he was presently preaching. He was downcast. 'We are hoping to break ground on some fine Pasadena realty, but first we must overcome escrow.' Then he brightened up. 'But until that joyful day we are worshipping the Lord over yonder,' and he pointed to his garage and changed the subject to gardening. 'Might I suggest a trimmer cut for your lawn? And some close work on your roses – for they are very old roses and need special attention.' I invited Mr Goldsmith and his 'number one' son on to my property to inspect these roses at closer quarters. They came timidly; Beefy was lunging at them from my bedroom window, but I assured them he was a peaceful soul. As they bent to the roses I mentioned my piano playing and hoped they didn't mind the noise and the raw state of my blues. 'We only perform gospel in our home,' said Norton Goldsmith. 'Only gospel.' I was very impressed. I was keen to tour the Goldsmith home, to see what books they had, what paintings . . . but the offer was not forthcoming.

After the rose inspection they walked back to their property and up the driveway to their front door. I followed, making small talk about comparative religion and the connection between gospel and rhythm and blues. I seemed to be doing all the talking at this stage. At the front door Norton Goldsmith turned and faced me with arms folded like the gentle genie guarding Aladdin's cave. 'It's been a pleasure visiting with you,' he said in his wine-dark voice. At this moment the front door was opened by a woman, very black indeed, wearing a primary-coloured shift, with her head covered in yellow plastic curlers. While Mr Goldsmith was introducing his wife 'Tam-Tam', I was able, by leaning slightly to the left, to sneak a glimpse inside their house: I saw two big couches set at right-angles, a thick high carpet and several upright lamps. All were protected by clear plastic coverings, making the place look as if they'd just moved in or were just moving out. I saw no books. 'Thank you very much,' I said and backed away.

I wished I'd struck up a closer friendship because I was feeling in need of neighbourly contact – perhaps coffee and cake and a chinwag. Tommy's disappearance had driven me towards the idea of the healing powers of the family. I was feeling isolated; although mostly I missed Tommy's cooking – simple fare, but always tasty and filling. Now I was reduced to heating up macaroni cheese dinners from a packet, although I did add a bonus: a pair of sliced-up hot dogs mixed into the goo. And all the while Beefy sat patiently on the threshold waiting for his pal to come back.

*

Three weeks later the prodigal returned, when dawn had scarcely touched the East with red. Beefy ran round and round in circles, crying out loud, and I was pleased too. 'Yippeeeeee!' sang Tommy, dancing with the dog. 'Congratulate me – I won the jackpot!'

He produced a bottle of champagne and as we drank he explained that he had been away in Hollywood on the T.V. game-show trail where he had selected 'All Star Secrets' as his best bet. In horn-rimmed spectacles and one of my three-piece suits, he'd won the major prize: a trip to South America and $2,000 cash. Where was the money and when was the trip? They would notify him 'in good time'. Surely he meant 'in due time'. He growled, 'Whatever.' I was making waves again, so soon.

Later in the day Jack Wontner called to invite me to dinner. I told him that Tommy was here and that I'd made a sort of date with Beverly. I also told him about Tommy's fortune. ('Skill, skill!' Tommy hissed. 'And tell Jack I've read all his books.') 'Bring everybody and we'll celebrate at the El Padre.' This was a Mexican restaurant, near Eagle Rock police station, where Jack always got special service and they served a strong margarita. At dinner Tommy embarrassed me by ordering the most expensive item on the menu (Lobster Thermidor Mexicali), and Beverly immediately followed suit. When I protested, Jack cut me off with, 'He's the king tonight – let him rip!' For some reason Jack's wife was absent and, maybe because of this, Jack was overflowing with ebullience, encouraging Tommy to join him on this plateau. As the margaritas were downed, so Jack and Tommy grew more and more patriotic, singing U.S. Marine hymns and vilifying Jane Fonda. 'Throw her body to the illegal aliens,' said Jack. Pedro, the owner, laughed loudly. Jack whispered to Tommy and when they shouted in unison, 'What's the best fucking country in the world?' 'America, America!' answered Pedro smilingly, as if on cue, and the waiters clicked their heels. I was watching Beverly closely, making sure she stuck to soft drinks – I was determined to get some sex in the bedroom when we got home.

95

But when we three entered the hallway we were greeted by a bouncing dog with a tuft of shag in his mouth and a battleground behind him. He'd torn up the carpet and torn down the curtains. I called out to Christ a lot, and Tommy roared with laughter. Beverly tried to talk me down with soothing phrases like 'poor baby', but after a while she gave up and joined Tommy on the dining-room floor (no shag carpet in there) for a game of Scrabble. Beefy watched the play with them. I heard them arguing about whether '*Ech*' qualified as an expression. Wondering what I was doing in Southern California at my age, I read some more Homer and then went to bed.

Life for Tommy continued to improve. He received his game-show cash a few days later and immediately was off to the stores, returning with fancy underwear, silk pyjamas and a red velvet jogging suit. At night he went to 'boogie' in San Fernando Valley clubs and, with his cash, he soon had a string of girl-friends. There was Peggy and Lisa and Franny and Mike, and they were always calling in the dead of night, waking me up, demanding in their shrill monotonous baby voices that they speak to Tommy. He was never there at dead of night but in the daytime, when he'd pop in for a shower or a snooze, I'd keep reminding him to pay his phone bill so that I could get some peace. Under these circumstances I felt no conscience prick when, roaming around his bedroom one afternoon while taking a break from my book work, I found and read a letter from Franny, aged sixteen. She said she loved him so much she'd named one of the jets in her hot tub after him.

Meanwhile – to work on the house! Or, to be honest, to pay professionals to work on the house. Altadena Lock & Key installed dead-bolts and locks on every window big or small, all with separate keys. The re-carpeting was dealt with by one of Herb's contacts, a wax-moustached Lebanese called Julius Caesar, directing a crew of Nicaraguans, recently arrived in America. Only Mr Caesar spoke English, but once I had chosen a plush carpet of light grey his men got down to cutting and nailing at top speed, singing Nicaraguan chorus songs as they worked. When they reached the living room Mr Caesar halted them with upraised hand and, calling me to the centre of the floor, said, 'Sir, you have, under the shag, very nice hardwood floor, very nice indeed; they don't make them so nice any more, they make this floor when America was top of the world after the war against the fascists. May I talk you into having this floor expertly finished with varnish, and polished, and then you may decorate with Persian rugs.' I felt he was right, I trusted his tone. Soon a Panamanian crew was scraping and varnishing and polishing and buffing and singing their own national songs. I went out to Sears Roebuck and bought some imitation Persian rugs, described as 'Kismet-style', made in Belgium.

Next I turned my attention to the bedroom, nailing up a print of the famous Waterhouse oil painting of Narcissus stretched out in countryside that resembled the Suffolk I had roamed as a child, and a more modern print of imagined Dorset fields where my mind could make me a Bryanston schoolboy seeking a copse for the secret snacking of cold pork and beans straight from the can, before darkness and prep and the sex talk in the dormitory. To complement these English scenes, I visited a local lamp store and bought a charming metal bedside lamp with a shade decorated with huntsmen drinking stirrup cup before the great chase on a crisp morning.

The garden needed Anglicizing badly. Left on its own, Far West nature went horridly arid, suggestive of the landscape of the Bible minus the milk and honey. Herb had hired me a new gardener (the Japanese, Benjamin, had quit after Tommy had called him a 'Jap'), and I confided in him my dream plan for a rockery (like the one Captain Manning had commanded at Newlands, my prep school) and for clumps of ferns and stands of silver birch trees (like those on Wimbledon Common, near Wildcroft Manor, my home). Leonard, the new gardener, said, 'Si, si' and got on with his motor-mowing and then some leaf-blowing, all of which made a terrific commotion.

After the workers had gone and Tommy was out clubbing with one of his girls, I sat on the concrete back porch in my beach chair, nursing a glass of California chablis and contemplating the way ahead. Might there one day be thriving on the brown stubble in front of me a garden of heavy-laden fruit trees, red daisies, blue myosotis and burning orange Siberian wallflowers? What adventures lay waiting for Beefy and me in the steep blue mountains beyond my concrete slab back wall? And now, with a satisfied 'Harrumph', Beefy came and lay down beside me. It would have been an evening of ancient peace had not the neighbours to my right been holding a barbecue. As the evening wore on the music – all rhythm and blues, soul and hot gospel – grew louder and the bass dug deeper, while the voices of the guests – initially so measured and refined – uttered howls, whoops, hollers and cackles. I knew this was the very stuff that formed the foundations of American popular music and that I, as a musicologist, should be appreciating the experience; yet at this moment, sitting in the grounds of my new castle, I found myself cursing my fate to be remaindered out West in alien corn.

I went indoors and put on a record of Flanagan and Allen singing 'Round the Back of the Arches'.

*

'Oh to be in England, now that April's here!' I flew to London in that month, to renew myself with friends and family, to bathe in my own culture pool. In my Altadena kitchen, on the bulletin board, I had left Tommy a note: 'Please keep your home tidy; try to train the dog; don't let any flaky people in; try to get a proper job.' When I returned two months later I was greeted by a shipshape house and a welcoming and well-fed dog. But Tommy wasn't there.

Three weeks later and still no Tommy. I was more than worried, I was lonely. Beefy howled at night, and little girls telephoned. There were a few bills addressed to him. Everywhere I went I took Beefy and slowly we became firm friends, especially at dinner-time. Luckily some work took me outside the house; I was invited back to a re-formed Mayfair Music Hall to perform my act provided the songs were cleaner. A week's contract. At the weekend, on my way to the theatre, I visited Curlew Worthington, the T.V. soap-opera director with the impeccable taste in house and garden decor.

Curlew had invited me to admire his latest addition: a swimming-pool done up Art Nouveau, all twisty and twiney, with nude statuary at each corner. For a few precious moments I stood still, with a glass of real French wine, inhaling the tranquil scene – the still, brown water in the wavy pool, the terra cotta tiles, the bank of tasteful flowers behind, the trickle from the mouth of the Greek god by the cypress hedge. Presently Curlew joined me, wiping his hands on his apron. 'Cutting pasta on the new machine. I have a small working dinner tonight and everything must be *al dente*.' I congratulated him on the peace and beauty of his garden and pool. 'Thank you,' he said, smiling. 'We must also thank *Star Wars* – after seeing a preview, I immediately bought stock in Twentieth Century-Fox.'

Emboldened by the environment and the confidentiality of Curlew, I poured out my troubles. 'The situation is untenable,' he said. 'Get rid of the dog.' I thanked him very much and didn't tell him I would do nothing of the sort. During Tommy's absence I'd grown close to Beefy and he to me. Whenever I took my afternoon siesta he'd sashay into the bedroom and with a sudden flying leap, join me on the counterpane. Then with his paw he'd lift up my chin and bore into me with those turquoise eyes. He seemed to know everything I knew, and a lot more besides. Where's Tommy, good dog? Of

98

course, he wasn't omni-clever. I stopped his farting by changing his food from Kal Kan supermarket meat to Avoderm, an avocado-based gourmet mixture from a New Age pet shop. After his nocturnal meeting with a skunk I worked tomato soup into his coat and the nose-biting stench gradually faded. I was acting on advice from a wonderful local vet, Dr Shackleford. Beefy never appreciated his doctor, cowering under the table, peeing on the floor, tugging me away at top speed from the Teresita Animal Hospital. I soon learned that slowly chanting the name 'Dr Shackleford' was an effective incantation when Beefy had done wrong. Like the time he bit through my car seat belts front and back, after I'd left him in the car to perform my music-hall act. The doctor's name made him cower and shiver. But the damage was estimated by the Ford dealership at over $400.

Tommy had been gone almost a month when the phone woke me around 2 a.m. 'Congratulate me! I'm gonna be a star!' he said, voice rather slurred. Explain, please. *Please*. While I was away in England he'd joined an actors' workshop where he'd been spotted by a woman talent scout, a relative of Cecil B. DeMille. She told him he had star potential, that he had the James Dean-Marlon Brando-John Travolta 'danger' quality. He had *explosiveness*. 'Wow!' Where was he now? 'We're all in Las Vegas celebrating. Champagne, caviare. Everything is flowing.' When would he be back? The phone went dead.

Next evening, returning from the Mayfair, I noticed that some of his clothes had been removed from his room and that there were tyre-marks on the lawn. I wondered if he had been telling me a tall story; I desperately hoped he had been. Because I was jealous, dead jealous. Flashing into the future I saw Tommy as a bright new star, cashing in on his sullen look, his sudden violent movements, all his body talk; the misunderstood young man, a neo-Hamlet. And what was I but a long-forgotten fallen star now reduced to singing silly songs about laughing policemen at a fake British music hall?

With the help of Curlew I got the talent agent woman's office number. Yes, said the assistant, Mr Conway had been seen at the workshop – yes, he had potential – no we have not been in Las Vegas lately, that is not our territory – no, we have not dined with him, nor even had a coffee with him. Days went by and I took Valium to sleep. Then Tommy called from, he said, Redondo Beach. He was 'strung out on coke', he had been gambling and whoring and scoring coke. Was he ever intending to come home and lead a normal life? He was very, very sorry and he'd be home tomorrow night.

99

'I'm so sorry, please forgive me,' he said, with a face spotty and puffed. 'I'm really sorry.' And he said he'd tell me the details in a couple of days, after he woke up. He'd tell me about the black bit-part actor who'd befriended him, how they'd driven to Nevada in his Cadillac and hired a famous hooker at a famous ranch whorehouse, and how they'd talked philosophy over a bottle of vodka. I told Tommy to please get some rest because my birthday was coming up and we would celebrate with a party and everything would be O.K. again. He pinned a note to his bedroom door: 'Warning! De-tox-ification Inside – Stand CLEAR!!' Then he took his rest for several days.

And now I was able to relax a little. In the late afternoon, after book work, I took to lying back in the vinyl-covered reclining chair, the Barcalounger. Tommy had christened this chair and Beefy had made it a regular sleeping and snorting place. Now I could, with cool mind, inhabit the creaking chair and peruse a favourite book, *Our Island Story*. We used this as our history textbook at Newlands back in the early 1950s, and I still loved the simplicity of the story of Britain as told in this book. Here was a picture of 'Early English at Breakfast' (which I had changed to 'Early at Breakfast'), and here was King Charles hiding in an oak tree. Peace at last! The world laid out in anal order. . . .

*

My birthday party was not a great success. In fact it came near to disaster. Afterwards some of the guests phoned to say they'd had an 'interesting evening'. Tommy and I had spent much time setting up the affair, renting white chairs and tables, buying carnations and candles and lots of liquor. The cooking went wrong, but Jack Wontner and his wife came to the rescue by bringing in lasagne from a local take-out joint and giving me a set of British china plates as a present. My big mistake was to invite friends of mine who had nothing in common except me. They were clearly hostile to one another but were trying to keep at arm's length for the duration of the party. Dr Ronald disliked Vik, Cherie Nussbaum though both of them were too worldly, Beverly was jealous of Cherie's influence on me, and both these women were uneasy among the homosexuals. All of them despised Herb. The latter, dressed in formal cowboy costume, had brought along his date, a buxom beauty called Carol McTavish, scarcely out of her teens and very flirty. Tommy, already flushed with drink and developing a satanic face that had most of the guests slightly scared, soon made a wobbly beeline for Carol McTavish. During and after dinner, and especially when I was showing old films of myself as a rock star, he thrustingly courted Herb's date. They made a temporary soap-opera triangle: Carol in the centre of the couch with Herb and Tommy on either side, both holding one of her hands. While I was singing 'You Turn Me On' on the screen, Tommy made his big play, nibbling Carol's ear and tweaking one of her ample breasts. Herb pretended to ignore this rudeness, applauding my performance by banging his knee with his spare hand. Luckily my other friends were too busy snubbing each other with barbs and grimaces to notice this drama, apart from the Wontners who seemed very interested in the state of play on the couch. Jack was probably making mental notes for a new novel. At least, that's what I hoped.

The party ended early, but Beverly elected to stay behind and comfort me. She even offered to sit on my face. But I was too overwrought for any fooling around – I was waiting for an empty house so that I could read Tommy the riot act. So after she'd gone I searched the house for him, eventually finding him in the garage, hiding. I told him his behaviour was disgraceful, that he was not a gentleman. He apologized over and over and then started crying. I made him agree to renounce alcohol and to go 'on probation' for the next month. If he fell off the wagon, then I would ask him to leave the house. Tommy passionately agreed, suggesting a blood mingling to seal the pact, 'like the heroes bold of old'. I said that would be overdoing matters, but he reminded me that I had talked about these heroes when we'd first met back in the 1970s. Beefy was watching us at the garage door. I ended the evening by saying that the hour was late and that my birthday signalled a new beginning. 'You always have a word for it, don't you?' said Tommy. The words I had concealed concerned Carol McTavish; I wished it had been me nibbling her ear and, even more exciting, weighing up her fruity twin tremblers.

*

I was terribly relieved when Tommy landed himself a job with a local car dealership, Tri-City Autos. He would be selling used cars for a certain commission. At last peace would reign again and I could get back to my book research. I set up my office in the study at the back, lighting little Dutch cigars as a way of starting the typing of notes, gradually working into the actual creating of the book page by page, and at the end of each page – even if I was in the middle of a sentence –

stopping for a break. Now came those blissful moments when I took Beefy for a walk, and we explored the neighbourhood.

One afternoon we strolled up Santa Anita Avenue to see Cherie's house, the communal mansion they called 'The White House', home to the 'Ishi people', whatever they were. In a few minutes we were standing outside a long high fence made of black metal spears, topped with barbed wire. Behind, set back quite a bit, was a large turn-of-the-century brick mansion with heavy eaves and sun porches, very solid and solemn. I searched for a gate but the fence was relieved only by a big black box. Suddenly the box spoke, a rhythm and blues type voice, low and full of authority: 'Can we be of assistance?' I said I was looking for Cherie. There was a pause. Then, 'We think you mean Yolanda Essence. Wait, please.' A few minutes later Cherie appeared from under one of the sun porches and crunched down the gravel driveway. She was wearing black pyjamas. 'You may come and take tea, George says. Indian or Chinese?'

The inside of the mansion smelt of overcooked cabbage and needed a good tidy-up. Women and children, all white, were running to and fro. I examined a wall of hideous abstract daubs. 'George's work,' said Cherie. 'He's a great ball player, too. We call him Master, but you don't have to.' I certainly had no intention of doing so, and Beefy's ears were pricking like mad. Cherie gave us a quick tour of the house, all much of a muchness, like a Sixties hippie pad. Two dozen women lived here, said Cherie, holding their 'old life' possessions and children in common, and with only one man ruling their new life: George, the Master. Cherie had clearly given me up as a man – there was ice in her eyes and her speech was too clear and precise – and I felt like a visitor from another planet. We reached a door marked 'Club Room' and I asked whether there was a bar or piano inside. Out of a gloomy corner loomed a tall black man with shiny hair braided in corn rows and a dark hole where one eye should have been. Cherie introduced me and Beefy to her Master and added, 'The dog is quite safe, no need for the corner.' 'Yes, but is the man O.K.?' said George and laughed deeply. Then he invited us up to tea in the communal lounge, and he put his arm round my shoulder.

During tea George smiled a lot and even stroked Beefy, but he hardly said a word. The women bustled about him, refilling his cup and plying him with cookies. I must say I was put off my food by his empty eye socket – he was sitting next to me and I felt I could look through the socket right into his brain. Out of nervousness I blathered a lot, mostly about ragtime and old popular songs. Cherie said they were into 'free improvisation' here and she slipped on a cassette of their house group to demonstrate. It was excruciating stuff – I'd heard such messing about during the Fifties when free-form jazz was the In Thing at Bryanston. Only Cherie's soaring cello was pleasant, but this mellifluousness was undermined by an electric bass stuck on one drone note. I asked Cherie if she needed such a drone. 'Really, Ian! Can't you leave your mind-set at home and realize that we're achieving a mantra effect of complete inner harmony by concentrating on one note? Everyone comes round to that note at the end of the piece – even my cello.' But what was the point of such monotony? I saw George furiously gobbling a cookie, but I had to go on – some demon inside me. 'The point, my poor soul, is that the drone takes us to the essence of *meaning* – to show us the *oneness* of the world. Something you could learn from in your present unfocused life.' She had a point, I must admit, and I told George so. But then a little girl of about thirteen skipped into the room and Cherie asked whether I remembered her daughter from her first husband. Before I could answer George told the little girl that there would be a meeting in the Games Room that evening and she was expected to attend. The little girl's response was to run scared to her mother's trailing skirt. 'No, Sandra,' admonished Cherie, 'You must go through initiation with the Master.' I felt George's smile was lascivious. Maybe he caught my expression . . . anyway he suddenly clapped his hands and Cherie hustled me out to the driveway. 'Goodbye,' she said softly but firmly, 'and don't get any wrong ideas, Ian. We live on a different level from you. I'll call, let *me* call *you*, and we'll meet for breakfast.'

As I walked Beefy home I mused on Cherie's communal lifestyle. At least she was leading a life of purpose now, however strange, and had submitted herself to an authority doing battle with the universe's indifference. Was the air meatier up here in Altadena?

*

My immediate duty was to Beefy and Tommy. The latter didn't stay long off the booze; within a few weeks of starting the Tri-City Car Sales job he was rolling home, plastered, with young salesmen buddies, equally plastered, and a string of girls. I was never properly introduced to any of them; they barged down the corridor and into Tommy's room and . . . click . . . the door was locked and the howling began. When I managed to apprehend Tommy in the kitchen, mixing a drink, and told him he'd broken our agreement, he fixed me with an eye that seemed cold and evil. Where was the clumsy bungler who shouted 'Yippee'? Out loud I mentioned Dr Jekyll and Mr Hyde. 'Culture, culture! I got it up to here!' he growled thickly and gestured me to get out of his way. Thoroughly humiliated, I put on my dressing gown and slippers and went outside to make sure they'd locked the front gate (part of the new fortress, fence and gate, that Herb's men had built). Of course they hadn't bothered to lock up, so I clicked the padlock and was ruminating by moonlight when, to my horror, I saw dark figures clambering up my new fence. I demanded to know the meaning of this. 'Fuck it,' said a male voice. 'Sounds like the old guy Tommy warned us about.'

Matters came to a head a few days later when Tommy came close to death. In the middle of the night I was woken by a loud thump, followed by a thud, and then a gurgling. I unlocked my door and went to Tommy's room – lucky he hadn't locked *his* door. There he was, lying on the floor, gurgling in his own vomit. None of his pals was around, he could have drowned, like rock stars used to. I yanked him out of that gunk. His last meal looked Mexican, but that is my image of vomit – in England we'd called it 'sick' and the image was tinned mixed vegetables. I finished my duty by rolling him on to his mattress, where he lay spreadeagled with head to one side, tongue lolling out, like some primitive folk Christ. I told him he should enroll in Alcoholics Anonymous; I would give him two months' notice; he must be home by midnight or ring to tell me where he's staying. . . . I could have rattled on in this vein except that his snores got the better of me.

Tommy's response was spread over the next few weeks: he stayed away from the house. Meanwhile Cherie followed up on her promise to breakfast me; we met in a charming 'garden restaurant', all potted greenery and salads, in historic South Pasadena. And I gave her my troubles. She asked me to come walk with her along the nearby railroad track because the grass growing between the rails and the nearness of the old brick buildings made her feel safe and comfortable. 'A neat therapy,' she said. I started in again on my troubles but she soon cut in: 'Do I appear troubled? Of course not! Yet only yesterday my ex-husband passed away from an icky coronary, blood gushing from every orifice. But I study and I meditate and I obey the rules of our world. Life is only a passing shadow.' I tried to back her up by quoting the old Ernest Dowson poem about the days of wine and roses not lasting long, and life being but an interval between misty dreams. She interrupted me. 'He got it wrong. It's life that's the dream.' But I wasn't about to join the Ishi people, even if I'd been the right sex. Still, the breakfast had been excellent and the walk along the railroad

104

track would be worth repeating, with Beefy.

An empty house became anathema (Beefy was still only a dog). I called up Simon Witham, and after much persuasion he agreed to make the expedition if I'd send him a map. 'Will I need an elephant gun as well?' As usual, he did the un-American thing of insisting on parking his car in the garage. Then we drove off in my car all the way to Hollywood, where we ate Japanese and saw a horror movie. When we got back to the house he expressed regret that Tommy wasn't around. 'He's most amusing.' Why? 'After hearing about you two I like to climb in between crisp sheets in my high-rise apartment and chuckle over the mess you've made. Most amusing.' I asked him when I'd see him next. 'You might as well be living in Timbuctu. If you're ever down in Los Angeles, look us up! Now please lead me to my Jaguar. . . .' Oh, funny, very funny. I turned to Herb for help.

He suggested the Hutchins and their friends. Enough mourning time had elapsed, and the couple were ready to step into the old homestead once more. But I can't cook! 'Hell, they'll bring supper up in stages!' said Herb. What magic was wrought when they arrived! For the house became a home again, bright and silvery, like a Christmas greetings card brought to life. Mrs Hutchins ('Call me Gertie'), a pert little woman with glasses and a wide hat full of fruit, was first over the threshold, sallying in with a bowl of lime Jello salad. She was followed by a merry band of friends, all marrieds and all positive-thinkers and all bearing bowls and dishes. Old man Hutchins brought up the rear, clutching a brown paper bag, looking around him, fingering the doors and the walls. Once inside the living room I told everybody to make themselves at home. 'It *is* our home!' said Gertie lustily, lighting up the first of a long line of untipped Camels. Everybody else started lighting up too and old man Hutchins dispensed liquor from his brown paper bag. Gertie was clearly in charge of the evening and was soon commanding the wives in the kitchen, while we men discussed sports and electronics in the living room. My accent was the topic for a while: 'Say that again,' said a friend of theirs. 'It's different.' Another friend asked me, 'Which side would you be on if England fought America?' We all laughed. Pretty soon Gertie and the women marched in with plates of steaming food – everything piled together family-style, the Jello, the mashed potatoes, the stew, the squash, the cabbage. Suddenly Herb appeared, whisked off his ten-gallon hat, grabbed a plate, squatted in a corner and started in to eat without a word. 'Well, I declare!' said Gertie and we all laughed. Beefy, in a red ribbon, made his rounds from guest to guest and was much petted and allowed to eat the leftovers. After hot pie and ice-cream they gathered round the piano and I sang them songs of the Gay Nineties and Roaring Twenties. Gertie said such music was even before *her* time and how on earth did I know all those songs? We toasted each other through the evening and when the end was reached I told the Hutchins and their friends that they were my friends and to please come back any time, any time at all.

And so the house was becoming warmer through the heat of these good souls. A week later I received a red-hot bonus: Dr Ronald Bund wrote to ask whether I would consider taking him in as a lodger. Would I consider! I was thrilled and touched. Now we could have heady discussions and Wagner evenings and maybe some fascinating visitors. I told Witham the good news and he said it could be bad news – he'd already had calls from some lawyer asking about Dr Ron's whereabouts. 'You should always keep people at arm's length and never invite them to stay – especially Americans. I think you're going native or loco. Or both.'

Dr Ronald arrived promptly at the cocktail hour of 6 p.m. carrying one smallish portmanteau and a briefcase. He was immaculately turned out in a good broadcloth suit with striped college-style tie, but there was a hollowness to his face and red rings round his eyes. With a 'Greetings, my gracious host!' he rushed in and sat down on the sofa. He had never cared for pets, but soon he was wiping Beefy's coat with a rapid motion while tossing back sherry with the other hand. I told him I'd make him as comfortable as possible, but I bet he was sorry to have given up his elegant Hollywood apartment, I would miss those soirées of Wagner and hock and cream cake. 'We must look to the future, my friend, using the past mainly for recreation.' Suddenly the door-bell chimed and he nearly jumped out of his suit. 'Tell 'em I died last week,' he said with a mechanical laugh, and he dabbed at spilt sherry with his hankie.

Who should be at the door but Tommy! But why the chiming? 'Big announcement – gala night – made big car sale . . . congratulate me. .. .' Slurred words. Dr Ronald leapt up and handed his sherry to Tommy. 'Thy need is greater than mine,' he said and turning to me, 'Would it be remiss if I retired to my room? I rise at dawn to begin a new job and a new life.' I led him to the T.V. room, next to my study. Vik's studio couch pulled out to make an acceptable bed and, of course, he should feel free to use the T.V. 'I'm not a viewer – perhaps the lad would enjoy it.' It took mere seconds for Tommy to install the set in his room. 'I appreciate your change of attitude,' said Tommy with remarkable clarity. When I went to say goodnight to Dr Ron his door was shut and no sound came from within. But I got into bed full of happy anticipation of musical evenings conducted by Dr Ron. Why, we might even start a literary guild!

But such was not the case. Every day Dr Ron rose early, went to work in his battered old car and retired to his room as soon as he got home. I did learn that his job was writing instruction manuals for Arabs at a multinational corporation in Pasadena, but I never found out the cause of his recent trouble. No mail came for him and he never used the phone. Sometimes I'd apprehend him in the corridor, tip-toeing to the back lavatory, and I'd try and strike up a conversation. But he'd never respond. He seemed flustered, even embarrassed. Of course, this may have been because I had caught him in his long underwear – and he being such a fine dresser in normal life. Perhaps my dream of starting a salon was doomed because we were living too closely-quartered, but at the time I didn't see the situation in this light.

I took to spying on him. It wasn't hard because he'd often leave his bedroom door ajar – so tired-out from work he'd become forgetful, I suppose – and I'd peek inside and take an inventory: a mountain of soiled clothes in one corner, the drip-dry shirts hanging on the cup-board door, with a wash 'n' wear suit in a cellophane case; books and magazines scattered all over the floor (mostly on Western history, and I saw one called *Great Cities*); once I saw a book resting on his chest, *The Gold in Real Estate* – that was when I caught him collapsed on the couch and fully-dressed, poor devil, with the anglepoise lamp burning into his face and his clock radio droning away to a 24-hour all-news station. I never stayed long, just enough time to satisfy my in-terest – besides, there was an odd smell always, a woody musk, but I never found any bottle of cologne or aftershave. What I loved was that in the morning he was always transformed: up with the lark, turned out immaculately in suit and tie and swinging his briefcase. He'd shut his bedroom door behind him, sealing off the squalid world which I had spied upon. Did he suspect anything? He was always the epitome of politeness when our paths crossed, he off to his Arab manuals and me, in gym kit, to the Y.M.C.A.

Tommy was tickled pink by the new set-up. He told me he liked living amongst his 'elders and betters', and now that he had two 'spiritual mentors' he was sure we'd never let him 'go astray again'. For a while he kept his drinking down to a minimum – a few sherries after returning from car-sale work. He also copied Dr Ron's style of

107

going to bed at a reasonable hour, round 10 p.m. To amuse him I retired to my bedroom at the same time. And when we were all in our bedrooms Tommy would holler out, 'Goodnight, everybody! Goodnight, Ron, goodnight Ian! Think about me in your dreams!' He was a creature of habit and these were decent new habits. I was quite touched.

Usually I'd only pretend to be going to bed. After a while I'd sneak out of my room, fix myself a stiff drink and then sit reading in the drawing-room, stroking Beefy. Or else I'd creep around examining my house, niches and all. I liked the bell chimes safe in their place in the hall, and the fruit cluster pattern wallpaper in the kitchen, and also the huge chunky old Frigidaire that shuddered and whined at self-appointed intervals. I liked Beefy's grunting as he flopped down on the Barcalounger or the sofa, and then I liked his hyperventilating. And in the background there was Dr Ron's all-news radio station droning on about world-wide disasters, and there was Tommy's T.V. blasting out bang-bang cop shows and the canned laughter sit-coms.

On these nights I was contented, as much at peace with the world as ever I'd been in Southern California. I was a home-owner with a full house.

*

'You're a boarding-house keeper!' stated Jack Wontner, killing any other view of the matter by lasering deadly blue eyes at me and grinning with perfect teeth. We were drinking British ale at the John Bull Pub in 'Old Town' Pasadena. He continued his lecture: 'Avoiding the responsibility of marriage and children. Attempting an extension of school life, with you as headmaster!' Well, I knew he was right, deep in my heart, and I also knew there was more to it, much further down. I smiled. I knew he wanted me to disagree, to shake my head and bluster and stutter. Telling 'home truths' was his meat and drink – the British ale was just a pose – and his victims must be made to squirm when faced with his bitter truth. He was 'telling it like it is', police style. We members of the public were all pathetic nerds ruled by primitive passions and base motives: emptying bladders and bowels and sex rigs; pushing the other fellow down or being pushed down. All atavistic, all mechanical, no love and no nothing after death. Seeing some of his fans move in with books and pens, I took the opportunity to escape his clutches. I knew Jack loved me.

There was good old Herb, leaning against the bar, near the pickles and pies, with his trousers tucked into the top of his cowboy boots.

Sipping a Budweiser – much better than a Watneys. 'When you're through with ya first set of toons, I got some gals I'd like ya to meet.' Just what the doctor ordered! I'd been wearying of Beverly's appetite for expensive dishes followed by lack of appetite for crude sex. So after I'd done my stuff at the pub piano (I'd been hired for the evening as a ribald music-hall entertainer) I joined Herb back at the bar. He was lying slanted at the same angle and, out of the side of his mouth, he said, 'The gals are lined up and primed.' First I was presented with a Mary McTavish – lithe, springy, athletic, blonde, early twenties. The older sister of the buxom Carol, whose bosom I had longed to nuzzle in ever since my birthday party. I said hello and we exchanged pleasantries, but I could see there were no flies on Mary and that, agile in mind and body, she would be a hard one to land. She faded into the crowd and after a short grace period Herb introduced another possibility, a much older girl – a woman – with a big nose and a skin problem, compensated by a compact body and aggressively protruding breasts. If I couldn't get to Carol's breasts through knowing Mary, then this woman might provide alternatives worth climbing. Such were my hideous thoughts in this British pub in Old Pasadena.

When I started talking the woman looked at me sidelong, slyly and sexily, even greedily. I asked what was her business and Herb, behind her, made an O-sign with thumb and forefinger and slid off into the darkness. 'I'm studying chiropractoring.' Pause. '. . . With a special interest in lower back problems.' We exchanged phone numbers and just as she was saying goodbye I realized that, in the excitement of our body language displays, I had forgotten to get her name. 'Elaine . . . and if you have any problems, call me up.'

The evening's highlight was the arrival of Dr Ronald leading a party of Marines, fresh from Camp Pendleton, complete with their own guard. The latter, an older man wearing a leisure suit with flapping flares, was a T.V. producer specializing in 'physique instruction' videos which were shot at his Laguna Beach condominium, according to the breathless Dr Ron. From out of the gloom materialized a tipsy Tommy and almost immediately he got into a slanging match with the Marines, with Dr Ron refereeing. 'You got yourself the elements of a good soap opera here,' said Jack Wontner to me. 'But don't count on Alistair Cooke as host.'

*

At the house, life became lively but not chaotic. My daytimes were

109

blissfully placid; Tommy was out selling his cars and Dr Ron was involved in some sort of deal with a group of Filipino businessmen and negotiations kept him in their territory, a faraway ethnic suburb of L.A. Sometimes Tommy would cook up a 'Conway Special' in the evening (as an apology for being behind with the rent; on one occasion when I asked for the full amount his comeback was, 'What are you – some kinda loan shark?'), and we would have fun picking up every scrap of food in the house, tossing the lot into a big saucepan and flavouring with herbs, spices and particularly ketchup. As Tommy stirred and the flavour spread so Beefy and Dr Ron would be drawn from their lairs to stand about expectantly, the dog whining and the man lecturing about the great cuisines and chefs of Europe. Happy with the situation, I would pour myself a glass of jug chablis and repair to the front porch where, from my beach chair, I would admire the sunset. Some evenings, to get the effect of an English country garden in the rain, I would rig up the hose and sprinkler so that the water fell just in front of the porch. With Percy Grainger on the gramophone, these were indeed moments of poignant nostalgia. There I sat till chow was up.

The night of my first date with Elaine, the chiropractor, I didn't take a chance with one of Tommy's cook-ups. I gave her wine in the study and then we set off for a decent local restaurant. As we were leaving I had to stop and savour a little of the pre-dinner lecture coming from the kitchen: Dr Ron expounding to Tommy on the subject of Utopias. 'In the Arcadian ideal one finds moderation and restraint – a little more paprika, please, in the stew, if you have such an item – but I would guess, judging by the amount of sherry you're adding to our dinner, that the Land of Cockaigne is more to your liking.' 'You fascinate me – tell me more.' 'It was a poor man's heaven – ham and egg trees growing by a lake of beer.' We left a happy house. . . .

Dinner was a great success; Elaine agreed to come back to the house. Fortunately no one seemed to be at home, except Beefy who ran round us in circles, jumping and licking. After showing her the family and school photos on the bedroom wall, I turned to the subject of sex. She wagged her finger at me and said, 'Now, now!' Even while I was kissing her and removing her clothes she continued to admonish with the 'Now-nows' while admiring the print of the wet Dorset fields. Under her suit was much lace and frilly stuff, beneath this were many petticoats, but her brassière was modern and see-through. Eventually we stood naked and in a trice we were at it hammer and tongs, still standing, she shrieking and convulsing, me ramming away while hop-

110

ing the house was truly empty, wondering if the neighbours could hear, and where Beefy was. Oh, here he was! Jumped-up on the bed, licking us all over. 'I had six orgasms before I stopped counting,' said Elaine when it was all over.

Elaine was dressed and in the hallway when Tommy came bumbling through the front door. He wanted to 'visit' with her, but she grew frightened and headed outside. We agreed to meet again. She looked back at the house oddly.

I was sneaking into my bedroom when Tommy buttonholed me. 'Ronald's inspired me. Let's talk life direction, let's talk goals,' he said, a bit slurred. He went on to tell me that he'd taken out a life insurance policy, with me as 'benefactor'. He explained, 'See, if I get killed in a James-Dean-style car crash, then you stand to make some money,' and he bear-hugged me. I replied that his plan sounded like a B-picture. Down slumped his head, he moped out of the room, and then I heard his bedroom door slam loudly. What a fool I was!

Two days later Tommy got fired from Tri-City Motors for reasons he refused to disclose, but he announced to me brightly, 'Now I'm free to pursue my artist goals! Yippee!!' In my mind I brought up the name of Jesus. My sex life was moving along quite well and I hoped Tommy's new life would allow me to proceed peacefully in a clean house. Mind you, I had begun to be irked by Elaine's physical blemishes. When I met her by daylight they showed up: one cheek smooth, the other crinkly like a dinosaur; a bottom that was crowding out the rest of her body; different-coloured eyes. The trouble was that just as I was turning off her, so she had started turning on to me. 'Are you thinking of me?' she asked as we drove to a fish restaurant. Actually, I was thinking of whether to have the orange roughy or the swordfish.

After dinner, as we were turning up the driveway my peace of mind was broken by the sight of a strange car by my gate – a creamy M.G. parked at a crazy angle. Once inside the house I tried Tommy's door, but it was locked; I knocked but there was no reply. But as I stood there I heard a gruff, deep voice and then a high, tittering one. My feelings were mixed: I was glad he had a girl-friend, but who was the male? What were their names and backgrounds? The idea of complete strangers in my home upset me. When Elaine had at last finished in the bathroom and we were in the bedroom, I discovered that our new bottle of massage oil had vanished. I went to the kitchen for some consolatory wine and found that there was only a drop or two left of my recently-purchased chablis. I left Tommy a note telling him to mend his ways. In bed, after the action, Elaine asked me

111

quietly why I put up with such a 'rude and thoughtless' person. I said that he and I had been through a lot together and . . . and I was frightened of him.

Tommy knocked on the door, apologized and asked whether we'd like some macaroni cheese. I asked him about the strangers but he wouldn't fill me in. 'Anyway, they've gone.' As I was trying to get Elaine off in her Volkswagen she started in on my 'lifestyle'. She said, 'I think you should change it. You never pay me any attention, especially when I'm talking. You treat me like a doormat.' My reply was to kiss her. Then I asked her about her orgasms. How many tonight? 'Ask Tommy – I'm sure he was listening outside the door . . . *you guys*!' And, gunning her Volks, she was off.

*

For the sake of variety and sanity I started dating the healthy blonde, Carol's sister. Fresh as a daisy and with a bounce in her walk, Mary McTavish was also keen on athletic sex – we made it on our first date. 'Golly, I'm surprised at myself,' she said, gently removing me. A triumph for yours truly, but not a very comfortable fit. Mary was training to be a registered nurse and enjoyed treating my body as a clinical specimen. 'You have skin that's the texture of a new-born babe's, including the extra layer of fat . . . Let's see – your butt cheeks are bubbly and the balls sling low – but I need to deal with that big zit on your back . . .' We got on to the subject of Tommy. 'He's been bothering my sister Carol, but she's a big girl and can deal with him . . . The question is – can you handle him? I think he's certifiably psychotic.' What evidence did she have? 'Those angry looks. And when he squeezes Beefy so tightly the poor animal screams. He's the kind of lug who can't handle a delicate creature like, say, a baby, without destroying it. Doesn't mean to, but can't help it. This guy is a Sherman tank, he's no good, you should throw him out.' I didn't dare tell Tommy.

But I did tell Dr Ronald. The matter came up while we were dining off nut cutlets at The Good Earth, a health restaurant in Pasadena. Ron had chosen the place because he was trying to slim down for Christmas – when he would be competing with other 'johns' outside the gates of Camp Pendleton for the attention of kid Marines as they marched out for their winter holiday break. My friend was kind enough to put aside his exciting holiday plans in order to concentrate on the administration of my boarding-house or, as he liked to put it, 'The Camp'.

'The vortex of your life,' he said, laying down his knife and fork with deliberation, 'has a tendency to suck in both the good and the bad – that is the nature of your charm. Tommy is – or was – *tabula rosa*, but I fear that his sybaritic inclinations are leading him down stygian paths and you may have to show him the door. Who knows? You may have to shutter the whole camp. It's up to you, my dear friend. Can you face the world alone? I wonder. There's no problem for me – for I find that – present company excepted – human-kind is trite, stupid and boring. Youth is even worse – but at least the decorative ones are good for fucking.'

The sound of Brenda Lee singing 'Rocking Around the Christmas Tree' on the restaurant's mood music system caused Dr Ronald to abruptly change subject. His head shook and his face grew florid. 'How I loathe and despise Christmas!' (I love the season – a time to be back home in England, safe with family.) 'Invariably I break out in a rash and often develop a yeast infection in the mouth.' His voice grew louder and he cast around as if giving a sermon. 'As you know, this is the high period for suicides and, in general, Yuletide is a bad time for the world – the year is ending and people feel depressed because they haven't realized the dreams and schemes they started at year's beginning.' I asked whether he had family to be with at Christmas, but he didn't reply, he just picked up his fork and attacked the slab of nut cutlet smothered in tomato sauce. Such was his fury that he allowed the sauce to dribble down the sides of his mouth as he chewed.

*

Of course, I was determined to spend Christmas in England with the family. I didn't believe that a proper Christmas, with all the trimmings, could be enjoyed in America – and certainly not in Southern California. It wasn't only the fact of rudely sunny weather, it was also the people: the wrong people.

Before leaving for London I had words with Tommy. Bad ones. We had a major row about his not pulling his weight around the house – his leaving dirty dishes in the sink, and cigarette ash on the carpets, rugs and couch. 'Anything else, *sir*?' he sneered and threw an evil look. I brought up his continual polishing off of my whiskey, wine, champagne, brandy. Might I have to start marking the bottle levels? Later I found a note pinned to the kitchen bulletin board: 'Your present attitude is NOT ACCEPTABLE.'

And then, out of the blue, on the night before I was to leave, I found a large package on my bed, gift-wrapped in gold tinfoil. Suddenly there he was standing in the doorway, holding Beefy gently by the collar. 'Open it,' he said. The present was a box of glasses – all shapes and sizes, for sherry and brandy and wine and champagne. He ticked off the functions. 'Sharp, huh?' Then he pulled out a red satin ribbon and tied it to Beefy's neck. 'Merry Christmas, my friend – and a prosperous New Year, as Charles Dickens said.' I hadn't the heart to read out the house rules, I was quite moved. When I said goodbye to Beefy he turned away and pretended to be interested in a bowl of artificial flowers. Pretty soon the house was sound asleep, and even Dr Ronald's radio was silent. But what tomorrow? Well, all's one for that, as Richard III said on the eve of the battle of Bosworth.

*

Into the Eighties! I returned to Altadena in the spring, when I should have been in England. The front lawn was a deep sickly green, mostly crab grass; Beefy was smaller and thinner, his ribs stuck out – if he'd eaten a pork chop, it would've showed; the kitchen window was broken and rain had soaked through the back corridor ceiling, streaking the wall and soaking the carpet. The whole house seemed blue and bare, too many empty walls – I needed to buy more prints of English scenes. And where was my lamp decorated with the merry huntsmen?

I found the lamp in Tommy's room. While inspecting there I turned up an exercise book called 'My Career – KEEP OUT'. Of course I examined it because I'm a writer and so nothing's sacred. 'Will Agents Open Doors?' and 'Pancake Make-up Tips' were two of the headings inside. There was a reading list that included Shakespeare and Stanislavsky. But then I heard voices and I quickly exited. Tommy was talking to a total stranger, a black youth, at the front door – and now he was inviting him in for a drink. I saw red. Tommy introduced me to Leroy. 'He's soliciting funds for his future education – he wants to save enough money to research his roots in Africa.' Leroy came up very close to me and started lecturing me on Afro-American culture and the fact that Beethoven was black. I showed him the door. As he went out he called me an asshole and I threatened to flatten him, but the door had shut. Tommy roared with laughter and suggested I needed a drink. Jet-lag, jet-lag, I explained. What was I doing back in this God-forsaken area, where the mountains are crumbly and every room is dust-laden, and the sun never ceases all day long?

Dr Ronald materialized, I suppose from his room, dressed in a

114

Brooks Bros suit, cool and calm. He congratulated me on not looking a day older and sounding, in the hall with Leroy, 'on splendid form'. We all went off to Jack-In-A-Box, a local branch of a fast-food chain, and I treated them to cheeseburgers and onion rings, etc. Tommy disclosed that he had enrolled in an acting class at Pasadena City College, and I pretended to be pleased and surprised. But Dr Ronald caught me unprepared; he was taking up a post as a writer of instruction manuals for an American construction company building cities – *in Saudi Arabia*. 'One must follow the dollar,' he explained. Why, oh why, couldn't my friends stick to regular nine-to-five jobs, coming home in the evening to communal suppers, to some yarning, to maybe a record recital, and then off quietly to their respective rooms? I could hear Jack Wontner over my shoulder: 'Can't express your feelings, can you? Won't commit yourself to life and its promises, frightened of diving into the dark lake.' What do you know about life, Jack? Safe behind your iron-gated walls in your burglar-alarmed mansion, far from ethnics, pampered by maids and flunkeys. . . .

Within a week Dr Ronald slipped away and, I supposed, soon took up his new position in Saudi Arabia. For over a year I had no word from him, but much later a rumour reached me that he was dallying with kings and princes. I would peep into his old room from time to time and linger sadly. The only souvenir of Dr Ronald was a pungent aroma. Was it a perfume, an aftershave cologne, or perhaps simply Dr Ronald Bund himself?

Meanwhile, Tommy too was preparing to do a bunk. The reason, he told me in a doomy, quavery voice, was that his beloved grandfather was 'failing fast' and he 'must needs hasten' to Minnesota to 'comfort my sinking loved one'. Tommy's natural histrionics had not been affected by his Method acting class at Pasadena City College. We had a farewell dinner the night before his departure at The Hamburger Hamlet on Lake Avenue. Mary agreed to join us but she warned me that her current feeling was that Tommy was a sociopath. 'I wonder if he has compassion for anybody, any time.' What evidence had she? 'Just feelings,' she said. At the Hamlet, over jumbo margaritas, Tommy warmed to the subject of death: 'What do you tell a dying man?' I suggested you tell him that you love him, but Tommy was off on a flight of fancy: 'A curlean photo – I want to take a curlean photo of my grandfather at the actual point of death so's I can catch his aura. Did you know you lose weight at the moment of death? That's because your soul has flown away!' I listened politely, not wanting to antagonize him, but Mary started pooh-poohing notions of soul and after-life. 'Hey, I'm a nurse, and after the stuff I've seen in emergency ward I ditched any beliefs I might have had in reincarnation and such. Nature doesn't care – when you see a pulverized head, crushed, you know, in some car wreck, you understand that what we have here is dust, nothing more, nothing less.' Captain Sorrell, in *Sorrell and Son*, the book I was currently reading, voices the same sort of nihilism but I kept quiet, not wanting to seem as if I was ganging up on Tommy and his fancies.

We arrived back at the house to find Beefy weaving around in the driveway, frenziedly pleased to see us. I screamed and tore my hair while Tommy laughed. Mary took me into the bedroom to calm me down but, as before, we were not a good fit sexually. However, I did achieve a decent moment of transcendentalism – I believed I was up in the heavens and talking with God. The sex act had put me on a railway to the Godhead, but when I told Mary she simply smoothed my hair and said, 'There, there.' During the night we kept bumping into each other and I made a mental note to buy a bigger bed. The Kalifornia King, they say, is bigger than the normal King.

Next morning we saw Tommy off to Minnesota at L.A. International Airport. I had lent him my pin-striped Italian gangster suit and a suitcase; I gave him the change from my pockets. Afterwards Mary pointed out that there was far too big a knot in Tommy's tie – but I was concerned with how Beefy would react to Tommy's disappearance (there were strange butterflies in my stomach). 'I think it's dumb to have such a neurotic dog,' said Mary. So sensible, so practical, so right. But she was drumming her fingers on her leg and that leg was going up and down, up and down.

For several days I didn't hear from her, and I decided not to call her. I was determined to spend 'quality time' on my own, in my own home, in my castle. Just Beefy and me. On a lazy afternoon I would stretch out in the lounger, dozing and gazing. Sometimes – and special times they were – I could doze myself back into the country of the past, where I felt again the tingle of excitement of a summer afternoon at Newlands – lying inside the friendly grass, listening to the faraway tick and tock of the cricket match, anticipating lemonade and a tea of doughnuts with no hole but lots of jam in the centre, and then the swim in the big bath, concealed under boards in the gym. A world on its own, with no mention of the H-bomb. But it wasn't always pleasant in this other country. Sometimes I'd find myself once more alone in the sea of desolation. Millions of miles from Wildcroft Manor, conveyed by taxi, train and bus, deposited in a big cold schoolroom of polish and bells and two older boys already on the bare floor fighting. That night I lay still under stiff sheets, completely puzzled. On Sunday we wrote postcards home. Home! 'Newlands, Seaford, Sussex, Sept 23, 1949. . . . Dear Mummy and Daddy. . . .' Then a smudge and after that: 'He simply couldn't carry on, but he seemed perfectly all right at the time! Yours sincerely, Capt.T.D. Manning, Vice-Head-master.' I had been abandoned by my parents but I didn't ever, not ever, blame them because they had sent me to boarding-school for my own good and they were sad too: my mother would cry, I knew she would. Everybody was sacrificing all round. Unpleasantness was goodness and we had recently gone through a terrible war. But the fact was I no longer existed. On the Monday we stood in our patrols in the Big Schoolroom waiting to march into breakfast. 'Otters alert!' I wanted to go biggies and I wanted not to cry. Standing next to me was Bumstead, a real storybook schoolboy, well-knit and handsome, looking straight ahead and biting down hard on his lower lip. 'Right turn! Quick march!' But now he was crying. Why wasn't I? As we marched the panelled hall a huge red man in a wall of tweed and clouds of smoke joined us and boomed, 'Hello! I'm a new bug, too – so we're all in this together, eh!' But he'd come out of a different door, and at breakfast he produced his own pot of jam. Later I was to experience the nasty kiss of his slipper. Why, sir? 'Truculence, that's why.' Just before lights out, even later, the dormitory head popped in. 'You, you – and you! All come right now to H.M.'s study for a caning.' Why, Adams? 'In your case, you imbecile worm, because you're always laughing and singing those stupid songs.' H.M., standing tall in his tobacco-rich study with its walls crammed with photos of Gallipoli and the Somme, selected a cane and then said kindly but firmly, 'This will hurt me much more than it will hurt you.' Next morning in the showers they cooed at the blue stripes on my thigh. 'Some of us simply don't know when to shut up, do we?' said the master in charge. Soon I had my own gang, the Magpie Gang, and then I formed a lavatory-paper-and-comb band which hummed current hits like 'Red Roses for a Blue Lady', and after that I wrote and drew a comic called *The Bumper Fun Book*. And one Saturday morning, about half-way through the term, a miracle happened: my mother and father reappeared in the private hall by H.M.'s study. They were alive, they weren't dead after all, and they were carrying presents – an American air rifle and Kid Colt comics. 'Take it easy, old boy,' said my father. It was worth all the pain. . . .

Dozing in the drawing room. And gazing. . . . At the bowls of dried flowers I'd bought on an impulse at the local supermarket; at the slick green waterproof curtains, a Hutchins legacy, with my safety-pin holding together the split; at the dull mud colour of the once shiny hardwood floor. Resolutions made: new polish, new curtains, real flowers cut from my own garden. Responsibilities faced, like my father would have faced them. Must get a proper wooden fence, a tall one. Beefy can jump the wire thing Herb put up. Make supper. Wander into kitchen in St Michael underwear, followed by dog. Open fridge, we both inspect. Plenty of ice-cold jug wine. Canned tuna fish topped with melted sliced cheese on a toasted English muffin, rounded off with instant coffee laced with Irish Whiskey. Satisfaction at last.

With Whispering Jack Smith singing 'Lily of Laguna' I lay on the couch and read a biography of George Formby. More spiked coffee. A perfect three-ring circus. A peace that passes understanding.

About 2 a.m. one morning I was woken by the phone. Immediately I was on the alert, a school habit. Hello? Then a voice, like it was calling from the very next room, speaking in a loud hissy stage whisper. 'He's gone, gone, gone! He died in my arms!' Then Tommy hung up.

Another week or so slipped by, in reveries and book research. One afternoon Mary dropped by. She looked lovely and fresh. 'Did you know Beefy burrowed under the fence and was running around in the street?' I tore at my hair and shouted at the ceiling. 'Oh, come on!' she said. 'I got him and put him in the yard.' She put her hands on her hips and surveyed me. 'You should get your life in proper perspective. Things aren't as bad as a soap opera.'

To cheer me up she offered to treat me to dinner at The Pepper Mill, a local restaurant with a good salad bar and plenty of soothing senior citizen customers. While I was enjoying a cocktail she said, seriously, 'We have to discuss our relationship.' I was wondering whether The Pepper Mill served its onion rings in loaf form or individual curly-crispy. 'I'm not sure,' she continued, 'about where I stand with you, and whether there's any future. . . . So I'm dating someone else as well as you.' This was a bit of a blow to my ego, but then I remembered Beverly and Elaine – I could always re-call them. Besides, Mary and I had never been a snug fit.

Eventually, after a dig in the salad bar, I asked about this extra man. 'He works for the police department, in a helicopter.' God! A snooper with a searchlight, roaring and shuddering over us citizens like a bird of prey. Wontner calls them 'Sky Pigs'. Mary laid down her fork. 'He's the same age as you, but he's overweight, has heart problems, and is balding fast. . . . But he loves me sincerely, and he pays attention to me. He's *involved*.' I said I see. 'He's very jealous of you – and even now he may be lying in wait for us with his light.' She giggled. 'Sex-wise, though, I'm holding him off till I find out your position on commitment.'

As we exited the restaurant, Mary suddenly clutched at my arm and pointed up into the night. 'Can't you hear him?' She flattened us against the ivied wall of the Tudored restaurant. Despite the usual din of the city I could make out a roaring noise, quite near by and getting closer. Craning out from our hiding-place I saw a big dark shape hovering near a high-rise office building. At least he hadn't turned his searchlight on to us. As a gesture of defiance I shook my fist at the shape. It hovered some more and then, with a cheeky victory roll, whooshed away into black night.

*

In April I put up new curtains – a light green in my bedroom, and so I now had more bath towels. I also accepted an offer from a local rock radio station, KROQ, to host an early morning show on Saturdays. Why not? The job might get me out of the house for a monetary reason and put me back in the current swim. So much time spent alone lately. . . .

In the middle of one night, a call from Tommy: 'I'm in emergency – Nevada Memorial Hospital.' How, why? 'Very long story – I got attacked and badly wounded in a Thai restaurant in Las Vegas.' But what were you doing in Las Vegas when you were supposed to be in Minnesota and coming straight home? 'Those Thais, man! They're murderous. They could've killed me!' I asked no more because it was the middle of the night, a horrid time, and I didn't want disturbed dreams. There was the book to consider.

He came back. The cat came back. When I opened the door to his chimes he quickly bypassed me, head bowed down in shame. There was a big white bandage wound around his head like a turban. 'We'll look at the hospital photos later,' he mumbled as he entered his room. Next day he surfaced . . . I knew he was up because of the vase of roses in my study.

His story just didn't ring true: on the way back from his grandfather's funeral he'd stopped in Las Vegas for a meal at a Thai restaurant. The food had made him feel sick, so he asked to be excused payment of the bill. Suddenly he was surrounded by a gang of

Thais who proceeded to beat him about the head with blunt instruments. 'See the photos.' These were head shots in clinical colour showing scars running everywhere, cross-hatching, zig-zagging, as if somebody was trying to scratch Tommy out. These merciless, loveless, objective photos, taken from many angles, were giving off a scent of the truth, a peep into a possible scenario of the future. And I sloughed them off. What could he have done to provoke such a vicious attack? 'I told you.' The truth of the incident remained a mystery. But I was glad to have part of my family back alive, and Beefy, of course, was thrilled to death.

Life was back on course again and I sailed away on my book work. Tommy was off on a slew of job interviews and, at the weekend, I employed him as an accountant, filling in my income tax returns for $50. He finished the job remarkably fast. 'When you hire a Conway you hire the best!' he said as I counted out the cash. 'Let's celebrate with a banquet – you buy and I'll cook!' While he was out getting the ingredients I inspected his room and found a new list of good intentions: 'DAILY ACHIEVEMENTS: 6.30 a.m. – Wake Up!' and 'LONG-TERM GOALS: To Stop Living in His Shadow'. I didn't care too much for that one, but then I realized he was right. Perhaps the best thing would be for Tommy to leave quietly and make his own way in the world. But who would fill the void?

Mary brought her friend Kathy, a fellow nurse, to the 'banquet'. A sexy girl with a roving eye. Tommy attended so closely to her that he neglected the chicken and so Beefy gobbled up the bird, leaving his red rubber ball at the site as a mark of his achievement. A new chicken was purchased and eventually Tommy grandly paraded his *coq au vin* to our applause. There was an awful lot of vin on the coq and, together with two bottles of local champagne, we all grew pleasantly sloshed. Tommy and Kathy left the house to Mary and me.

But who had to clear up the mess next day? And who had to take Beefy to the vet when he cut his tongue open on one of Tommy's broken beer bottles? During the night Beefy was at the vet's I woke several times full of the dread that he had died of his wound. But when I picked him up he was full of beans and jumping all over me in his glee. He seemed to have taken to me at last. 'They take to anybody who feeds them,' said Mary when I called her. She had something unpleasant to tell me: Kathy had spent the night with Tommy and now she couldn't find her diamond ring. I promised I'd speak to him as soon as possible, but when, eventually, he returned he was in such high spirits I hadn't the heart or nerve. 'What a position!' he raved, 'Maître d' at the Kerkorchian Arms in Temple City!' An Armenian with a taste for Olde Englande had hired Tommy as a waiter. 'There's a costume and everything.' I congratulated him and went off for a swim at the Y.M.C.A.

I came home to find him entertaining a girl I'd never laid eyes on before. Some of my rarest old records were scattered on the floor and the record player was blasting out the first Elvis Presley album. These items were precious to me, and I'm afraid I lost my temper and let the topic stray from rare records to broken beer bottles and wounded dogs and a diamond ring that had 'disappeared'. 'Who is this guy?' demanded the girl, surly. I was furious that Tommy hadn't informed her as to who owned the house. 'There you go again,' said Tommy. 'Me, my, mine – you're self-obsessed and you should seek counselling. Think about it!' And he left the room. A few hours later, from my bedroom, I heard a door slam and a girly voice say, 'Fuck on a first date? You gotta be kidding. I'm Westside class, not Valley shit!'

Quietly I crept back into bed and resumed my Proust. Pretty soon Marcel had done the trick and sent me off to dreamland. But in the middle of a deep dream of happy seaside days in England I was woken by much banging about somewhere outside my door. Then slam! went the front-door . . . and that jolted me into action. Hastily tying my dressing gown, and with Beefy at my side romping, I rushed out and down the moonlit garden path just in time to see Tommy marching down the drive. He was wearing a brown suit and a fedora hat, and he was carrying a small battered valise. Were these heirlooms left him by his grandfather? An image sprang to mind – of an All-American kid hero setting off at dawn from the family homestead in search of fame and fortune.

I asked where he was going, but he didn't answer. Beefy and I trotted along beside him as he strode dowm Alameda St (a street with no pavements, but there was no traffic at this time of day or night). As we trotted I repeated my question and, after many yards, he answered, with his head pointed straight ahead, 'I'm going any place that's far away from Altadena and its culture.' I turned round and started running home, but Beefy had decided to travel with Tommy. I had to drag the dog by his collar to get him back, and there was much howling. In bed I couldn't stop my brain pondering, and after a little while I found myself dressed and driving down the street looking for him. Beefy sat beside me, hyperventilating.

He was at the intersection of Altadena and Lake, sitting with early morning workers on the bus-stop bench. I felt embarrassed questioning him in front of this audience of real working people, family men all, I felt certain. But I had to know: why are you going? 'To earn the money to pay off my debts to you and to buy a new car.' What happened to your old car? He left the bench and took me away from the workers. He whispered, 'They repossessed it in the night. Don't you notice *anything*?' How will you earn this money? He led me slowly back to the bus-bench. 'I'll win big in Vegas.' But that was where the Thais attacked you! 'Can't you understand this feeling?' and he smote the roseate-hued dawning. 'You're a writer. Try to understand.' Then the bus arrived and he left with the sensible regular workers and none of them smirked, none of them paid a bit of attention – and why the hell should they?

To kill the ghosts I invited the Hutchins and Herb over once again. They jumped at the idea and arrived pronto, laden with food – chicken pot pie, lemon meringue pie, pans of mashed potatoes, boats of Jello mould – accompanied by plenty of friends, one of whom was in a wheelchair, and there was much jolly strategy-making as we negotiated the enormous all-electric, fully-computerized machine through the front door. Once we were all gathered in the drawing room I told everybody to make themselves at home. 'It *is* their home,' said the man in the wheelchair, snatching up a handful of mixed cocktail nuts and downing them in one angry munch. Al from El Monte was his name, and he commandeered the evening, lecturing me on stereo systems and the superiority of quadrophonic sound as he whirred around the room, pointing with his spoon to where I should place the speakers I would be buying. Meanwhile Gertie Hutchins smoked and served, smoked and served, and Herb said not a word but made much noise as he swiftly worked his way through plate after plate, and the other friends chattered and laughed and declared with a sunny affirmation, and old man Hutchins repeated any remark that tickled his fancy. Everybody helped with the washing-up, and wheelchair Al did a spot of juggling with my best plates. Such a happy time – and then the house was silent once again, except for Beefy's breathing and grunting.

*

I was getting into my Y.M.C.A. kit at seven-ish in the morning when Tommy rang. He claimed he was speaking from a suite at the Stardust Hotel and Casino in Las Vegas. So far, he claimed, he'd won $200 and when he'd amassed enough money he'd be back to pay off everybody. 'You, too.' He certainly came back, striding in at the week's end with never a word and locking himself in his room. For several days I didn't see him, but he somehow sneaked a note to me. It was on the kitchen table, propped up against Beefy's red rubber ball. 'Detoxification again! No, but seriously – I've missed my little Altadena World!'

At the end of the week I ran into him in the Dr Bund Memorial Room (the one next to my study). He was watching T.V. Immediately he switched channels – from a cop show to the national news. After an item about violence in Lebanon he turned to me: 'Comment?' He was so anxious to learn but he wanted it fast and simple. My lecture on Lebanon was soon interrupted. 'Notice anything new about me?' I said that the scars looked better. 'Not that. See, I'm not wearing glasses any more, am I?' I'd never been terribly aware of his glasses. 'I've taken to contact lenses because I intend to climb that ladder to celebrity once more and you gotta look right. Why did *you* give up the race? What happened?' I said something about being an author, and being too old to be a rock and roll star. 'Yes – but don't you want to be a success?' The subject was dropped by my suggesting we go out to a cheap Mexican 'family' cafe. During the meal he started ordering the waiter around in a loud, officious voice. I told him to 'ssssh'. He told me to stop acting like a 'fucking teacher'. Diners turned their attention to us – family people, real people. I quietly reprimanded Tommy. He screamed, 'All I was trying to do was order some champagne! It's OUR ANNIVERSARY!' I felt myself blushing, soon to go up in smoke.

*

I never saw any of the money that Tommy won in Las Vegas, and he went back to his job as a waiter at the Kerkorchian Inn. Peace reigned again, I tapped my book along, Beefy lay at my feet most of the day. After two pages I always took a rest, lying on my bed, looking out of the window at the top of a tall poplar tree somewhere across the way. The poplar reminded me of Potter's Bar and golf-links and staying with my kindly common cousins. One afternoon when I was lying and dreaming, safe in the past, the phone rang. A bright, clipped and cracked adolescent voice wished me a good day and told me he represented the A.I. Collecting Agency and was this Giuseppe Aeillonissi he was addressing? *Certainly not!* If A.I. was not paid by next week, then legal action would be taken. *How dare they accuse me of being in debt! How had they obtained my unlisted number?* Unfortunately my steamed-up state had made my indignation come out peppered with stutters. Said the young whippersnapper, 'So – you're a cripple, are you? Can't say your letters? Do the world a favour and get some help!' And he downed the phone while I was stuttering a riposte. I took a Valium, called the police, they called the company and round about cocktail time I got another call. The boss of A.I. Collecting Agency shot out machine-gun style: 'Listen, buster. If you want privacy, move to a desert island. We can get any number we fucking well want in order to get the job done, see?'

Mary kindly agreed to come up for dinner; a nurse was just what I needed. We talked about 'relationships' again, and she explained that the reason she never climaxed with me was because I refused to 'cuddle' during the build-up period. Isn't that what you do *afterwards*? She hinted that her dating with the helicopter policeman might cease to be platonic. I was frightened that the next subject might be engagement rings, but no. . . . 'Ever see *Play Misty for Me* with Clint Eastwood?' Yes, I had seen this film about a psychopathic woman who stalks Eastwood after he spurns her. Why? 'Tommy reminds me of her. Get rid of him.' I changed the subject by talking about the fracas with the collecting agency. 'I'll bet this Giuseppe they're after is really Tommy,' she said matter-of-factly. The idea was unbearable. 'Do you mind if I search his room for Kathy's diamond ring.' I said I'd do some piano practice. A little later there was a sound of keys jangling at the front door. Mary and I found ourselves panting in the bedroom. What were we getting scared about? I went out to face him. He wasn't alone; he had a fellow waiter with him, a skinny, hollow-eyed shrimp. 'Hey,' said Tommy, swaying and with sweet breath. 'I'm pretty close to you now, workwise.' How's that? 'Well – I'm a waiter and you're a writer – waiter, writer, writer, waiter. They almost sound the same.' The skinny shrimp laughed and laughed. 'This is Doug and his lover just kicked him out and he has no place to stay.' And I found myself saying that yes, Doug could stay if he was quiet and tidy. 'Thanks, man,' said Doug. 'I'd like to suck you down to the gonads but. . . .' And he crashed on to the couch and Beefy licked him.

Back in the bedroom Mary told me I was crazy. Yes, but did she find the ring? 'No.' What a relief! 'But I did find a whole bunch of credit cards, and they're not Tommy's or Giuseppe's. Where did you say he works?' After sex I went to the bathroom. All was clear inside the house. As I was washing my hands I heard a retching noise and, looking out of the window, saw Doug being sick into one of my best bushes.

Tommy's hours at the Kerkorchian Inn were odd. Many days he didn't go there at all (so he had no need to borrow my car), but instead was picked up in the morning by some new girl and off they'd go to the ocean. He called this 'jaunting'. Every now and then he'd return for clothes or a shower, etc, and leave what my diary reported as a 'touching note'. But life at the Inn wasn't always as smooth as his jaunts; one night I found him bashing the furniture about and when asked what was the matter he said that Mr Kerkorchian had fired him. Next morning I phoned Mr K. and asked about the problem. In a thick accent, he said, 'Yes – true I get kicked down my own stairs by customer. I not deny it. But this boy go crazy and call not just ambulance but police and fire persons and I am not hurt. I have wife and brothers. Why he call fire persons? He should be in theatre. Besides he's rude and big-headed and he takes pills.' I reminded Mr K. that Christmas was coming and eventually he agreed to give Tommy one more chance.

On the strength of Christmas coming I decided to give myself a present by having a proper wooden fence erected – to replace the flimsy wire affair. Herb recommended a local building contractor, a thickset fellow with no neck, and he recommended a redwood fence accompanied, perhaps, by a Scandinavian-style hot tub, set in a surround of decorative brown half-bricks, the whole deal increasing the sales value of my property. I agreed to these improvements because I was still keen to make my house into a home. After signing some papers agreeing to let the work be done while I was in England over Christmas, I strolled up to the Post Office with Beefy to see if I'd had any cards yet. There was a registered letter from the International Revenue Service demanding thousands of dollars. What the. . . .? Then I remembered that I'd paid Tommy to do my American tax returns. I'd have a word with the family accountant when I got back to London.

Tommy had a shock for me later that night. 'I told that greaser Kerkorchian to take his job and shove it!' The world upside down again! 'Relax – I just got the tickets from the game show I won. Remember? "All Star Secrets"? So I'm off on December 14 to South America with $1,000 expenses – yippee!' And he dashed around the house, punctuating with leaps to the ceiling and jabs at the furniture and walls, pursued by Beefy, extremely high-tailed. Beefy and I saw him off at the airport; he was wearing a new blue suit he'd bought, but he was carrying one of my suitcases. He shook my hand, hugged Beefy long and hard, then shook my hand again. 'I'm nervous – pray for me.'

When we got home I padlocked the front gate and dead-bolted the front door. For some reason I was filled with a dread that I might be murdered some time soon. Assassination was only for those who were world-wide stars. Modern stars were too involved with real life. Were George Formby and Max Miller ever endangered? They inhabited comfy worlds of bar-room snugs, thick with tobacco smoke and the fumes of fried food; four-ale bars, cardigans and scarves, tip sheets and multi-coloured socks and co-respondent shoes. I determined to give up my quest to be a star again, to be an earth-shaker and trend-setter; instead I would study songs and perhaps become a local pub singer of comic songs. I went to bed with *Film Fun, 1945*.

A few days later, just prior to my leaving for England, I had a collect call from Santiago. Tommy said he had been robbed of all his traveller's cheques and I must wire $200 at once to the O'Higgins Bank of Chile. 'Then I can be back the day you leave – and so the house and dog won't be neglected. You see . . . I do think about you!'

*

There's not much to report on 1981. Life had become repetitive, as it does when one ceases to take action. A little violence now and then can be a good thing.

After the usual, and very agreeable Christmas festivities with family and friends, I went to lunch with the family accountants on a blue steel day in early January. My mother came too. Over coffee and chocolates I asked the chief accountant for a little more money, to tide me over till the rock book was published and selling like hot cakes. He wearily agreed, after a glance at my mother, and added with, I felt, a certain amount of acidity, 'You've certainly had more than your share of bad luck recently.' I said it was longer than 're-cently' but that some changes would be made and at once. 'That's the spirit,' said the accountant.

My mother was woken up early one morning by a call from Tommy. 'He seems a very excitable young man,' she said, as she gave me the phone. Tommy wished me a 'very, very happy Christmas and a truly prosperous New Year.' There was a long pause. 'Did you hear Beefy talking to you? We miss your spark – the house is dark.' I was touched.

To my surprise I was met at L.A. Airport by Beverly, very enticing in tight black P.V.C. trousers and flaming orange hair. 'I'm your New Year gift. Call me New Wavy.' She was driving a smart blue Honda Prelude, with a dash that was like the control panel of a moon rocket.

I determined to buy such a car – another new leaf. As we purred the thirty miles to Altadena I struggled to make conversation, always rather a task with Beverly. I did discover that she was, at present, selling cosmetics from the boot of her car, driving around the San Fernando Valley with her samples. But she never ventured into Altadena. 'No Jews and too many blacks,' she said with a shiver. This didn't help the depression brought on by jet-lag.

As we rounded the corner of Christmas Tree Lane and entered Alameda St the usual dread shot up like sick from my stomach to my throat, and then stuck. What disasters awaited? But I was cheered to see a sturdy bright redwood fence guarding my house, a healthy, bouncy Beefy at the front door, and on the back patio a hot tub with decking and half-brick tiles. Standing on top of the hot-tub lid was Tommy, in a grey suit, grinning and brandishing a champagne bottle. 'I'm worth $4,000!' he challenged me. How's that? 'Game show, game show!' I couldn't believe that one win on 'All Star Secrets' had turned on such a tap of prosperity, but I shushed Beverly because I didn't want to spoil the New Year so soon. I even agreed to let Tommy lead us through the snaps of his South American trip. 'The travel bug has bitten me now. Know what I want to achieve next? To be shot into outer space – the ultimate challenge.' I said I had lots of phone calls to make and that Beverly might enjoy some backgammon. Later she and I sat in the new hot tub, playing with the jets and watching Tommy knocking about the house with a drink in his hand, followed by Beefy. Now I was seeing the house from a godlike angle, a philosophical worm. How absurd and pathetic we all were! Beverly rubbed her foot on my crotch and said, 'When are you going to get rid of him?'

Next day I bought a hatchback Honda Accord and Tommy gave me $1,500 for my Ford Granada. Within the hour he was off to San Diego, saying he had a series of important parties to attend.

Alone again. Of course I had old Beefy – he was becoming more faithful to me, he seemed to understand, and he let me plod on with the blessed book – my hoped-for hot air escape from this circus – but every so often he'd wander into the study to check up.

After work I'd treat myself to a hot-tub dip, and from the steam I'd again play the godlike worm, viewing the pathos of my brown lounge and weedy garden, trying to whip up deep thought summaries about existence: Life is . . . this or that or just a riddle or just a bowl of cherries. Writers through the ages have had the confidence to make such pronouncements but I was damned if I could make a contribution.

Did Beefy's red rubber ball tell me anything? Except that he wanted me to throw it into the back garden? Which I did . . . and then went indoors and knocked out a new song at the piano, inspired by Tommy's telephone line about the whole house missing me:

WON'T YOU COME HOME?

The car won't work, the birds don't chirp,
The toaster's on the blink,
And dirty dishes sit there in the sink.
The cuckoo clock won't cuckoo,
Dear old Rover seems insane,
Won't you come home and start our world again?

The plants and flowers look droopy
Though I've watered them for days.
The cockatoo's gone loopy,
You should hear the things he says.
The L.A. sun just isn't fun,
I long for London rain.
Won't you come home and start our world again?

The fridge froze up last Friday,
Now it's merely lumps of ice.
And no day's ever my day,
You'll admit it isn't nice.
We miss your spark, the house is dark,
Though sunshine floods the lane,
Won't you come home and start our world again?

It's a funny thing, but every time I sang the line about the spark and the dark and the lane I got as close to tears as I'd been in a long time. It was a good feeling. Nights could be blue and fearsome – maybe the result of take-out dinners of fried chicken, macaroni salad, baked beans and onion rings – and once I had a vision of a vile place of worship above the corridor by the bathroom. A radiant white light of great force lanced down and some invisible evil landed, hovering outside my bedroom door. A noiseless voice told me that life's answer lay waiting in that strange land above the corridor – layers of floors with many rooms. I shouted 'George Formby!', got out of bed in a muck sweat and headed for the bathroom. The lavatory was flushing merrily. But nobody was in the house. After a check I dressed in my gym kit and went to the Y.M.C.A. for a work-out and swim, followed

128

by a full breakfast including Polish sausage. That did the trick.

Mary called for a meeting. At The Pepper Mill she took the chair, telling me to order the filet mignon if I so wished. We sat in the middle of the restaurant and for a long time she toyed with her shrimp salad. Then she said that though at first she'd been infatuated with me she'd soon discovered that I wasn't a natural hand-holder, cuddler or listener. Her cop was all these things. I agreed with her and added that, in truth, I'd always had a crush on her younger sister Carol, ever since my birthday party. Tears started rolling down Mary's cheeks, right in the middle of The Pepper Mill. People were passing by with their salads. Mary said it was always the same old story: her boy-friends fell for Carol. I said that I hadn't necessarily *fallen* for Carol – but I had to have someone, and Mary had given me up for the cop. Still, we'd had some laughs, hadn't we?

I called Carol. Like her sister she lived with the parents in a man-sion in the better part of Pasadena. Yes, she'd come out on a date, she was between boy-friends. After a very liquid dinner at Monahan's, the 'Oirish' place, spooning in a booth behind closed curtains, she agreed to join me on the couch at the house. When we got into heavy necking Beefy jumped up and tried to interpose his body. Perhaps he was on Mary's side? I locked him in the Dr Bund Memorial Room, telling him not to worry. After a few vodkas-and-orange I started tell-ing the voluptuous Carol how I'd always been crazy about her. I was surprised at my ardour. She responded with deep kissing and we seemed to be well on the way to the bedroom when I changed the record and put on Whispering Jack Smith singing 'My Blue Heaven' in 1927. This broke the spell: Carol actually burst out laughing while our lips were pressed together, not a pleasant experience. I asked why, oh why. 'Those lyrics! "When whippoorwhills call and evening is nigh . . ." *Come on*! And the guy's high-pitched voice. The whole thing is like . . . like an old black and white cartoon!'

Well, that put me in a bad mood all right. I had to start up the old Lothario routine from a new tack. Where was that Barry Manilow album they'd given me at the radio station? But before I could get us racing again, who should burst into the lounge but Tommy, wearing my leather jacket. 'Uh-oh!' he said leeringly, then he cackled and went off to liberate Beefy. 'If you ask me,' said Carol, 'that guy's in love with you. You know he only wants one thing from girls.' I didn't ask whether he'd ever got it from *her*. No, I saw Carol to her car and then buttoned up my shirt and trousers.

I looked in on Tommy and Beefy. The T.V. was playing but

Tommy was deep into a book. What was so engrossing? Shakespeare, James Clavell? 'I'm reading your diary.' And that was all he said.

*

In July I enrolled at the University of California's class in Speech Therapy – my stutter had lately developed a side effect: the back teeth were cutting the sides of the tongue on certain tense days. The University applied electronics to the ears and suggested slow, steady breathing and even slower speaking, like a record at half-speed. I felt like a bloody fool, especially when ordering a meal.

One evening, returning from speech therapy and thinking slow and calm, a Rastafarian in a beaten-up old auto ran a red light and smashed into my new blue Honda Accord. The hatchback was crumpled like a used Kleenex but I was O.K. physically, though shaken and furious mentally. Trying to remonstrate with the black youth I bit my tongue and drew blood. After a black cop had taken the details and calmed me down I drove the crumpled Honda home, poured out a full glass of wine, lay back in the lounger and watched the news about the Pope getting shot. Next thing I knew was Tommy tumbling in, high as a kite, and full of histrionics: 'Hey, hey, hey! What happened to your car? Anybody get killed? Shall we call the paramedics?' There was glee, too. Three times he asked me how the accident happened, and three times I told him. He started laughing and asked me again. Finally I was forced to take action . . . No, I simply lost my temper – and hit him in the face over and over again. He fell about the lounge and then the hall and then the bedroom, he flopped and flapped like a rag doll. Then he crumpled on to the floor. Two crumples in one night. I picked him up. He wandered back into the lounge and sat on the rug. 'I could've hit you but I didn't – I could've killed you. But . . . *no way*. I'd never hit you, ever. I just wanted you to get your anger out – because you're angry with the universe, aren't you?' I felt like hitting him again, and then I wanted to hug his blood-streaked face to my thigh and to tell him I was so very sorry and could he ever forgive me? But I resisted. Tommy, by contrast, started crying loud and long. 'You have no heart,' he said, somewhere between the tears. 'You're still a very proper Bryanston boy.'

That weekend Witham condescended to drive up to my 'jungle residence' and take me out for a Mexican dinner. 'Tell me your news' was his opening gambit and I knew that in order to keep him amused (and to keep our friendship) I'd have to launch into a descant of my recent woes. After spinning the yarn, with me as the luckless victim, he ordered another Tecate beer, sat back and said, 'Frankly, I count you as a lucky man – lucky because you don't have to work.' But of course I work, I spluttered. I'm writing a book and it's extremely hard work. He sniffed. 'You're doing what you enjoy doing – real work is the opposite. You're still a scrimshanker, a slacker pursuing the same hobbies you were pursuing at school.' I told him he was being unfair, but I didn't get up and walk out or anything like that. Nothing he said to me could ever break up our friendship, for Witham was an important silver cord between me and the values and beliefs of my class and background; of the England both of us had known briefly in those few precious years between the end of World War Two and the coming of the Beatles.

Witham, holed up in his West Hollywood castle in the air, with a sea of dope dealers, transsexuals and threatening ethnics swirling below him, had protected himself from catching the savage virus of the L.A. natives. He had his Wisden, his card cricket, his Bass Ale and his *Daily Telegraph* (monthly in bundles). I had chosen, it seemed, to live among the natives. And I was paying the price. I likened my present position to that of Jesus Christ himself.

Witham let out an embarrassingly loud hoot of laughter, slapped his cavalry-twilled thigh, waved away the waiters who were rushing to our table and then, after composing himself with a cough, said 'There's no doubt about it – you're tremendous value! You're bathos unbounded! And I must say – you're never a bore. *Jesus Christ indeed*! . . . what a great idea!'

To calm him down and to show him that my life wasn't utter chaos, I invited him back for coffee and brandy. He expressed disappointment that Tommy wasn't around to amuse him; he didn't seem very interested in the comparative tidiness of the house. Suddenly lightning and thunder struck, a semi-tropical storm. 'Only up here in jungle town,' said Witham, sipping sedately. But Beefy, locked outside, barked vigorously at each thunder-clap. 'Why don't you get rid of that fucker?' I said I certainly wasn't going to abandon my best friend – steadfast, straightforward, incorruptible, devoted. Then I realized what I was saying and stopped. Witham said, 'You just have to be surrounded by fans, don't you? Hardly the Empire model!'

*

The break in the weather was followed by a lucky break in both my writing and my social life: the book started rocketing along and Tommy got a new job. He slammed down the phone, yelled his usual

'Yippeeee!', galloped about the house and then danced with Beefy. After I'd settled him down with a glass of wine I asked the nature of this job. 'Six weeks' work at $4 an hour making wooden loaves of bread as collection boxes for a religious organization.' At times he could be very articulate. And so, for a while, I was left in peace to get on with my writing.

Between pages I took to sitting at the piano and pecking at novelty songs I might use in some future night club act. The best – the most cathartic – concerned Tommy. I called it 'Cup O'Noodle'. Recently he'd been reduced to eating snatched meals from a heated styrofoam cup containing noodles and flavoured objects. These cups, with their bone-dry contents, were obtainable at cut-rate stores for a few cents, and were marketed as 'Cup O'Noodle.' Flavours ranged from beef to chop suey. The printed ingredients ran on for ages. Now here was Tommy with his heated styrofoam cup and there was I, out with friends like Witham, supping off rich, strange and expensive foods. My conscience pricked . . . and I wrote the song.

CUP O'NOODLE
(Sung to the tune of 'The British Grenadiers')

1. 'My name is Cup O'Noodle 'cos that is what I eat.
   I sometimes work in waiting, and sometimes on the street.
   Or else I'm a telephone salesman, or selling ancient cars.
   But mostly you can find me now – hanging round in bars.
2. I wear the finest clothing from Whitcombs' Haberdashery.
   The stuff is made in London, but it's kept next door to me.
   On Monday I don Irish tweed, on Tuesday slacks for sport.
   On Wednesday, I'm in pin stripes, and on Thursdays I get caught.

All my friends loved the song, especially Jack Wontner. 'You're quite the poet,' he said. But when I sang it to Tommy he grew surly and stamped about. After I apologized he told me he'd been fired from the religious job and the holiday season was approaching and he had no money. 'I did so want to purchase a Christmas tree with all the trimmings.' Never mind, I told him, something seasonal is bound to turn up, and in the meantime he should have a good feed on Thanksgiving Day next week. 'Who'll feed me?' I reminded him of his many girl-friends and he started to make a list.

I celebrated Thanksgiving with Witham at yet another Mexican restaurant. 'Anything to avoid turkey and pumpkin,' he said. A span-

132

gled and wide-hatted singer, working the tables, stopped by for requests and Witham tipped him $10 to sing a traditional Mexican num-
ber which involved imitating a rare bird with a very high-pitched trill.
This amused Witham enormously and he hacked at my shin to rub
home his joke. Afterwards, drunk, he roared off in his Jaguar to the
safety of his West Hollywood air castle. At a loose end, I decided to
drop in for a nightcap at the British pub in Pasadena. Imagine my surprise when I saw that both Elaine and Mary were there, drinking with
friends in separate corners. Like a referee I brought the two women
together and soon they were sparring. Mary said my jeans were so
tight you could count all my change; Elaine said the tighter the better;
Mary said she preferred me with no pants on at all. Encouraged, I invited her for a drink in the back alley nearby, where I asked whether
she and the sky cop were still friends. 'More than friends,' she replied
slyly and pointed up into the night where, as if on cue, a blinding
white light splashed down on to us and a whirring assaulted my ears.
'It's heaven to me,' she said.

I came home alone and for a while I sat in the darkness listening to
Vera Lynn singing 'Up the Wooden Hill to Bedfordshire'. This
always took me back to childhood days, but the sweetness was tinged
with sadness; still it was pleasant enough. Then slam went the front
door and Tommy lurched in. I asked how his Thanksgiving had been.
'Lousy.' He had been with a new girl and her family. 'Her mother
slapped her in the face and she slapped the mother. We had turkey
roll instead of whole, fresh-cooked bird. I called up my family in Minnesota, but not one would speak to me. This is always a bum time of
year.' I told him to look on the bright side – after all, he had a roof
over his head and a faithful dog. '*Your* roof and *your* dog.' He came
and stood over me and the Barcalounger. 'Disasters always come in
threes, you know that.' What did he mean? 'I mean that William Hol-
den just died and so did Natalie Wood. Who's next?' And with that he
stepped out on to the patio for a think. He never ever went into the
hot tub.

Luckily there was no third death to upset our own Altadena world.
Jack Albertson, the actor, died somewhere else, and so the folk myth
was satisfied. Fate let Tommy land a seasonal position as Santa Claus
in a Temple City shopping mall. And the back of my rock book had
been broken, so I was feeling relieved. I managed to entice Beverly
up to Altadena with the offer of a pre-Christmas dinner. 'It's not
something we Jews celebrate,' she said, 'but I'll overlook it.' She had
Cornish rock hen and German chocolate cake at the Oirish place and

after a rest on the couch the door-bell chimed. I adjusted my clothes and opened up. 'Ho, ho, ho!' said Tommy, dressed in his full Santa Claus regalia, and clutching a big gift-wrapped parcel to his long white beard. 'Open please,' he said in a deep voice. The parcel contained dozens of glasses in all shapes and sizes and a cigar box. 'Happy Christmas to you . . . and many, many more,' he sang and then tripped off to his room.

Beverly and I repaired to my bedroom, but before resuming our activity she insisted on my opening the cigar box. Inside was one fat cigar, but it had been smoked and was almost a butt. I hoped this was not going to be typical of Christmas in California. This year I would stick it out in the land of sunshine because the book was tearing away and I was determined to finish it off by the end of January.

On Christmas Day, a hot and muggy one, Tommy tied a red ribbon round Beefy's neck to go with the tiny green plastic folding fir tree in the lounge. I'd had a lot of cards (mostly from family) but Tommy only got one (from a 'Mike' in Marina Del Rey), so I sent him a king-sized card. Beefy got one from our family Labrador in England.

We had an early dinner with friends of mine, a husband and wife team, ragtime buffs, at L.A. International Airport in its famous revolving tower restaurant. Tommy behaved very well. About 6 p.m. we went our separate ways. I went home and sat in the hot tub with a copy of *Country Life*, studying the estate agent advertisements, comparing their stately homes with my brown drawing room, seen through the window in front of me – an empty, silent set, scene of domestic drama and now enjoying an interval of order. Knight, Frank & Rutley of Hanover Square were offering a fine Queen Anne house set in mature grounds in Dorset, solid stone and seasoned wood, dressing rooms, a walled garden and lots of moss on the ornamental stone lions; flowing from the pile was a green-sea sward with rich insides – moist soil and friendly ants – girt by an ancient hedge. Somewhere over the hedge was a cricket pitch and on the boundary lay Smith and me singing songs as we watched the First XI play the Old Boys, eagerly awaiting the arrival of Captain Manning in his baccy-stained tweed jacket, packing his pipe from a dirty leather pouch, gig-lamps perched on nose, always the same wonderful routine on a hot summer's afternoon – the bulldog bark of 'Swimming for all you little wretches! All up to no good, I'll be bound . . . but the water will cleanse you of your wickedness, ha ha!'

My diary entry for New Year's Eve 1981 reads:

134

What an obstacle to refinement is the body! Wind emits from the anus, foul breath from the mouth, rotting smells from the armpits. We are lumpy hulks from an ancient sludge – so how can we be gentlemen when encased in this clobber? Oh, to be a spirit, a zephyr! Today I've been bothered by bowels turning to liquid – and no one could care less: Curlew Worthington showed annoyance when I mentioned my condition on the phone; Jack Wontner and wife ignored the subject as if I was showing bad taste in mentioning it. I celebrated New Year's Eve with them at the Oirish place, and just before midnight I asked what was their wish for 1982. 'We don't know what we'll be doing tomorrow, let alone next year,' said Jack. I said next year was coming up in one minute. 'Well, whatever,' said his wife and Jack changed the subject by telling her to walk through the crowded bar so that we could count the men and women ogling her.

*

For the first time in ages I made no New Year's resolutions nor lists of 'Aims and Goals' in my new diary. In my mind I resolved to deal with Tommy one way or the other, but first I had to finish my book. 'Get rid of the dog, I say,' said Witham on the phone. 'Keep the boy – he's the source of endless amusing stories.' Fat lot of good my friends were.

January saw me start a series of bad colds that continued on and off for the next few years. My medicine was an old family remedy, the 'jollop': honey, lemon juice and lashings of Scotch. But the new Scotch bottle was empty and I'd only had a few sips . . . Tommy must have swigged the rest. When at last I confronted him I informed him he wasn't going to be able to take advantage of me for much longer. He didn't reply but just stood there swaying in the lintel of his bedroom door, staring straight through me. In the privacy of my bedroom I felt a sharp pang of meanness.

He vanished for many days and when he returned he said he was being trained as an 'assessor for an Orange County electronics company, with blueprint copying as my speciality'. The work would be at night-time. So I enjoyed evenings alone, dining off take-out fried chicken and hamburgers, and watching a lot of educational television. David Attenborough shocked and saddened me with his news that we had developed from worms and jellyfish. So I went channel-grazing, eventually settling on Connie Francis, erstwhile hit-maker of sorrow songs to a chink-chink beat, a heroine of mine. But tonight

135

she was talking about the consquences of being raped in a motel, and I didn't want to know so I changed to a Lassie film.

One of the advantages to my disc jockey job (on Saturday mornings on local station KROQ) was that the music policy called for sweeps of up to forty minutes of non-stop rock, and this allowed me to relax: read the paper, walk the dog, have breakfast, talk to the listeners on the phone. Many had to be told to bugger off if they didn't care for Vera Lynn or Al Jolson. But some were girl fans and a few seemed anxious for a date. I agreed to rendezvous with a sexy-voiced caller at a certain Chinese restaurant in Hollywood. Fortunately I took the precaution of arriving early and positioning myself at a poky booth in a dark corner. A few minutes later a vast shape darkened the doorway, waddled up to the bar, asked for me, turned and scanned the joint. Detailed by the overhead spotlight was a garish butterball covered in turquoise jewellery. I slunk out of the back door.

Unfortunately there was no relief to call up: Beverly had announced her engagement to Irv, the jeweller with the penchant for anal intercourse; Elaine was too busy chiropractoring and 'finding' herself; and Mary was in the clutches of the flying policeman. So when I received a letter from a KROQ listener, a girl called Kris, stating that she loved me and my show and, in particular, a song I'd recorded called 'Oh! What a Beauty!', referring to a marrow, and was she correct in understanding that a marrow was shaped like a banana and did I own such a thing, I was most definitely interested in meeting her and checking her out. I rang her and arranged to rendezvous by daylight in the the parking lot of the Oirish place. If everything checked out fine then we could repair inside to a snug booth, draw the curtains and get to know one another.

She beat me to the punch. I was standing in the parking lot peering around when I heard a 'beep-beep'. A girl in a jockey cap was sitting in a Volkswagen Beetle and smiling like Shirley Temple. I approached warily and she got out. She was very small, very young and extremely well put together. Black tights and a clinging sweater revealed exciting curves; she spun round like a model, showing an ideal bottom. 'Hi, I'm Kris, but you can call me Biffy.' I said I had a dog called Beefy whom I loved greatly and she gurgled out a baby laugh. I wondered how the table talk would be.

This I remembered: she was 20 going on 21, and lived with her parents in Anaheim, a part of Orange County, over an hour from Pasadena; but she never minded driving because her 'Volkswaggon' was her life, and she was a 'Volks Freak' and belonged to 'Volks

International'. Of course she also loved KROQ and British accents in particular. Her laugh was punctuated by a tiny 'EEEK' that rose from her chest to her head and then ran away like a frightened mouse. As the 'EEK' left I got a good view of her teeth and saw that, unlike those of most Americans, they were irregular, like broken battlements, and stained swimming-pool green. 'I've been in jail, y'know,' she said and hung her head. 'Only possession of coke . . . but my dad was real mad. He's a stockbroker.' I told her I'd be kind and considerate, but I was longing to handle this exquisite toy. 'My last boy-friend was moody. He beat me up, pushed me through a plate-glass window. He was from the East Coast.' Such a fragile art object! What did she do about this violence? 'I took pity on his underprivileged position and bought him a car – only a beat-up Chevy. He lived in it for a year. Sometimes we made out in it. Eeeeeeek!!'

She agreed to follow me home. I was shivering with excitement – an over-40 with an under-21! Why, I could be her father! I found Beefy locked in my bedroom. From Tommy's room came the sound of two different kinds of snore.

Kris stripped off slowly for me, and she was a teenage rock song: perfectly-proportioned body, a dinky toy Playboy centrefold, a living doll. I couldn't wait to get inside her, like easing into a hot bath after a rugger game. The explosion came fairly fast and she, for her part in receiving the goods, made much moaning which fortunately was not as piercing as her eeeeking. She left about midnight.

*

Tommy, despite the offer from the Orange County electronics company, started working as a 'trainee house insulator', and I started seeing Kris fairly regularly. The hot tub was a perfect trysting place, and that first twilight among the bubbles and foam I examined her body in detail as, wide-open-eyed, she gazed at the stars. A perfect body and I was her owner, but I'd never break her as I had my other toys many years ago at that birthday party. She levelled at me her Mia Farrow eyes and I reassured her over and over. After the hot-tub examination I bought us the best-selected breasts from Pioneer Chicken take-out and we ate from the couch to the music of World War Two.

On this second date I let her stay the night because she wanted to join me and Beefy at KROQ for the radio show. I warned her this meant a crack-of-dawn departure but she nodded eagerly, kneeling in a praying position on the bed, squidgy breasts stuck out waiting. What a decent fit she was! I pulled her on like a marshmallow sock and as she came into close-up her mouth hung open like a fish and her eyes widened almost down to that mouth. But afterwards, at sleep time, I realized yet again that a larger bed – the Kalifornia King – must be purchased and at once. I liked to thrash around in my own rangeland and strangers bothered me. Kris liked to cling and touch and murmur. 'I just love everything English, everything,' she said at some stage of the night.

One evening, at her invitation, I went to have dinner in her part of the world, in Anaheim, Orange County, home of Disneyland. To get there I had to drive down unknown freeways, amidst fleets of white-shirted businessmen coming home after an honest day's work, between rolling velvet hills and beautifully laid out tract home waves, until diving down to earth close by an enormous scalloped stadium.

Anaheim turned out to be a disappointment – too homogenized, too mathematical, all the same shops and restaurants you can find wherever you stray in America today. I longed for remainders of the past, of orange groves and ostrich farms, of beef kingdoms and the rugged free-wheeling spirit of the German pioneers who had founded Anaheim. The closest place to my wants that Kris could find was a great barn called Stuart Anderson's Black Angus, but this steak establishment was part of a chain, too. Still, the dim walls were decorated with tinted photos of 1920s life in Orange County and I examined them with interest, blocking out as best I could the 'foreground atmosphere music' of Neil Diamond. I flew into the flat, open fields, the tilted barns, the rows of spiky little fruit trees. Over against the lonely railroad station was a sleeping Mexican suitably cloaked and sombreroed. The past as refuge . . . but not strong enough tonight, so I ordered a double margarita on the rocks with no salt. Kris had a wine cooler. I had a T-bone steak, but she only had a salad. Conversation was limited; I was shocked she didn't know who Jack Nicholson was. Then I was disgusted by my shock. Why the hell should she know about some sybaritic self-satisfied film actor? She reached out under the tablecloth for my knee.

After dinner we drove around the neighbouring hills looking for a lonely spot with bushes, where we could make out. She knew the area since childhood and soon we were heading for the undergrowth. But round the bend came a pick-up truck and it screeched to a halt. A gang of youths in the flat-bed stood up and cheered us on. I was fiddling with my fly buttons. Out of the driver's cabin poked a mass of heavy-metal curly hair and it gravelled macho, 'Gotcha, Kris! I'll be back later for my piece of your ass – but don't give the old fart a coronary!' And off they roared down into twinkling Anaheim.

From then on I kept my affair with Kris strictly to the house and its environs. I was starting to feel protective towards her, she was my toy child. Now I knew what the songs meant when they sang about 'dolls'. Each time she presented herself to me for a date she wore a different outfit. But the style was always the same: 'California Heritage', picked from thrift shops – ruffles and lace and ski-caps; blood-orange slacks of the Forties, wide-fanned frilly skirts of the Fifties, stiff like lampshades. She stood there, trembling, for my approval. Always she was clutching at my hand and I let her hang on, even in public. Such behaviour wasn't my style but I had pity for her because she'd told me about her asthma and how incidents in her childhood had set off the asthma, so I let her hold me and cough. Pity surged around inside me like a hot drink before bedtime, I loved pity. When she had a paroxysm of coughing I asked whether there was anything I could do to help. 'Just be near me,' she whispered. While practising my comic songs at the piano I'd let her sit up beside me. As I sang and strummed she would show her contentment by emitting a kind of whirring and purring sound.

*

On Saturday February 20, 1982, Kris arrived at 5 p.m., wakening me from the Valium-induced sleep I always took after my KROQ radio show. She stood by the bed and then from behind her back she produced a gift-wrapped package. I hate having to tear off gift wrapping in front of the giver, it's so embarrassing. I don't deserve anything nice. I wanted to get the 'Thank you, thank you' over even while tearing the slick bright paper. The present was a coffee mug printed all round with a piano keyboard and filled with jelly babies. 'Thank you, thank you!' And then I went to my study to get the cash I'd left in the drawer of my desk for our dinner and movie date that evening. There wasn't any cash. I thought of Tommy.

I'd deal with him later. I'd tell him off in front of Kris.

It was long past midnight when we returned and the rock blare could be heard from the road – each beat bash a hammer on my skull, and also an insult. *You wait.* But my keys wouldn't work because the front door was chained from the inside. Locked out of my own house! There was another way to enter, but it was a humiliating way. I crawled in through Beefy's 'doggie door,' a square hole with a rubber flap cut into the kitchen door. The flap flopped on my face. Where was the party?

139

There wasn't one. I switched off the stereo in the drawing room and then went round switching off lights. There was food on the floor and some beer bottles. I let Kris in through the front door and she said, 'Egad!' I just cursed. There were burns on the carpet in front of his room. I knocked. No reply. I banged. No reply. I tried the handle and, surprisingly, it turned. And there they were – he and his girl, whoever she was, tangled up on the mattress, zonked out, drunk or drugged or both, making disgusting heavy breathing noises.

I went over and shook him violently. No response. I yanked him out of the tangle, off the mattress and on to the floor, and I kicked and kicked at his naked thigh with the pointed toe of my cowboy boot. I shouted to him to get out, to be gone by tomorrow. Then I left.

Minutes went by. Kris and I lay on my bed; she was looking at me but I was looking at the ceiling. Then there was a knock on the door, quite polite. I didn't answer. But the door opened and he stood there, in his silk pyjamas under the lintel and glaring his killer glare. An evil cold-fish eye – but I wasn't about to give in, what with Kris clutching at my arm and mumbling. I told him to get out of my room. He continued to glare. Kris said, 'Egad, egad.' I sat up straight and said that if he wouldn't get out then I'd have to make him. He just glared. *You fucker*. I got out of bed, in my underpants, and went up to him and punched him in the head as hard as I could. It wasn't a prep school punch at all, it was intended to smash his fucking skull in. Then, as he stumbled and turned, I punched him in the neck, the shoulder, the ear. Why wasn't he fighting back? He could've easily whipped me.

He turned and faced me, tottering, glassy-eyed now. I started punching him again and my punches, growing longer and more accurate, eventually sent him staggering from the bedroom, across the corridor by the bathroom and into the drawing room where he collapsed floppily on to the hardwood floor. I stood and watched. After a few moments he sat, up, crossed his legs, put his elbows on his knees and his fists into his cheeks and went pensive.

I walked back to my bedroom, shut the door and got into bed. Kris was sitting up with the bedclothes wrapped round her; her teeth were chattering. I told her that all I'd done was what had to be done, and she agreed and smoothed my brow. For a short while we had peace in the house. Then . . . a dreadful bellowing from next door. And banging. Splintering. The wall shook and a school picture came down. 'I'LL KILL HIM!' we heard Tommy say. 'Easy, easy,' said a girl's voice. Then there was more racket – banging, splintering, thudding, shouting, cursing, screaming.

I locked our door and called up the Altadena Sheriff's Department to report a disturbance.

In no time at all they were there, in force, in my front garden. But Tommy was with them too . . . weaving around the moonlit lawn, accusing me loudly of attempted murder. There was blood all over his face. Two cops listened, another took notes. I felt that, as property-owner, I should make my presence known.

I stood on my front porch in dressing gown and slippers, and they told me that serious charges were being brought against me. I asked whether I could make a phone call. 'Your privilege, sir,' said one of them. At the far end of the lawn Tommy weaved around, nursing his face.

Beefy led us down the corridor. The cop, lumbered down with weapons and whatnot, almost knocked off one of my framed album covers. In the study I called Jack Wontner; it was around 1 a.m. and I'd woken him up, but he was quite together. I asked whether the police had any right to be on my property. 'They have no right.' I turned to the cop and told him what the best-selling ex-cop author had said. The man looked daggers . . . but he backed off.

He sent his men home through the front gate. Tommy was sitting by the flower-bed. The cop looked at us both with contempt and said, 'We'll leave you guys to sort out your own domestic affair.'

The girls were in their rooms, all was quiet. I put my hand on Tommy's shoulder and apologized. He held out a hand to show me some more blood. 'But you hit me! *You* hit me!' Again I apologized and he suddenly burst into tears. I didn't like that. Then: 'Sure I'll leave in the morning. I have to make my own life. I understand. . . .' He got up and held me. 'But . . . I'm so scared.' I assured him that he didn't have to leave absolutely at once, he could take his time, we'd talk tomorrow. I couldn't bear to have my world turned upside down like a wastepaper basket.

But next morning, Sunday, with its church bells and neighbours in dark suits and bright dresses, Tommy was in a very aggressive mood. Kris and I passed him in the kitchen corridor. He said as he moved, 'I'll never forgive you. You hit me in front of her.'

Kris and I excused ourselves and went off for a drive. It was nice clean weather and we tried to enjoy ourselves, but when we came home he wasn't there and nor were his things. My leather jacket was missing too. Kris said she had a Volkswagen Club meeting and she left me about 6 p.m. It was then that I developed a hole in my stomach, like the one I used to get on the first day at Newlands.

I rang Jack Wontner to apologize and he invited me to dinner at The Panda, a local Chinese. Luckily he was alone, so I felt bold enough to empty myself. I said I was experiencing a great void now that Tommy had gone. 'Fill it with a parakeet,' said Jack; he didn't want any details. 'Look, the kid was a sociopath and you're well rid of him. If he'd been in my life like he was in yours, I'd have gunned him down long ago.' I thanked Jack for everything. He shook his head and pulled out his credit card.

But the house was terribly empty now . . . the corners where his stereo speakers had sat, the piece of carpet where his mattress had lain, the wall above it where he'd hung his collection of Samurai swords. There'd be no more home-cooked dinners with his writing out a menu and leaving a blank for me to fill in with the 'Entry of Your Choice'; no more folding of paper napkins into wigwams so as to pretend they were fancy serviettes; no more front-door-knob being fiddled-with noisily and then the banging of the door, the clomping of boots and the call of, 'Eeeeee-Unnnnnn, I'm home!'

'We miss your spark, the house is dark . . .' The line from my song kept running through my brain. His line really. I talked a lot to Beefy and waited for the call that never came.

His girl-friend called, though. She had some facts to tell me: Tommy was often stuffed with $100 bills and she didn't like to guess where they came from; he used to give her clothes – like a nice pair of Italian-made sweat pants – and she was pretty sure they were mine; the day he checked out her car was choked with all kinds of articles. 'He was no good and you were taken. I'm real sorry.' By any chance did she have his current number? 'Why d'you want to talk to that asshole? Oh . . . you want your sweat pants, O.K.' She gave me a number in Venice.

He was very cold, but there was a party in swing behind him and I felt sure someone was standing next to him. He picked his words carefully. 'You know what? I'm very proud because I resisted my impulses on Saturday night. I could have snuffed you out just like that.' But he called me back to apologize. There were waves breaking in the background, nothing else. He said, 'I'll always love you.' And that was when – I couldn't believe it – I actually cried. I hadn't cried for years and the tears tasted acrid, but then I suppose they'd been stored up there a long time. He waited and then he asked if he could come over soon to pick up some of the things he'd forgotten. 'I'll never forget you,' he said.

Afterwards I sat about and thought. It became clear to me that

142

Tommy was beautiful and dangerous and I loved him. But nobody was to be told.

My friends were very understanding when I told them my version of recent events . . . all except Cherie Nussbaum. She was cold and terse, she who had got me into this house. 'I haven't got time to deal with your life. We're in different spheres.' There was a click. 'That's the call I was expecting. *Ciao.*' I called back to say I was very fond of her, and why was she acting this way? She laughed and hung up.

Now I grew angry – especially when I remembered that I'd lent Cherie's daughter my old gramophone several years ago. Only *lent*. There was a space in the drawing room which needed filling. This time Cherie was ice: 'Sandra left our community. Do not bother me again.' But she did give me Sandra's new number and Sandra said sure, come pick up the stereo any time, her boy-friend had a neat new system. When I mentioned her mother she blew an 'Uh-oh'. I dashed over to her apartment in North Hollywood to fetch my property and get the story. This is it: 'The White House', home to 'The Ishi People', was part of a conglomerate called Rainbow, Inc. which owned and operated other mansions in Altadena and also in Santa Fe, New Mexico. George, the man I'd tangled with, was a senior vice-president. Somewhere, usually sailing the Caribbean, was the Saviour, the boss. What was he saving the women and children from? Sandra said, 'The coming Armageddon – and also other men.' I stayed for coffee and cake. Sandra said that every night, and some afternoons, George's enormous cock was worshipped; in the Games Room were held lesbian orgies – Sandra had been initiated into dildo manipulation whilst ostensibly playing ping-pong. 'Live While You're Living Because You're Going To Be a Long Time Dead' was the house credo; the basement held an armoury of assault weapons, including a bazooka. Why hadn't the police stepped in? 'The White House' was off limits to the authorities because George had been most helpful as an arbitrator between the police and local gang leaders and drug czars. Sandra warned me that her mother was best left well along. 'She's nuts.'

The bizarre nature of Cherie's life put my problems into perspective. What did I have to worry about? And now I was free. I should be feeling supremely happy.

Kris came over often. She was the easiest girl I'd ever had, and I wished I could fall in love. What was love? Bumstead biting his lip; or winning the nod from Captain Manning so you could sit on the edge of his morning bath and talk with him? Kris apologized for not knowing who Norman Mailer was; she sat on my lap as I read her a Jeeves story. She stroked my arm and crooned. Whenever Beefy ran away she helped me find him, and she patched up his mouth the day he came in with a cactus in his mouth, dripping blood on the Belgian rug. We kept ourselves occupied and it was great: washing up, opening cans of dog food, finishing the rock book while she sat under my feet. Listening to her: Volkswagens don't all look alike, there are many differences like different windows and window-catches and hub-caps and cigarette lighters. She had a terrific body. One night she woke screaming. 'Sorry,' she said. 'I was dreaming my Volkswagen had been stolen.' The sex was lubricious. I had the feeling I'd brushed past God. 'I like you best of all the disc jockeys at K-Rock – because you're English and your name is Ian.'

*

Alone on a Monday morning. Tommy rang. Could he come and see me? Of course – 6 p.m., cocktail time. I forgot to ask about my leather jacket, etc. He arrived on the dot, in a pale blue suit and holding a cardboard box. Could he step inside? Did I mind if he smoked? He was so polite, so calm. We had some wine. He told me he'd had a fight with the Venice girl and was moving in with another. After twenty minutes or so he said that the hour was late and he shook my hand. He shut the garden gate so carefully. Inside the carboard box were two of my tennis rackets, three albums I'd made when I was a rock star and the kitchen bulletin board.

Next week he rang again. He wanted to borrow $65 to rent a room at the Pasadena Y.M.C.A. Heavy March rains were falling when he arrived. I gave him the cash and he shook my hand; he didn't come in. As I was closing the front door I remembered about the leather jacket and the Italian sweat pants. I ran out into the driveway and saw him being driven away in a red Mercedes. I never saw him again, except in dreams. The first arrived within two weeks: Tommy's army of friends, all male, were angrily approaching me in a field. They were each wearing a piece of my wardrobe. Tommy, on horseback in the rear and bursting out of my best Harris tweed jacket, was laughing demonically. As we went in close on his face there was a dissolve. Another face . . . it was my brother.

I ordered the biggest bed you could buy – the Kalifornia King that I'd been promising myself. Kris said she'd been looking forward to testing it and, if I liked, she'd move in and take care of everything. I said I'd take a rain-check if that was O.K. with her. But thanks very much.

I had decided, at this juncture of my life, to return home to England. Kris said she'd visit the house and take care of Beefy. I told her Beefy was going to a highly-recommended dog hotel. She wished she could be with me every second. I said I was very fond of her. She sighed, 'Oh, well.' When we said goodbye she was sitting in her Volkswagen wearing the same jockey-cap she'd worn at our first meeting. She looked very sweet and I felt sorry for her. I said I'd not be away long and then we could start all over again. 'Oh, well,' she said.

On the morning of my departure for England I decided to visit my neighbour Mr Goldsmith, the businessman and preacher. I'd not socialized with him since the early days, and it might be wise to pass a few pleasantries because I was leaving an empty house. He came to the door in a three-piece suit. 'We'll keep an eye on your property, be assured. But will the older gentleman be coming to stay?' What gentleman? 'The African-American in the red Mercedes – he seemed to be an associate of your room-mate's. . . .' Go on, please. 'Well, he'd always arrive within a few hours of your departure.' How long would he stay? 'Oh, sometimes for weeks. Can we be expecting him?' Certainly not. 'I'm happy. He was too fond of television and jazz. And so much partying – all through the night.' But why didn't you complain? Why didn't you tell me? 'Oh, it's not in our nature to make waves.' He stuck out his hand. 'Now you have a good time back in your homeland.'

*

Back home again in Wildcroft Manor, in my own room once more, I shuddered to think what a fool I'd been. The jet-lag wore off by 7 p.m. and soon I was sitting in the lounge at the old bridge table eating pork chops, while my mother had fish fingers. We followed the latest Falklands War news, and then after supper we talked. My mother agreed it would be a good idea for me to borrow her car and drive down to the West Country to give that talk. Was I being paid for it? I hadn't written to the school yet, give me a chance!

The West Country meant Dorset and there, deep in hundreds of acres of rolling greenery, dense shrubbery and dark woods, magnificent in its blood and bandage stone and brick, standing square and resolute at the end of a two-mile drive, was *Bryanston*! Just saying the name filled me with the old fire and for a delicious flash I was in that ideal state again – a boy in a boy's body, albeit pear-shaped. I saw that

145

gang of friends not far away, down in the meadow, near the river, and I ran puffing to join them so that we could all watch the arrows fly over the hill, following them for ever, but for now we wander by the racing green river, discussing Yeats and Wilde, laughing at the skimming Eight, at those thighs pumping foolishly to megaphoned orders, those hearties who get more food than us arties, and then, at tea-time, our gang rushing back through rustling beeches to the yellow lights and the ringing and banging and shouting and mystery, and me telling jokes all the time.

Bryanston! *Et Nova Et Vetera*. Grey shorts and grey open-neck shirts. Runs in the early morning, runs in the afternoon as punishment, no caning, no fears, all sweetly reasonable, first names from the masters, artistic natures encouraged. The perfect stage for my melodramas: hysterics in the tuck-shop – pork pies thrown and dippens too (the nib quivering in my best friend's brow); revolution in the Art Room, centre of my world, with 'Action Painting' currently the rage and me pinning up my latest poster statement, still wet and dripping, in the Main Hall, then the Beak coming up against my art and getting paint on his jacket and telling me it's neither art nor funny, and me telling him he's a Philistine and marching off in a huff, running when he tells me to stop, and when I'm cornered he says, 'You'll be expelled for such outrageous behaviour!' Expelled! By a headmaster famous for his progressive ideas, his spirituality, his burning bow!

I faked a mental breakdown and they sent me to the sanatorium and summoned the school psychiatrist. Outside the window they were off on a cross-country run; by my bedside was a common-sense man in cardigan and tie. He said, 'Think of the Cyprus situation and Sir Hugh Foot, our Governor. Think of his terrible predicament – Greeks and Turks and us, as usual, stuck in the middle. I'm sure that your problems with, arguably, this century's greatest headmaster will shrink to their proper size.' After supper I said I was feeling better and could I see the headmaster.

He sat me down in his comfortable study and offered me a cigarette; we both smoked in silence for a while. On the shelf behind him I saw a copy of his book, *Manhood in the Making*. Then he said, 'If the volcano has cooled and we can expect you to behave like a young man and not a spoiled child . . . by all means stay on here. And try to be creative.' For several minutes we talked of acting. 'I'm told your impression of King Lear – not to mention a scoutmaster – is quite funny. I shall be there at the school revue tonight . . . and I wish you every

146

success!'

I was a success, a real howling one. It was the high point of my life. Everybody was transformed and they loved me. Never a prefect, never in any Eight, Eleven or Fifteen, never even a *Junior Colt*; taking lonely walks through the woods to find a spot where I could read a comic as I ate from a tin of pork and beans; hearing, after lights out, shocked reports from my thinner friends about getting raped in those same woods, of cock against cock and mouth over cock, and how do they think up such things, it's disgusting; but my best friend, Bill, told me off, saying I must open to the variety of life and accept that love of boy for boy could be the finest expression of love, and even if I didn't understand such feelings then at least I could respect them; respect them, indeed! Never panted after, never sent notes, never involved in any leggy-leggy under the library table, my only thrill in sliding down the ropes in the gym but these days I was getting too fat for that. But now! Now, in the dark and fusty gym – a place transformed into a theatre of magic – I was getting their attention, there was laughter and cheering and clapping. 'Good old fatty!' yelled somebody. 'You're an ass, but you're a funny one!' Backstage a junior, helping with costume changes, whispered as he gave me my scoutmaster gear, 'I wish I could be like you and yet still be a prefect and responsible!' After the show I was happy to receive the throng of boys and masters who came to congratulate me. I was the very centre of the circle. But at the back, standing by the bars, almost hidden in the shadows, was a jolt from home. It was true my father resembled George VI, right to the shyness, but not the stammer; he was looking at the gym floor, fingering an old felt hat. After the crowd had paid their respects he came up and shook my hand. 'Well done, old chap. Very funny. How d'you remember all those lines?' Oh, Daddy! 'And you never stuttered once.' Daddy, if only I could tell you how much I love you, but the words won't come out. 'Well, must be getting along. Got a long drive back. Well done.' If only we weren't in this gym, in this country, on this planet. Daddy, there's so much to explain. . . .

The reason he'd been able to see the school revue was because he was passing through Blandford on his way back home after selling some bricks and tiles in Dorchester. He was a builder's merchant, but my mother had told us years ago to inform the other boys that he was an architect. The second-hand 1939 Bentley helped too. My maternal grandfather paid, silently, for the schooling. I wish my father could have lived to the time when I made the U.S. Top Ten in 1965. But he had died in the winter of 1962, suddenly but peacefully in his sleep, one evening after a round of golf. At the graveside, just as we were leaving, my uncle tossed in Daddy's old felt hat.

*

I'd always hankered to return to Bryanston in another blaze of glory. And now I had good reason – a certified rock star, a pin-up for some. I would show them how 'fatty' had worked himself into a hunk. And Mr Ellis, who had never stopped to sit by my bed when saying good-night to the dormitory, would be riveted!

I wrote my letter to the Da Vinci Society, the arts appreciation club at school, and I catalogued all my achievements – all the records, books, T.V. and radio shows – and I suggested they might like to have me down as a guest lecturer.

An Alan Blease – not a master during my time – wrote back at once: 'Certainly! My predecessor, Mr Ellis, died several years ago and I, for my sins, am now in charge of the Da Vinci. Do come down and strum some of your ditties. Can't promise an honorarium but you'll get a hot meal and a clean bed. And – who knows? – there may be a few "in harness" staff who remember you!'

Just across the Dorset border I had to pull over and stop. The powerful countryside here – trees, fields, hedges, smell – mainly the smell – had knocked me for six. Over in that dark copse . . . what promise of irresponsible lust! The thick bunched trees are heaving together!

I got lost finding my way around Bryanston. There were so many new buildings, new rooms, new departments and divisions. But I pretended to be at home as I didn't want to seem like a dirty old man. Eventually I located Alan Blease in the shiny metal Modern Science building; he was skinny, drab and mousy-haired. Pulling himself from an array of test tubes he said in a light North Country accent, 'Can't shake paws till I get this goop off with some H_2O. D'you mind vegetarian? Wife and I are both veggies. Juicers too. Sorry. Come. . . .' On our way out he showed off Bryanston's new video control centre. 'Electronic classroom. Keeps 'em hooked. All mod cons here. Hi, Caroline!' A bosomy girl in a tight fisherman pullover bounced past us. 'She'll be Head of School next term if I have anything to do with it!'

As we crunched down the drive in the darkness from the Science building to Alan Blease's house, I knew we must be passing the playing fields and I knew the river was not far away. They were quivering in the blackness. And I flashed back to my time, before coeducation

148

and enlightenment, when the world was enclosed, dark and mysterious and puzzling, and pregnant with stinging thrills. I flashed to 'Penis' Parker patiently talking me through the rudiments of masturbation near the boathouse, and to the two seniors who drowned at the weir after seeing the White Lady, and to that first-term chorister who hanged himself by the river after they'd accused him of stealing sixpence from the church collection plate – and especially to Bill, my study mate and mentor. Bill, red-haired and Wildean, reading to me in a tight monotone of dappled things while joss-sticks burned, and only at my urging did he let me in on the secret of Mr Ellis's jealousy of Philip's special attachment to Bill, and then 'borrowing' my Grundig to tape gurgly conversations with Philip where they discussed High Church liturgy, classical music and the debauched mind of Mr Ellis. How I had fought to get my tape back from Mr Ellis after he'd confiscated it from Bill! 'Have you no morals?' he screamed. How I had longed to be an object of desire or attention, or at least to win approval from Bill for my drawings and stories! But all he said was that I still had a lot of learning to do.

'Why so gloomy?' he asked me that last summer term as we lay on the long grass under rustling trees near the Greek Theatre, mugging up for our English A-Levels. I said I couldn't find the right words, but it was just that all of this, this Bryanston, this beauty, would be gone when the term ended and we left. 'Don't brood. Live and love and burn with a hard gem-like flame!' said Bill, laughing. Laughing Bill, who left under a cloud and cut me out of his life, I never knew why. Moving on, I suppose. But what drove him – only a year or so later – to jump to his death from that hotel in Spain?

'All change but not decay at Bryanston, isn't it?' said Blease breezily. 'That's the nature of this place, same with your pop game no doubt. I'm a Brian Eno man myself.' After hot vegetables and cold juice we walked to a building called Darwin. Spanking new classroom with theatre-in-the-round seating. A sprinkling of Da Vinci Society members, boys and girls, mostly in blue denim. The last time I lectured the Society was back in the days of Bill and Philip, when my subject had been 'British Music Hall'. How they had teased me for dwelling on boiled beef and carrot songs while they were immersed in Auden and Pound! Now, here in the Eighties, I was to talk about the Sixties and screen a telefilm of my appearance on 'Hollywood A-Go-Go', a syndicated T.V. programme from the days when I was at the top of my pop fame. What a sweet, tousled lad I looked then! If only Mr Ellis were here! After singing my big hit, 'You Turn Me On',

I went into 'Be My Baby', my version of the old Ronettes hit. Woweee! In that fisherman's sweater and with that tumbling hair, I looked as appetizing as Carolyn, the may-be Head Girl. If only Bill and Phil were here too, plus the bully who made me run naked through the changing room so's he could laugh at the jelly-wobble bottom. . . .

'Be My Baby' ended and was followed, on the telefilm sound track, by the squealing of mix-Sixties teen girls. In Darwin, the lecture hall, there was a stony silence. I saw a cigarette drop. 'Any questions?' asked Blease. A big blond brute with a mane of heavy-metal hair, and what looked like Carolyn nestling in his arms, said from his sprawled position, 'I've never heard of your song and I'm a Sixties fanatic. But I've certainly heard – and still hear – 'Be My Baby', a true Phil Spector classic. And you ruined it! I think your act is *pathetic*, absolutely *pathetic*!' There was another silence – and then I heard the old familiar bell and I couldn't stop the sweet pang that went through me. Blease consulted his watch and said, 'The hour is late and I know some of you have mock A-levels coming up. So I'll just thank Mr Whitcomb for coming all this way on behalf of the Da Vinci Society.'

As I pounded down the black school drive I walloped the steering wheel and vowed aloud never to return ever again to this benighted Bryanston. My memories, the earlier ones, would be preserved, though. 'The trouble with you,' said Bill once long ago, 'is that you cannot bear much reality, to quote the poet.'

*

One afternoon, as I was mooning at the piano in Wildcroft Manor, I got a call from Dr Ronald Bund. What a super surprise! Where was he, and what was his news and was there a chance he'd be returning to Los Angeles? 'Hold on, mon ami! May I treat you to a meal of your choice at my hotel, where we can take quality time to catch up on our different worlds?' He was staying in a Georgian terrace house in a quiet Kensington cul-de-sac. Third floor, 'The Orangery'. I was a bit taken aback by his costume: a tight, wasp-waisted maroon suit, a flowing wide tie and a Tyrolean hat. The costume appeared even odder because he was bursting out of it, his stomach resembling a beach-ball. 'Friend, I have ordered a brunch of champagne, poached eggs and kippers.' His accent, too, was strange – clipped and guttural, like a German who had been to Eton. But what's the news?

'In the final analysis Saudi Arabia and I did not agree. Some trouble with the son of a prince, the details of which I shall not bore you with. Suffice it to say that I still have both my hands. But let us concentrate on the gleaming future. I have plans, oh I have such plans!' While working in the desert Dr Ron had amassed a 'veritable fortune' which he was now going to spend liberally on the arts. 'I have learned from you, my friend, and I intend to become a media personality.' He would start by hosting his own television review of the arts and to stoke his brain he had bought, on a recent shopping spree at Foyle's, 'most of the great books of the world. In hardback.' These, together with a collection of 'erotic male drawings' he'd gathered in Hamburg, would soon be shipped back to Los Angeles, 'that other desert'. Dr Ron was flying high again, cheering me up tremendously. 'I will create a cultural heaven in L.A.' I told him that, of course, he could have his old room back – better than that, he could have Tommy's. I was a boarding-house keeper once again – but no longer the head man.

*

Kris was at the airport to meet my plane, but she turned away to avoid my full frontal kiss. What was up? I soon found out: stuck to the centre of her steering-wheel was a snapshot of a boy with an oafish, oval face framed in Beatle hair. When questioned about her present un-sexy mood she answered glumly, 'Strange things have been happening.' Who is this fool on the wheel? 'We can't make love any more.' After a few minutes of pleading I knew she meant what she said. The tedious sex shopping would have to start again. It was often this way when I returned from England. Anyway, who's the boy? 'He's Ian, my Ian.'

He was Ian Nokes, her pen-pal, and he writes to her every day and he cares about her and he's flying over to see her in August at his own expense, and probably she'll marry him. And what exactly does this Nokes do? He's a fry-cook at a naval depot in Portsmouth, and he loves her. I was flabbergasted at her lack of taste – and I told her so. She hung her head. I told her to watch the road. We stopped on Lake Avenue for a last meal together – hamburgers and onion rings. I ate most of hers. She dropped me off at 'home' and we gave each other a last peck.

I never saw her again. She did marry the fry-cook and they were living in a Portsmouth maisonette when last heard of. She wrote me from there. 'Ian's family can't believe I'd swap the sun and surf for rain and runny noses – but, you see, when you're as happy as I am you can live any place in the world!'

151

Meanwhile . . . I looked forward to the return of Dr Ronald. On the recommendation of Herb I hired a Mexican woman to clean up the house the day after I arrived back. She was so kind, so motherly; even though she didn't speak a word of English, she conveyed her love with a smile. Afterwards I rang her husband to thank him for lending her. I said she was very affordable and had been like a mother to me. He said brusquely, 'Gimme a break, man!'

At the dog hotel I collected Beefy. His ribs were sticking out and his eyes were hollow; he didn't want to know me, and I felt like I hadn't a true friend in the world. But when we got to the house I held him by the collar and hugged his coat. The old poem says everything connects, even the waves clasp each other, so why shouldn't I kiss you and hold you. . . .

Thank God for Dr Ronald's return! 'Well-met by sunlight – if it wasn't for the smog,' he said when I answered the merry notes of the front-door chimes. He was wearing a black shiny trench-coat, tightly belted, and a Hitlerian hat with a bright feather sticking up rudely. Under both arms was a bottle. 'My friend – a time for celebration, for you're looking at a fine wines importer – and here's some vintage Bayreuth hock to start with.'

I conducted him to the spruce guest room, mentioning that I hoped it would stay spruce. 'No doubt, my gentle liege.' We opened the hock and went to the drawing room. Ronald soon expanded, going so far as to stroke Beefy (he'd never cared much for animals before and had said so). He was stroking and smoking and taking erratic gulps of wine, now wiping the glass coffee table with fast palm movements. All the time he was talking fast and furious. 'We – and I am not necessarily speaking royally – we are on the edge of a crock o' gold! Let me amplify: I am currently involved with Bob Rinducci, a 350-pound debarred lawyer from Las Vegas, but don't let that put you off. He is an expert in the laundering business and knows the ins and out of money. We're going to import rare wines and Rolls-Royces and so forth, to sell for a quick profit. And then – oh joy! – I shall be in a position to devote my time to the pursuit of the arts. . . . Meantime, let me express my darker purpose. . . .'

He stood up and started pacing the floor. 'On Wednesday I take delivery of the first Rolls. Prior to resale I shall be using this glorious chariot – a triumph of your country's engineering skills – for the transportation of, er, carnal delight. Do you mind candour? What a fine wine! Now – one Private Wendell Oatsacker, a nineteen-year-old Marine, superbly equipped by Nature, will be conveyed in the Rolls from the gates of Camp Pendleton to your stately home. *Voilà!*' I chipped in to say that, much as I enjoyed company, I hoped that the present order of the house would not be disturbed.

'No sweat!' said Dr Ron violently wiping the mantelpiece. 'I am anally-fixated in more than one way. Dusters will fly! We will put Oatsacker to work – and, anyway – what are Mexicans born for?' He spun round and roved his eyes wildly as if searching for a safe port. 'Now . . . to work! First I must purchase a rubber sheet and then a supply of Heineken beer, the Marine's favourite. My stars, but I'm excited! I must take a pill!'

True to his word Dr Ronald made sure the house was spick and span. Private Oatsacker, muscular but with a putty face, washed the dishes, vacuumed every room, walked the dog and called me 'Sir'. There was no need for Mexicans. In return Dr Ron hung up the lad's state flag, Oklahoma, in the front porch and provided him with constant quality beer and premium snacks. My framed album covers were removed from the main corridor. 'I've told him you're a noted professor. Try to enter into the spirit of things.' During a break from the bedroom Dr Ron and the Marine took brunch with me in the kitchen. I asked the boy what were his long-term goals. 'Upon leaving the Corps he intends to enter the ventriloquism business,' said Dr Ron. He would have given a demonstration, only Ron suddenly jumped to his feet, wiped his mouth and announced rather brusquely, 'Private Oatsacker and I are now going to watch home movies.' I noticed that Ron had a good deal of talcum on his face and rouge on his cheeks – a bit like Dirk Bogarde in *Death In Venice*.

After the weekend Private Oatsacker returned to base and the flag came down, my albums went back up and the quality beer and premium snacks disappeared. The only souvenir was a large tub of industrial-strength petroleum jelly on Dr Ron's night table. 'Never fear – it will, like all things, pass,' he said, cupping a hand over the telephone mouthpiece. He was spending most of the day on the phone to his partner, the debarred fat lawyer now living in La Costa, a resort down the coast. Hadn't I read about some Mafia figures moving in there recently? 'Quite right, my friend – but art knows no borders as you know, being an artist yourself. What price the Mona Lisa?' I said that was fine as long as my house was left inviolate. 'Don't worry – I shall be away soon, back to your homeland to buy more Rolls and wine.' This was a surprise, and not a pleasant one. Alone again. When would he be departing? 'Next week – and now I must away to La Costa.'

Slightly distracted, I took to rummaging about his room while he was gone. Luckily he'd reverted to his normal untidiness so my excavations were unlikely to be noticed. In the middle of a heap of culture books, nude boy magazines and 8mm porno movies, I dug up some interesting reading matter: financial statements addressed to Bob Rinducci (the Rolls and wine mobster lawyer) and also to 'Dr Robert Rind' and to 'The Reverend Robert Rindland'. Between a make-up kit and a brochure on face-lifting I found a bulky file marked 'Classified – The Faisal Project'. I couldn't resist getting into this. Here were Dr Ron and Dr Robert representing themselves as 'Creative Marketing Inc.', a company with 'offices in four major metropolises and access to telex'. A letter on gold-lettered CMI-headed paper hailed King Faisal of Saudi Arabia and offered an expert public relations campaign for the upcoming Olympic Games in Los Angeles: 'Let us outline a plan befitting these troubled times of international terrorism and a wayward press: (1) a documentary on the lines of the famous German film *Olympia*, with staged displays by the Saudi athletes and much showing of the flag. (2) a dinner at Koose-Koose, an Arab-themed restaurant on Sunset Strip where guests recline in cushioned comfort to eat traditional dishes (without benefit of flatware or cutlery). (3) a speech, at the end of the dinner, made by the King, stressing the spiritual zeal of Middle Eastern Youth as a moral lesson to the decadent and alienated Western Youth, mired in drug abuse and rock.' Someone signing himself 'Ricky' had scribbled a note on the Faisal proposal: 'My sister has a girl-friend who does one helluva belly dance. Worth pursuing?'

I snuck the material back between some long underwear and several copies of Alistair Cooke's *Civilization*, then wrote Dr Ron a note about cleaning up his room before his departure. He, in turn, left me a note assuring me that he and a 'serviceman' would make the room 'shipshape'. I replied with a long letter on how much I valued our friendship, and wished him luck with his foreign dealings. 'Not foreign to you!' said his final note. 'We are simply bringing a little much-needed culture to a benighted country called America.' And then he vanished . . . but the room *was* clean.

*

The previous Christmas my uncle and aunt had announced, via a greetings card, that they would be making a tour of 'The States' in order to visit friends and relatives. They'd promised to drop in on Altadena. And thus it was fortunate that when their arrival date rolled around I had an empty house and could pretend all was quite normal and entirely natural in my Californian world. For I was mindful of their piety: dedicated churchgoers of the fundamentalist kind, with a special interest in posting missionaries all over the British Isles in an attempt to, as my uncle put it, 'stop the rot'. Their church, showpiece of the South London Bible belt, was famous as the parish of 'Battling Eric Noakes', a reformed alcoholic and notorious holy-roller who had made a practice of heckling the sermons of the Archbishop of Canterbury. Last Christmas I had attended one of the Rev.'s own sermons, a fire-and-brimstone affair, and I will never forget his cry from the pulpit about there being 'more mosques than churches in Sheffield' and the necessity for a 'motor coach-crusade so that we may proselytize the onion dome into the soaring steeple!'

My uncle, a retired businessman, took particular pleasure in his position as Keeper of the Collection Plates. How proud he was to hand them out with gleaming eye and firm thrust! And then, at the climax of the service, to march triumphantly down the aisle holding aloft his tray piled high with cash. 'Let's hear it for the silver saliva!' hoseannahed the Rev. on the day I was there. Everybody knew what he meant and a great cheer went up. The church was an unusual one, a breakaway much feared by the Church of England, and every inch was kept spotlessly clean. My uncle was in charge of the cleaning, too. He liked to say that whenever he felt at a loose end he'd go and clean a room or two. He'd been to a major public school and had commanded a battalion in World War Two; my aunt, who had converted her husband during the Attlee regime, had been known to hiss at the mention of 'Pope'. They were an awesomely upright couple and I spent a good week cleaning the house. First I made sure that none of Dr Ron's boy books were lying around: next I walked slowly through every room spraying with an aerosol can of 'Mountain Fresh' in each hand; then I set to with paper towels and feather dusters, in the process discovering several hitherto unknown nooks and crannies, the graveyard of countless flies and hideous insects without name. After an hour I called up the Mexican woman and haggled a spring-cleaning fee as I'd had quite enough of anal therapy.

Uncle Jeremy and Auntie Iris were delighted with the house, especially its 'possibilities'. I put them in the master bedroom and I took Dr Ronald's (not yet daring to brave the ghosts of Tommy's room). A renewed burst of aerosol deodorant finally eliminated any lingering traces of an unhealthy past.

And on the first morning, as rose-tinted dawn lit up the East, I felt a

155

new world beginning. The flush of the lavatory followed by the pounding of the shower symbolized a fresh start, led by people of principle. Uncle Jeremy rapped on my bedroom door and ordered sunnily, 'Up and at 'em! Brekker in ten minutes!' This was to be the form every day – a full English breakfast followed by a briefing session on exactly what part of L.A. we were to cover that day. Maps were spread, and the locations of such strategic spots as Disneyland and Universal Studios were pinpointed. Every minute was to be accounted for. 'Planning is the secret of a full and rich life,' said my uncle. Los Angeles could be thoroughly absorbed and we could still be back in time for tea.

'A tip-top HQ is always essential', he liked to say. The kitchen was stocked with sensible foods – white bread, lettuce, tea, butter and lots of tins of baked beans. They shook out the rugs and washed the curtains. They put up a clothes-line in the back patio. Auntie Iris said Beefy's food and water bowls must be cleaned once a day. The regimented week went racing by and I was very sorry when they left – because my life had become much cleaner all round. Beefy positively glowed.

*

Boosted by the example of my relatives I launched into a strenuous programme of work: I won a commission from Books On Tape Inc. to record famous works on to audio cassette for the pleasure of freeway flyers with lengthy commutes and for marathon joggers and others. In the comfort of my study, with Beefy snuggled under the desk, I read Rider Haggard, C.P. Snow, Graham Greene and R.F. Delderfield into a microphone. Sometimes the work was frustrating – especially that of Delderfield. His books seemed longer than the Bible and sometimes he forgot the name of a character so that they became newly-christened. And, frequently, as I was picking up steam again after the shock, my recording would be spoiled by a police helicopter or a disco car or, especially, the screams and hollers of the children next door – the ones belonging to the Goldsmiths. And then I would slam my desk and shout, 'Bloody piccaninnies!'

One particularly sweltering October afternoon (why can't the seasons here change normally!) my reading of Delderfield's *God Is an Englishman* was halted again and again by these children, so I strode next door to lodge a complaint. Mr Goldsmith was away working at his business, I knew that, but I could see his wife peering out from frilly curtains as I rang the door-bell and heard the chimes ring out loud and clear. Eventually she deigned to open the door, and I caught another delicious glimpse of their living room: they still hadn't removed the plastic covers from the sofa – perhaps they had no intention of ever doing so; there was a new painting – a tall, imperious African woman wearing a cape and mortar-board and with a fiery mountain in the background.

Mrs Goldsmith, hair in rollers and body in a jazzy orange-and-yellow slashed shift, stood her ground, raking me up and down with eyes that reflected proud disdain. The stance and the raking . . . that's what set me off. Spluttering and stammering – my decent side fighting my indecent – I tried to protest about the excess noise. Did children *have* to scream and holler as they played? She held up an open palm. 'You're no father, so you can't understand. These are kids and this is their natural state of being – they roll with the flow of their emotions.'

I replied that I knew lots of children – English children and well-bred within a civilized society, children whose manners she could take a tip from. What on earth was I doing? I stopped in the middle of the next sentence, about-turned and beat a retreat back behind my tall fence and the protection of Beefy. For an hour or so I felt dirty and rotten, a regular mouldy fig. But aid and comfort was again at hand!

At a few minutes past 6 p.m., I was tapping at the piano and sipping on some wine when my blue mood was broken by the sound of a low-pitched chugging 'huh-huh, huh-huh' coming from the front lawn. A laugh I loved – I knew it of old, from back in student days at Trinity College, Dublin: I knew this cheering noise as the signature tune of my old pal Charles ('Chas') Sprawson.

He was standing amid the weeds and crab grass drinking in my circumstances through razor-slit blue eyes, eyes that knew neither fear nor conscience. He was dressed as usual in shapeless old corduroy bags and a much too tight white shirt open down to the third button, his massive chest bursting through, a Superman from the Chelsea Arts Club. But most impressive of all, an intense heat – a challenge to L.A. – radiated from his lobster face. Some might say that Chas seemed like a man about to succumb to a massive coronary, but to me he resembled – no, he *was* – a disturbing and disruptive figure from the days of Empire-building, *Four Feathers*, and the lash.

When his eyes hit me he laughed even louder. I was thrilled to see him, but I reprimanded him for not giving prior notice of his arrival. 'Don't be stupid,' he said and, kicking aside the welcoming Beefy, he guided me into the house and the wine. Soon we were yarning away, catching up. He was here on business, Fine Art stuff, and he would be staying he didn't know how long. A floor would do, or the garden. I put him in the Tommy Memorial Room because Dr Ronald had cabled that he'd be returning in a few days. I felt sure that these two characters would get along famously.

As we were standing in the Tommy room I became aware of a strong smell. Together with a lack of respect for animals, Chas and Dr Ron had this olfactory characteristic in common. But whereas Dr Ron smelled of Man's cleverly formulated perfumes and colognes, Chas smelled of pure untreated Nature. A very pungent stink, and one could see it spreading in a dark semi-circle from his armpits. As fast as a record by Frankie Laine I was whizzed back to the locker room at Newlands, not a bad feeling at all.

Chas had only one piece of luggage – a battered steamer trunk stuck with many torn labels (Karachi, Mandalay, the Golf Hotel of Bechuanaland) from the great days of Englishmen Abroad. Days of Empire, nights of Bridge. He was born in India during the last days of the Raj to a family which for generations had helped polish the Jewel in the Crown. A Sprawson relative had been Surgeon-General of All-India – I liked to use that fact as an opening gambit when introducing Chas, and he'd shake with modesty and go even more lobster. There was no doubt in my mind that Chas was shot through with real class, reeking of duty and decency, good form and good manners. Because of this he could afford to show an interest in perversion every now and then – he'd put on a satyr face for this. He was completely at home with himself. He made me feel a bit parvenu. Definitely a person to go deep into the jungle with . . . and thus a perfect companion for Los Angeles life.

'Much squash round here? Brought my racket.' I gazed at this shining example of sportsmanship, an endangered species. . . . We might try the Y.M.C.A. . . . . His barrel chest, flaming too, V-tapering down to a pair of rather small feet, encased in a pair of old-fashioned Dunlop plimsolls. . . . Again, that smell! Badger, perhaps – an unknown animal in Southern California. I said I'd leave him to himself and I showed him the back shower and lavatory.

While he was in the shower I spied in his steamer trunk. It was on the bedroom floor and open: a fine mess of rumpled sports clothes and such books as *A Short History of Swimming* and *The Encylopaedia of Sex Crimes*. I found his business ensemble in a separate compartment: a drab black sack suit, a Trinity College tie, and a moth-eaten leather satchel containing slides of old paintings and scribbled

158

notes on lined yellow paper.

Chas was a dealer in Fine Art, operating in the British Isles out of the back of his car. He was pretty successful – a nice house in the Cotswolds with royal neighbours – and his speciality was nineteenth-century British watercolourists, with emphasis on marine views. No matter that Californians knew or cared little about such art – they tended to invest in cowboys-and-Indians or else ultra-modern grid-and-glare work – for Chas was here, no doubt, to work the natives into a passion for storm-lashed China clippers, pebble beaches with grimy groynes, and even Early Victorian cricket pitches. He would create a market through charm and guile.

Public school and Trinity College, Dublin, followed by a stint as a swimming-pool attendant in a rough part of London and a job as a Classics teacher in Saudi Arabia, had shown him the ropes of the 'Varsity of Life'. Eventually, with a wife and children to take care of, he settled temporarily in Bristol as a pin-striped salesman for an established Fine Arts dealership. But being a loose cannon he was soon striking out on his own, motoring around Britain and Europe with a shooting-brake full of paintings and a long list of possible clients. Should such a client express a special interest not stocked in the car, then Chas would resort to a painter of neo-Old Masters with a Paris address. Did the client require a still life with bananas instead of cherries? Then bananas it would be! The Channel Islands proved to be a rich market and Chas became notorious among the local police for his zeal – jogging up a private drive, leaping an electric fence, wading through an ornamental pond, in order to surprise a tax exile with a gilded picture of fishing boats in trouble near Dungeness. The exile, a writer of bloodthirsty thrillers, later relented, called off the police and placed a standing order.

For his Southern California campaign Chas had brought coloured slides, to be followed – if interest warranted – with the shipping over of the actual painting. At dinner (The Middle East Café) he asked me if I had any rich contacts. Jack Wontner was into cowboys and Curlew Worthington was all Art Nouveau. Luckily, when we were back at the house, Dr Ronald rang to say he'd be returning imminently and with a chocolate-coloured Rolls. Right now he was in Paris. When I told him about Chas being in pictures he grew excited, talking of his connections at Paramount and Twentieth Century-Fox. But when I re-directed him he grew even more excited, talking of 'high culture in the low desert' and promising to come up with a list of wealthy doctors and lawyers crazy for England and 'class'. But for the time being

159

Chas was on his own. Never fear, he'd get results.

I asked if I could accompany him on his trips into L.A. and he said, 'All right'. That evening I felt excellent: somehow, I believed, the aura of Chas could laser to death any lingering badness in the house. And elsewhere. Chas was talking of the sights he'd see, of 'Sunset Boolay-vaaar', and I found the old song running through my head: 'Everywhere you go, sunshine follows you. . . . Children love you, they seem to know. . . .' Well, the general sentiment was right but the details were wrong: Chas loathed children, even though he had three beautiful daughters. Of course, he loathed most creatures great and small, and Beefy was to come in for a lot of ire. The very next morning he was toddling along to the back bathroom, night-gowned and sponge-bag in hand, when, not seeing Beefy curled up in a dark corner, he took a nasty fall. Awakened by the noise I rushed to the scene to find Chas sprawled and cursing and kicking at Beefy while the latter tried to lick his rubicund face. I said I'd repack his sponge-bag if he'd stop kicking the dog. I was pleased to see he had two matching tortoiseshell hair brushes, a round tin of tooth powder and a cut-throat razor.

Soon we were ready to get out and about in modern L.A. It was such a welcome change from the hothouse of Altadena life. At the Y.M.C.A. swimming pool he easily outpaced me, but at the Pie 'n' Burger coffee shop I was the boss, showing him the American way with breakfast. He ordered the entire works and more besides: three fried eggs sunny side up, with four rashers of bacon and the great pad of hash browns, plus a dish of canned peaches. Now in the normal way the canned peaches are a substitute for the potatoes – for those on diets – but Chas, despite the waitress's protests, insisted on having the peaches. She watched spellbound when he proceeded to stack portions of egg, bacon, hash brown and peach on to a wedge of toast and then slowly fork the creation into his mouth, head turned slightly sideways in the manner of old-time schoolmasters. 'Jolly good,' he said. 'Best breakfast I've ever had.'

This meal remained his favourite wherever we went and whatever the time of day. Hitherto I'd not given much thought to breakfast, but Chas made me see the possibilities of the American kind through fresh eyes. His whole approach to California was, I thought, more endearing than David Hockney's. As he raced me around in his compact rented car, he would point out such things as the different types of palm tree, and when I brought up the seat-belt law he replied, 'Don't be so wet.' He drove dangerously, often actually aiming at animals, always smoking untipped American cigarettes, attacking the environment with his eyes, and with his window down because he loved the traffic's roar and the toxic fuels and poisonous fibres one hears about in the media. He had no intention of visiting Disneyland or Universal Studios, but he did express an interest in dining at 'Grauman's Chinese'. I did nothing to stop his enthusiasm, but occasionally I'd point out local traffic rules, like the one for 'Stop' signs.

Most of his exploring was in the pursuit of Fine Art business. When it came to actual dealing he made me wait outside. Often his brazenness and charm would get him invited back to the homes of gallery owners. Did they discuss the dollar value of dead white European watercolourists? At breakfast next day I'd get a report. 'Why do homosexuals, almost to a man, like gold bath-taps in their houses?' he asked rhetorically one morning, flushing with anger or shame or mere exasperation.

Encino, a well-to-do enclave within the San Fernando Valley, over the hills from Altadena, worlds away, opened up exciting possibilities for Chas – and not only in art. A dealer he'd either met or accosted at a gallery had invited him to a party in Encino on a street called Judy. The house was a spanking new tract home – rustic stone facings and neo-Art Nouveau stained-glass windows – and the charge for entry was $25. Chas told me he'd only watched and wandered and I believed him, knowing his taste. 'Activities in every room – women making most noise – best place was the main bedroom. Blue light only – Vietnam veteran, in uniform, in wheelchair, with melancholy expression, watching wife on bed with several men – every orifice filled. After it was all over the men lined up by the wheelchair to apologize and to thank the veteran. Interesting. . . .' Any picture deals in the offing? 'Dealer says he knows a rich man in Malibu who buys paintings of Dr Johnson.'

We set off for the Malibu man, but the Pacific was too tempting. Chas insisted we plunge into the boiling late November surf. 'Last one in's a drip!' he taunted as we raced across the yellow sands. When we emerged from the angry foam we saw amazed faces pressing against the ocean-view window of Malibu's famed Beachcomber restaurant. The management wouldn't let us enter in our present condition, but I told Chas about a wonderful piano bar I'd heard of, within a Chinese restaurant near Universal Studios. 'Sounds incredibly exotic,' said Chas and so off we went.

The Far East Terrace proved to be a find. Both of us were well-catered-for: the elderly lady pianist let me sing an Al Jolson medley;

161

Chas sat at the back on a bar stool, eyeing the room and enjoying the way the customers told of their lives through the songs they chose to sing ('My Way', 'The Impossible Dream'), and most intrigued by the elderly man in tight designer jeans who, when moved by a song, would clamber on to a table and execute a hula dance. In turn, there were women of a certain age sitting around singly who were intrigued by Chas – and he responded nobly: lighting their cigarettes, standing them cocktails, asking them leading questions about their private lives. Hilda, a creased flame-head and veteran of many a marriage, asked Chas whether he was married. When he winkingly claimed he was single, she invited him to cocktails the following afternoon at her Studio City apartment. Many times had I sung to Hilda, but never had she come on to me, so I was a bit jealous even though she was a ratty old bag with a fallen front and behind.

Chas followed through with the date and, at dinner, over his usual bacon and eggs and peaches, he described Hilda and her odd living arrangement: the afternoon in Studio City was baking as only the Valley can bake but inside Hilda's apartment all was freezing and stygian, the air conditioning almost drowning out the music of Barry Manilow. Dressed in a casual Polynesian shift, Hilda showed Chas her tropical fish and then quickly followed with a tour of the bedroom, particularly the bed. This bed she shared with a female ventriloquist, currently supplementing her income by working at a photocopy place. The dummy sat forlorn, legs and arms dangling, on a shelf above the headboard. 'Oscar won't mind, will you?' said Hilda to the dummy as she patted the bedspread. Luckily, at this difficult moment in came Harry, from the apartment above, for a chin-wag and a highball. 'No standing on ceremony in the Valley,' said Hilda sulkily but she soon perked up after a couple of vodkas. Oscar sat with the party in the drawing room as they drank and chatted. Harry needed little coaxing from Hilda to tell, yet again, the story of how teenagers had robbed and murdered his wife a year and a month ago. 'Seems like yesterday, doesn't it?' he said to Oscar.

I was allowed to accompany Chas on his expedition down the coast to La Costa for lunch with his old headmaster, the Reverend Horace Shankleigh. My astonishment that the H.M. of an established British public school should have retired to La Costa (I had visions of the real Reverend crossing paths with Dr Ron's mobster partner in his guise as the 'Reverend Robert Rindland') turned to amazement when he strolled into our coffee-shop rendezvous clad head to foot in ecclesiastical garb.

162

Almost immediately H.M. and Old Boy dived into a discussion about some cricket technicality involving the bowling of wides. H.M. wanted his theory published in Britain and said that Chas was the man to effect this business. In vain did Chas try to direct the conversation on to his memories of schooldays. No sooner had he set the scene of a Latin class on the morning of the big match versus Eton when H.M., rubbing his hands high and with elbows out, announced with authority, 'Let's eat!'

He highly recommended the Monte Cristo sandwich and I was glad of his advice, for it was a winning combination: egg-battered bread slices mixed with ham and cheese and spread on top with strawberry jam . . . reminiscent of school tuck treats. Of course Chas insisted on his ruddy bacon and eggs, which didn't help his relationship with the H.M.

At a briefing in the car on the way down I'd learned how the H.M. had, through an unfortunate marriage, decided to leave his school and start a new life alone in America. He soon found himself drawn to the West Coast where he married a woman rich in oil money. She, in turn, gained an impressive clerical figure, very suitable for display at golf club and charity dinner. At important public functions she insisted her husband wear a thick brown wig. He was wearing a light straw-coloured one for our lunch today and Chas congratulated him. This seemed to fire up the H.M., for he launched into a breathless account of how he had invented a new sport: 'Throlf'.

All of the Southland, it seemed, was nuts for Throlf and Chas should be his publicist in England. 'What's the drill, sir?' 'Simple as pie. One throws a golf ball around the course – hence Throlf. *Quod Erat Demonstrandum* Q . . . E . . . D. Or – *Quite Easily Done*. Ha! Ha!' We laughed along. 'All for charity, of course. We get some big name celebrities to join in, chaps from Las Vegas and so forth, keen to contribute to good works, very keen.' Chas made another attempt to steer the table talk back to his schooldays by reminding H.M. about a class he used to give pertaining to Greeks and Trojans. 'Jolly good bit where you describe – in cricketing terms – the Trojans stealing up the Greek flank in the night. . . .' But H.M. didn't take the bait, instead he called for a slice of pecan pie. Chas tried bringing me into the conversation. 'He's a singer. Used to be in rock and roll.' H.M. perked up. 'Rotten Row? Singing in the saddle in Rotten Row! An urban cowboy, what?' Stepping in, I summarized my brief rock and roll career and H.M. became quite animated, humming snatches of obscure melodies and banging his dessert spoon to an odd beat. In

163

the middle of a sentence describing my demise he interrupted to inform us that he too had written pop songs, even a musical. 'An out-and-out assault on the abomination of abortion. You must hear a selection. . . .' While Chas and I tried to eat our pies H.M. sang in a high, piping voice of 'vacuuming' and 'scraping'. I gave up on my pie, but Chas braved on stoically. He picked up the bill too – but it was no use. H.M. was dead stuck on me; I was in 'Show Biz'. 'D'you think I'd have a sporting chance in your City of Angels?' he asked coyly, shrugging into his clerical cloak. As we motored away, waving, H.M. was standing stock-still in the parking lot, head high and singing a plangent version of an Irving Berlin number made famous by Fred Astaire: 'Heaven . . . I'm in heaven. . . .'

'Bit of a flop,' said Chas as we shot back up on to the San Diego Freeway, home to Altadena. He was smoking rather too heavily. We made up for the H.M. débâcle by having hot Scotches in the drawing room and I read aloud from a *Boy's Own Annual of 1919*. 'Very civilized,' said Chas, stretched out on the Barcalounger. After a while I shut the book, prepared more toddies and, in due time, opened up about the troubles I'd had with Tommy and about the string of girls I'd run through. His advice was: 'Try living alone for the time being. Find a decent servant.' I told him my eventual goal was a wife and children: the ordered life. He shuddered. 'It's your chaos and crisis that I admire. Sorry. Women are sexual receptacles to you. Not being rude or anything. Compliment.'

I did so want Chas to meet Dr Ron, but the latter's return from London had been delayed. Something to do with the effect of the current money market on Rolls and wine. 'But, my friend, I will definitely be back in your house – with a chocolate-coloured Rolls to improve the neighbourhood – at Christmas, that parlous season.' He sounded as if he was phoning from the next room, his room, and afterwards I checked to make sure he wasn't there. There was something fishy-sounding about Dr Ron these days. Still, he was a good and loyal friend. I told him I'd be flying home for the usual family Christmas in London, and Beefy would be going to the dog hotel. 'Ah,' said Dr Ron. 'Then you'll need a watchdog – and I have the perfect one. He's called Fred; he and I will guard the home front, never fear.'

So I shut up the house in a reasonably calm state of mind and turned my back on Los Angeles life for the time being. Chas and I travelled back together on British Airways, tended by stocky school-matron-like stewardesses serving tea and fruit cake. When we arrived at Heathrow Chas neither kissed his wife nor shook her hand. However, I knew they were great friends and that their life together in the Cotswolds was a great success. Perhaps England was the answer.

*

When I returned to Altadena there was a chocolate-coloured Rolls in the driveway, at an angle. Behind the gate Beefy was running round in circles, keening into the dark brown afternoon air. Inside I found paper roses adorning both drawing room and kitchen, but when Beefy jumped up on me in his glee I saw the traffic jam of fleas on his coat, like tourists in Yosemite National Park. Then Dr Ron emerged from his room, filling my eyes with red plaid golf trousers and permanent-waved curls in the Bacchic style. 'Welcome, friend – let's open the champagne at once.' He turned in the corridor and shouted, 'Fred!' Presently there appeared from the end bedroom a shambling, bucolic boy dressed in military fatigues with big splayed feet, and a comic book in his hand. 'Fred, say hello to Ian Whitcomb, the rock star.' Fred wiped his free hand on his trousers and gave me a weak handshake. 'I'll see to your every need,' he said, in a Southern drawl. 'He needs *girls*, Fred. Stick to your feather duster. . . . Meanwhile, fetch us the Spanish champagne and don't forget the frosted goblets.'

In my vulnerable jet-lagged state I could see old patterns returning to biff me again. As we drank our champagne in the lounge, and Fred busied himself with housework, I sweated visibly. 'Don't worry,' said Dr Ron. 'All kinds of leaves have been turning.' He told me of his latest cash-raising plans: a course at Pasadena College in screenwriting, T.V. 'deportment', public relations and World Culture. What about his business ventures with Rinducci? 'A parting of the ways. Sordid financial details, not worth soiling you with.' I thanked him for the house decorations, indicating the paper roses. 'Those were Fred's idea.' Was this the same Fred who once butlered for Ron – was this the ex-Marine who'd ruined a Ring cycle session, and who had been ejected into the streets of Hollywood? Then I noticed the jar of industrial strength petroleum jelly, almost hidden behind a bowl of paper roses. *Déjà vu, déjà vu!* God, don't let me keep repeating the mistakes of my life! 'You've seen the Rolls, I suppose? Feel free to use it – for trips to the supermarket, or for your radio show. . . .' His voice trailed off, and a few minutes later we bade each other goodnight.

*

February. A new year, a new life, leaves turning over, well no . . .

they're growing afresh, but you get the idea. The house blissfully empty, Beefy beneath my legs as I sit at my desk and write up my diary: 'No current projects. Rock book remaindered, says Double-day. Must write proposal for new book. Best-seller book. What? Still want to be a star again. Hollywood shimmies over the hills. Mean-while what about conditions at the house? Perhaps I should get mar-ried. But to whom?'

Excessive rain was thumping down when Chas breezed in through the front door. Saved again! Mind you, he hadn't even given me a by-your-leave – no call, no letter, no nothing. Still, was I relieved to see him! He was dripping and steaming, in his usual baggy cords, wide open white shirt and plimsolls. 'Hullo,' he said and laughed low.

His baggage included several gold-framed paintings of eighteenth-century horses with big drooping genitalia, and a couple of oil por-traits of Dr Johnson. 'For the Johnson fan in Malibu.' I helped him unload the magic lantern slide paraphernalia. 'Got to give a beastly lecture.' So my contact had paid off! Last year I'd given Chas the address of the Valley Hunt Club, a swank spot full of Anglophiles with tons of money. I'd suggested he might dig some gold out of them – and now he had a definite fixture: the club was billing him as a 'British investment analyst'. This was more likely to attract their members than references to 'Fine Art' and 'Old Masters'.

Dr Ron and Fred returned in the early evening from some assigna-tion or other. Introductions were made, explanations were waived, and soon we were enjoying more Spanish champagne, served up by Fred. At last my two great 'character' friends, Chas and Dr Ron, were on stage together! I was anxious to see whether they gelled. No sweat! After some eye assessment they got along famously and were soon developing ways and means of getting the best out of people. Dr Ron promised to prepare a list of doctors and lawyers who might be made interested in British art; Chas suggested a few promising R.A.F. stations Ron might visit the next time he was in Britain. 'Which may be soon,' said Dr Ron, 'for I am considering entering the world of Euro-American high finance.'

The rain continued to thunder on the roof and we, snug in my house, continued to drink and toast and yarn. Very Pickwickian. 'Almost,' said Chas. 'Another Ealing success,' said Ron. When we were all safely in our bedrooms (Chas content to doss down on a mat-tress in the dining room), I wrote in my diary: 'A full and cosy house, even a home! Beefy patrolling, storm raging. Everybody safe and sound. Peace of mind at last!'

Chas allowed me to accompany him on the night of his lecture at the Valley Hunt Club. We dressed up to the nines, both in Trinity College ties, and Chas managed to do up the top button of his shirt, but his face pulsed something terrible as if coronary time was nigh. 'Don't be so stupid,' he said.

During dinner though, he got an attack of the collywobbles and had to push aside his devilled crab. 'Please don't go sick on me,' said our hostess, Mrs Burton-Wilbransen, president of the Talks Committee. 'Think I'll look at the tennis,' mumbled Chas and sloped off. He re-appeared in time for the lecture, materializing slowly, a purple spectre, from the shadows at the back of the Churchill Ballroom. Only half the chairs were occupied and mostly, it seemed, by the dead and the near-dead. Mrs Burton-Wilbransen, up at the podium, lean-ing professionally into the snake mike, introduced Chas as 'a Britisher who will show us the way towards solid investments in oils'. Some of the twilight people stirred. Then Mrs B.-W. led a reluctant Chas up to the podium, handed him a slide-changing squeezer, and pointed to the snake mike. But Chas backed away, for he'd never been much of a performer. During his lecture he remained in the shadows, speaking in a soft monotone, face lit by his natural colour. As I was up front and knew his offhand style, I was able to follow much of his drift.

The first slide – a model of Pliny's house in ancient Rome – re-mained on screen for ages. Even I couldn't see the point. Maybe he hadn't got the hang of the slide squeezer. 'Collectors and connois-seurs,' he was saying when Mrs B.-W. moved up on him. 'Quite dif-ferent. Dr Johnson collected orange peel. The Duke de Vinchy col-lected executions. Not connoisseurs – but collectors . . .' Mrs B.-W. had reached him and was pushing him up on to the podium. 'We're all dying to hear what you have to say, so don't be shy.' Having placed him, she then swung the snake mike round so that he looked as though he was swallowing the thing. 'Now speak up, there's a good man.'

'I was watching a pornographic film the other day.' His voice boomed round the ballroom. 'In one scene there was a bust of Pliny.' Ah! The relevance of the slide! 'Pliny's house had a squash court.' Mrs B.-W. insisted the slide be changed. And now slides raced by like card trick flicks as Chas talked of a connoisseur who lived in a tower in Yorkshire and had an affair with a young baronet, and about Con-stable's obsession with rotting wood and pond slime. Even so, the twilighters and shades stayed slumped in their seats. Until the very

167

end . . . when on came a slide which brought them to life suddenly. Chairs clattered and banged and there was much noisy breathing. The slide was a graph, courtesy of the *Financial Times*, showing the rise in value of nineteenth-century paintings during the last decade. 'Notice how Victorian oils are doing well. Got a few of those.' Mrs B.-W. clapped her hands and called the lecture to a halt. 'Most instructional. Have you got any business cards?' 'Sorry.' Old people were clustering round the podium. 'Well,' demanded Mrs B.-W. 'have you got any oils with you in the car?' 'Only slides.' 'That's no good. Who wants slides when we can have the real thing in a gorgeous gold frame?'

Driving back, I told Chas that he ought to carry some stock around because the killings could be good here in Pasadena. He should learn from Dr Ron and become more pushy in this land of the super salesman. Californians really appreciate a good sales pitch; it's art. He looked glum, so we went to Hollywood and found a sleazy bar with a striptease. Soon he started cheering up. 'It's the palms I love, and the blue mountains behind your house in the evening. And then the pools and the breakfasts.' As the girl bumped and ground in front of us I confessed to Chas that often I found myself envying his peaceful life in Gloucestershire, in the tasteful eighteenth-century stone cottage, and his lovely Trinity College wife. 'She calls me a silly lizard and wants me to sell more beastly paintings so we can start a snail farm in Durham.' Well, his life was safer than mine. 'But it's the wildness I like, I keep telling you. The mystery, too.' What mystery? 'Last night. I heard someone walking around outside the dining room.' And? 'I said "Who are you?" and a voice replied, "No – who are *you*?"' Christ, I thought, who was it? Tommy?

*

I was very sad when the time came for Chas to fly home to England. For wherever he went in my L.A. life he cast his glow so that whatever had been depressing or maddening or frightening to me in the past now appeared trifling. His blue-eyed searchlight shrivelled my enemies; the landscape, too, seem bathed in a new clear and clean light. During his last days I started singing 'Everywhere you go, sunshine follows you'. But after a while Chas told me to shut up. 'I much prefer "La Bamba".'

On his last evening we went into Hollywood to have drinks at Steve Boardner's Bar, a dark and secure hangover from the early Fifties, full of grizzled sports fans, Joe DiMaggio on the wall and vintage

Sinatra on the tubby old juke-box. It was a time of double melancholy for me, because not only was I to lose Chas but also Witham, my bitter tonic.

Earlier in the day Witham had called to matter-of-factly tell me that his record company bosses were posting him back to London, there to act as European talent scout for likely rock acts. How would I survive without my guides, my keepers of the old culture? 'Dr Ronald offers a cut-rate service,' said Witham sharply. I was telling him the latest on Dr Ron's money-making schemes – hoping for a laugh – when he cut in. 'Of course, you speak without respect because you insisted on owning Bund, luring him into your lair and then, up close, examining all the warts and the joins and the jelly. Why can't you leave your illusions, your heroes, alone? Why must you own people?' Why was Witham being so nasty when I knew he really loved me? Must be pre-travel jitters. 'You say "Come into my parlour", then you tell the world how they've abused your hospitality. Poor old Ron! I expect you've already rummaged through his room!'

It was Witham who had suggested the rendezvous in Steve Boardner's Bar. I didn't tell him Chas would be present because I wasn't sure how he'd react. I'd brought my two friends together years ago in England, and the result had been a business deal: Chas had sold Witham a neo-Edwardian cricket team painting to civilize a wall in his sky-high Hollywood apartment, a work to exorcize the lesser breeds swirling around on the boulevard below. Trouble was, after the painting was up an American rock record executive pointed out that one of the players had three legs and asked, 'Is this cricket?' Witham was furious to be so humiliated and accused Chas and me of being in cahoots to flog him a dud.

But that last evening, at the bar, the two public school men forgot their differences in an intense discussion of England's chances in the next Test. I sat back and enjoyed watching my friends. We were interrupted by a vicious brawl: two swarthy men, each gripping the other's throat, were sinking slowly behind the bar. There was an ominous silence. Then they popped up in view hugging and kissing each other with a passion only found in these parts. 'Tristan and Isolde in Hollywood,' said Witham. 'I'm certainly relieved to be leaving this mess for the green fields of England.' 'Oh, I don't know about that,' said Chas. 'Yes, you do,' said Witham. 'You can slum away over here and then return to your peaceful Gloucestershire cottage, have a hot bath, some shepherd's pie and a good laugh.' He gave me a quick glance of pity. We'd both served in L.A. for many years, Chas was only a tripper. When Witham and I shook hands goodbye at the end of the evening, I said there'd be a big dent in my life. I think he appreciated that because he didn't come back with a crack.

Dr Ron was the next to go. He took me to a local health restaurant to break the news. 'Never fear, my friend,' he said, bending a spoon, 'I will return with a fortune . . . and then *what larks*! As Dickens so aptly put it.' Where was he going to? 'London – where else to traditionally make your fortune?' Spontaneously I said that I too would go to London and there, apart from seeing friends and family, seek a new book commission from my publisher. Biographies – they seem to be the current rage – I'll write a best-seller show-biz biography. 'That's the spirit,' said Ron, wiping the table furiously. Yes, but would the house and Beefy be safe while we were away? Would strangers invade as had happened before? 'Let me tell you about Fred,' said Dr Ron, putting his hands on his lap. 'He comes from a rough background, true. The child of lumberjacks; taken from behind at age seven. . . . ' The waitress barged in at this point to tell us about their dessert specials, especially the diet carob chocolate chip 'suicide' cake. Dr Ron gave her a withering look. 'Where were we? Well, Fred joined the Marine Corps and put his developing brain to rest. He has emerged the perfect servant, unquestioning and subservient. He'll be the right machine to take care of your castle while the knights are away at the wars.' I thanked Ron profusely. What would my L.A. life have been without him? And now, to turn to brighter matters – what exactly would he be working at in London? 'No, no, my friend. One must say *Europe* these days, for soon we will be one great culture and economy over there. And we will be able to challenge the power of barbaric America and gutless Japan. Germany will be united again! I'm sure that you too, in your field, have encountered Euro-Pop.' Slightly irritated, I told him that I'd been an author, and an author only, for many years. 'Whatever. Anyway, I journey to London to set up an H.Q. for the gathering of money at low interest rates to be lent in America at a high rate. *Voilà*!' I said I'd never understood finance but I wished him success so that he'd soon be back in Altadena. 'Fred will keep the house warm, never fear,' said Dr Ron gently.

In the autumn, with a contract to write a biography of Irving Berlin and a desire to work steadfastly, I returned to my house. Chaos greeted me.

I opened the garden gate and there was Beefy, thrilled to see me as usual, but very bony, and bald in spots. His left ear, once so high and noble, was flopped down and bandaged. Fleas hopped on his coat, his turds covered most of the garden, the rest was holes and cigarette butts. Indoors were more butts plus a layer of dust on everything, lots of insect corpses and a flea-dance on my bedspread. In the fridge was nothing but dog-food cans and a mound of potatoes sprouting branches and leaves. On the inside of the bathroom door was dried blood and big scratch marks. I found Fred in the back bedroom, curled up foetally on the floor in a corner, wrapped in an army blanket. Sex magazines were scattered around him, the T.V. flickered a shoot-out silently. Answering my call, he said, 'I'm sorry' and started to cry. After I'd worked off my anger he said, 'You better see the garage too, while you're at it.'

My Honda Accord was smashed in at the front and bent all out of shape generally. The front bumper was missing, as was the hood ornament that says 'Honda'. The left door was jammed and the window was broken. How had he got the car keys? How had Beefy's ear been downed? And the blood on the bathroom door, and the scratches? So many questions. I was speechless. What was I doing in this God-forsaken part of the world? Fred was still in his room, but now he was staring at the wall; he was more puzzled than me. Perhaps he had realized that life's riddle holds no answer. 'I put fresh flowers in your room, roses from your own garden. I did my best – but it was the long, hot summer and it was Beefy. . . .' He started to cry again.

I left Fred alone, but a few days later there was a phone call for him. I fielded it. How are you calling Fred? Don't you know he's phoneless? 'He'll be limbless soon,' snarled the caller. It was Bob Rinducci, the shady lawyer and Dr Ron's ex-partner. 'That bastard Fred stole $350 off me and I have proof. I'm a bad guy, very bad when I'm messed with. I know Ron put him up to the deal but I have connections, know what I mean?' I told him he was sounding off at an innocent party. This was *my* phone and *my* house. 'I can have his legs broken or his ears cut off. If I so wish I can have both jobs done!' Phone dead.

I took Fred to the Jack-In-A-Box on Lake and bought him an order of chicken strips and onion rings. He said he'd taken the money for Dr Ron because the money was owing to Dr Ron, who'd been like a father and mother to him. Just then it started to rain cats and dogs and I thought the little shack-box would tumble. Fred said, 'Time to go,' and shook my hand. What about his belongings? He patted his khaki parka. 'Goodbye, sir. I wish you – and the world – only good things.' I gave him a lift to the nearest bus stop. I never saw him again.

171

But later, over the next year or so, I'd encounter men at parties who could describe my house frighteningly well, and they'd talk warmly of the young military boy who lived there and how hospitable he'd been. They knew the hot tub and they knew Beefy. Whatever became of that nice young boy?

*

'I apologize from the very bottom of my heart,' said Dr Ronald, bowing deeply. 'I have been the father of your woes too many times.' Having concluded his business in London, he was back in Altadena and into new and exciting projects. 'Despite Mr Orwell we are going to make 1984 a gala year!' We two would live and work at our separate projects but under the same green roof. No more boarders. In my new W.H. Smith journal (bought over Christmas while taking the usual holiday in London) I had written: 'Time is of the Essence. Write Your Book'. Irving Berlin would get my full, undivided attention.

For his part Dr Ron was dedicated to new ways. No more Marines, he swore. All work and a strict diet from now on. Why, as of today he had a new partner, a local entrepreneur he'd met while buying his breakfast croissant at the Jack-In-A-Box on Lake. I didn't like to ask what schemes they were devising. Lately Dr Ron had been getting a lot of letters post-marked Las Vegas with legal firm names on the left-hand corner; his phone rang constantly and when, while he was out, I picked up a call a gruff voice demanded to know who I was. When I questioned them, the party rang off. I suspected Rinducci was behind the call and the letters, but I didn't probe Ron because . . . because it was a new year and soon the refreshing, life-renewing hard rains would be arriving.

'Let me take you to a Sizzler restaurant, a fine chain, to celebrate our new life on the right tracks,' said Ron. Of course, being his guest, I couldn't prevent him from telling me his latest money plans. 'My partner, Hal Rogers, has a wall full of framed degrees, and his speciality is comparative religion. But he realizes there's no return at present in that subject. So. . . .' And from the house to the restaurant and all during dinner I let him rip, which gave me the opportunity to thoroughly enjoy my Malibu chicken.

The gist of the scheme was this: shopping malls to be erected around a central giant car-wash, financed by Thai businessmen, who, seeking resident alien status in America, have been told that they can achieve this by investing enough dollars in their chosen country. 'Clever, isn't it?' I said I really hoped it would work, for all our sakes, including Beefy. I added that the dog was much improved. Suddenly Ron turned nasty. 'I fail to understand your passion for that animal.' Because I love him. Who do you love?

'I have attachments to nobody and nobody has attachments to me.' His voice grew loud and strident, alarming customers (and this was a family restaurant). 'I loathe everything about this decadent city, this nowhere-ville – no values, no honour, no untarnished beauty! And teetering on the edge of the abyss! They are coming to push us in! I mean the barbaric hordes from the Third World! Western culture has atrophied in this semi-tropical heat!' A fat Mexican busboy was in the act of whipping away Dr Ron's half-eaten sirloin. 'Vamoose, pronto! What to do about these illiterate invaders? Why, they are encouraged *not* to learn English! Even the rest-room signs are in Mexican!' The busboy was waddling off with his prize. 'Look at their revolting phy-siques! Note the sloping shoulders and amoeba ass! An insult to eyes raised on ancient Greece! I see no hope for Western civilization so long as present lax immigration policies continue. . . .' His voice, strangely, trailed away, as if by losing his sirloin he'd lost the battle.

Now Dr Ronald and I were living alone in Alameda Street, guarded by Beefy. The mountains of printed matter in Ron's room grew wider and higher until they merged into one great landfill, covering everything except the pillow end of his bed. At night he'd re-turn from his shopping mall/car-wash business and, after unctuous greetings, would disappear into the landfill room. Sometimes I'd peep in, just to make sure he was breathing (for he was my only talk-ing friend), and I'd be relieved to see the short back and sides haircut, the toothbrush moustache, the top of grey undershirt; and now here was the sharp-pointed snoring cutting through the all-news 24-hours-a-day radio station. And in the morning, crack o' dawn, he'd emerge from his underworld dressed immaculately in suit, tie and waistcoat, and exuding an unearthly fragrance. 'Good morrow, my friend. How do you manage to look so good in gym clothes at this hour and at your age?'

The house went to pot. Old meals piled up in the kitchen sink, the dust was as thick and even as in the bad old days, the corpses of flies and moths and unidentified flying objects collected not only in the usual places but everywhere else as well. From the study window I watched the back garden revert to desert. Soon wild mountain beasts were paying visits. Deep one night I was called from my bed by Bee-fy's cries; I found him in this garden desert, roaring around in a cloud of dust, trying to deal with an unspeakable creature, an un-nameable, a real flesh-creeper. This object, this hideous thing . . . like a bloated rat or a punk-haired piglet, with bared serrated teeth (rather like Chas's) and glinting anthracite eyes (not unlike Dick Gimbel's)* . . . stood stock-still, as in a movie freeze-frame, squatting fatly in the middle of my back fence, vile in the moonlight.

I gave Beefy the command. He barked, circled, feigned a leap, did some unconvincing *grrrrrhs*, went into reverse, fell over on his back and started kicking like an upturned beetle. Arming myself with a rake I approached the monster and took a poke, feeling the teeth sink deep into the fold of that horrid squishy flesh. The brute didn't budge. I, too, reversed and fell over. Finally, with Beefy barking encouragement, I made a charge and rake-lanced with all of my heart and with all of my hatred of the unknown. Success! The vile wretch tumbled grumbling into my neighbour's garden and disappeared from my life. Before getting back into bed I took a long shower, scrubbing every inch of me with all the fervour of a born-again Christian back from missionary work amidst the mosques of Sheffield.

Next morning I hailed Dr Ron as he was leaving his room, dressed for business battle. Half-way through the story he interrupted: 'Your first encounter with a possum, or oppossum, which our coloured friends treat as a delicacy. A harmless creature unless cornered. But then, aren't many of us that way?'

Dr Ron was away a lot, sometimes for days. Alone, unguided, my mind started racing down crazed pathways. I thought of the possum when, one Saturday afternoon, smoke and strong smells from next door told me my neighbours were having a barbecue. A coloured delicacy, Dr Ron had said! They were neighbours I didn't know much about – the gospelling Goldsmiths lived on the other side. But these were a couple who were generally quiet – rather bourgeois actually – with a B.M.W. saloon car and a baby and a Mexican gardening team who came regularly to blow leaves. However, as the day turned to night so came an awful transformation: the barbecue became a rowdy party with ceaseless tom-tomming pierced by shrieks and wails, and flames flickering above my fence and moving shadows looming up over my house, and me pacing the patio and wondering whether Dr Ron was right about civilization and that these possum-stoked savages were preparing to 'fit de battle ob Jericho' clean on to my property!

Next day, of course, all was calm and collected. Their front lawn

* The hot jazz cornettist in Part one.

shimmered and their B.M.W. sparkled. The husband wished me a good morning and invited me over next time to sample his famous barbecue sauce.

But my confusion continued and I developed cluster headaches too. I started banging my desk a lot, and then the wall. The house was only a wooden frame with plaster and it shook with frailty. And when, as a cure, I'd take to my bed in the daytime there were disturbing dreams: of finding dead babies in a bathroom I never knew was mine, of floors of rooms I never knew were over my house, and some of these rooms overflowing with partying strangers; night after night up the dusty trail from West Hollywood would come Tommy and I, trekking with all our belongings, and behind us the cries and the flames, and in front the house of dreams with a knocker of pearl and the bird of paradise waiting on the roof to greet us. 'C'mon, Ee-on! Not much further to frosted champagne and a plate of canapés!'

*

Dr Ronald, once again, tried to come to the rescue. 'I have just the man to take care of the running of the house, leaving you and I to ruminate on more important matters.' From behind his door he produced Ajax, a lug in flared jeans and a windcheater, with a sailor's drawstring bag slung on his left shoulder. I should have known better, but he had a firm handshake and a winning smile. 'He's ready, willing and able to work his passage – washing dishes, watering the garden, dealing with noisy neighbours – all in return for a room.' Ajax, the lug, backed up Ron's words with a vigorous nodding.

Quickly, too quickly, Ajax installed himself (in Fred's old room) and made his mark around the house. A fancy wire basket hung from the kitchen ceiling, filled with fruit, especially bananas. Soon a banana aroma saturated every room, and this was helpful when the lavatory got blocked by Ajax's zeppelin turds. All along the back patio and out into the yard were strung clothes-lines, and on these lines hung Ajax's multi-coloured bikini underwear, fluffy-ruffled shirts, silk trousers, silk scarves and flared jeans from many designers. 'He fancies himself as a clothes-horse and dreams of being a male model. Humour him,' said Dr Ron. I mentioned the need to diet. 'Oh, but he was a magnificent specimen when I first met him at the gates of Camp Pendleton!' Not another! 'Still . . . you'll find him useful round the house.'

But Ajax's idea of usefulness did not always jive with my life-style.

175

Often, after his evening chores, he'd saunter around in silk pyjamas and, when he'd found me, he'd try to advise me on how to succeed in the Eighties. For example, he'd flaunt in my face a magazine called *Gentleman's Quarterly*, pointing out the latest fashions and telling me that the right clothes were the way to fame and fortune. 'Ron tells me you deserve a break. Have done for years and years.' What a nerve! – especially from a general factotum. 'Let me tell you about neck-ties.' I sought refuge in my room.

As time went by the lug turned thuggish. By day he worked down in L.A., but the jobs came and went at an alarming speed. They were always in 'Security': guarding banks, supermarkets, shopping malls. Hadn't Tommy been a uniformed guard for a while? History repeating itself, and I was not learning its lesson. Ajax's uniforms grew more military with every new job; his face went from bovine to glowering. His boots grew bigger too and he'd clump into the house of an evening, slamming doors and thumping walls. Soon he was neglecting his household duties: dishes unwashed, breadboard left out and crumb-covered, cupboard doors wide open. When I upbraided him he looked at me as if I was a fool. Then off he clumped down the corridor to lock himself in his room with my T.V., roaring and grunting and slapping at an endless stream of game shows, sit-coms and cop pics.

'Show him the door,' advised Dr Ron one night as we stood in the corridor listening. But I was scared of a stand-off, for the fact was I was frightened of Ajax. He seemed to be metamorphosing into a monster, his teeth longer and sharper, his lips like inner tubes, his eyes like black squash balls set in a bilious sea. One night he left the front door ajar and Beefy ran out; it was hours before I became aware of his absence. At around 3 a.m., horrible hour, I drove the Altadena streets searching, panicking, for my one constant, reliable, steadfast friend. Eventually I found him miles away, running with a pack of wild dogs, howling at the moon with the worst of them – a gang member, one of the mob. I was shocked at Beefy and I told him so. But as far as Ajax was concerned, I simply didn't have the nerve to confront him. I just slipped a note under his door.

Christmas was coming and I would soon be returning to England and home. Ron would watch Ajax, I felt sure. And Ajax would take care of Beefy. Strangely the lug and the dog had a sort of affinity. I was telling Ajax how pleased I was with this affinity when he handed me a gift-wrapped package. 'Seasons greetings – it's the Playboy Diary – easy on the meat beating!' He sidestepped me and knocked

176

on Ron's door. 'I'll be in to give you your gift later!'

Next morning I asked Ron what he'd received and he went very sheepish. 'If you must know . . . he offered me a blow job.' I was flabbergasted. 'Well, he used to be a street hustler. Didn't I tell you that?' I must have looked upset because he offered to buy me breakfast. 'Oh dear,' he said as we got into the Rolls, 'I've done it again, haven't I?'

*

When I returned in the spring I found the house in reasonable order. I asked Dr Ron how his Christmas had been and he said, 'The professional house-cleaning company did a good job, eh?' Then he told me his tale of woe. Ajax had taken himself a girl-friend, black; they had thrown an immense Christmas party with a rock group and a Baptist choir; guests had thrown up in the house and garden, giving as their excuse 'partially-unfrozen fish fillets'; guests had camped on the property, some remaining for several days; the lavatory had been blocked by sanitary towels. But Beefy had been well fed, even enjoying the fish fillets, and the house-cleaning people *had* done a good job.

Ajax was now working as a strong-arm man for West Coast Detectives, Inc., and was carrying a revolver in a holster beneath his jacket. 'Sometimes I despair of our Constitution and its repercussions,' said Dr Ron. As for Ron himself, his business ventures had all collapsed and, what's more, he'd been screwed out of his Rolls by his most recent business partner, the expert on comparative religions. Now, to his chagrin, he would see his partner's teenage son gadding about the neighbourhood in the chocolate-coloured vehicle, 'when I, as often as not, am hurrying home with a take-out chicken giblet.' In order to survive he had been working part-time for a pornographer friend called Jack Skivvler who operated a sideline, or 'front', in the Christmas decorations business. 'Yes, I have been reduced to writing doggerel for Yuletide tree gift boxes!' What about his long-range ambition? The Great Cities/Great Cultures project? 'Not long! Just as soon as I get to Europe!' And he raised his fist towards the drawing-room ceiling . . . which was covered in black smudges. 'The party – they had an indoor barbecue.' I said I'd leave Ajax a strongly worded note. 'Throw him back into the street!', said Ron with some passion. 'Please – I want, as my final gesture, to help you. I who have been the root of your undoing.' Patiently I explained again that Ajax's function was to take care of Beefy. He shook his head and suggested dinner.

'I will introduce you to the latest foodie craze, an import from the South-Western states: the sizzling fah-heet-ah.' Only when we were ensconced in our booths at the Mañana Mexican restaurant did it sink in that Dr Ron had been talking about leaving me. The last link with old world values abandoning me to L.A. life! 'Understand, my friend, that for the well-heeled white middle class of Los Angeles, eating out, expensively and exotically, has become the substitute for the old culture you and I so cherished. Now let me explain the fah-heet-ah. . . .' He smoothed out the tablecloth and smiled at the hovering Mexican busboy. 'Spelled F, A, J, I, T, A, but pronounced fah-heet-ah because the myth goes that they're from old Mexico, re-dolent of castanets, capes and rippling guitars. But, in truth, this dish is the invention of a white Texan marketing man. Take a tortilla and fill it with tomato, onion, guacamole and sizzling chicken or beef. So simple, so clever! You have created your own sandwich, you feel that you too are an artist. A demotic dish, free of the chef-as-artist syndrome. A good invention, eh, Pancho?' The busboy smiled and filled our glasses with water. 'Can't understand a word and never will. Unlike those East European immigrants at the turn of the century who were eager to embrace the American way. When the language goes, then the game is up. Anyway, I'm departing this region in order to find a still centre in Europe.' He proceeded to expand heatedly on the subject of cars and phones and Third World peoples; he hated them all. What he treasured were 'integrated cities replete with plazas, squares, moot halls and promenades; and public buildings in the classical style, with fine limestone balconies from where strong leaders can address their citizens in stentorian tones. A sense of true community, of who's who and who has always been who, from time immemorial.'

I grew dejected, knowing that I was stuck in the Southland trying to put down roots in what appeared to be shifting, gibbering sands. But another kingsize margarita and another helping of fajita soon smothered my melancholy. Dr Ron, in his excitement, had let fajita splatter his cheeks. We ended with coffee and Ron indulged in a dish of fried ice-cream. As he scooped, he told me of his great D-Day plan: 'By 1990 I hope to have enough money to establish a beach-head in Britain, and there I shall purchase a modest thatched cottage on the Dover coast or, perhaps, in historic Bath . . .' He wiped the tablecloth with wide, rapid strokes. 'Well, my friend, shall we? . . .' And he rose. And I rose. And we returned to the mess. . . .

Back to sitting in my study, typing out notes on Irving Berlin's early days in Czarist Russia, gazing out of the window at tall straw which was once grass and at the unknown weeds like giant cauliflower, at the possums and racoons and coyotes roaming my property; and then back to my desk and the friendly fur underneath – Beefy harrumphing with satisfaction as he did knightly deeds in his dreams. A fat and sluggish fly stayed too long on the window-sill and got thoroughly soaked by my aerosol spray. I watched the complicated monster – such fine micro-mechanisms! – thrash out a ragtime dance of death. Afterwards I apologized and we had a burial at sea in the back lavatory. And so I returned to Irving and his connection with Rasputin, but I musn't forget the cheque for earthquake insurance, and the calls in search of a date and a fuck, and all the while, right into the evening, the sun shines down stupidly. Then: 'Hah, hah, haaaah! Ho, ho, hoooooooooo!' and a banging on the wall. Ajax is awake and watching his T.V. shows. Might as well give up and take the blessed dog for a walk.

Dr Ron was tip-toeing to the bathroom when I emerged from my study. He was always tip-toeing and there was really no need. 'I am fearful of interrupting the act of creation,' he said. He took in my grim face. 'Time out for you. Lay down your burdens and let us watch the Academy Awards – with the proper accompaniment of fresh popcorn and sodas. My treat!' Yes, but the T.V. was in Ajax's room and the idea of sitting among his squalor revolted me. Whispered Ron, 'Wait till he leaves for his nightly detective work. Then we'll sneak in and steal the set.' Good thinking.

The Academy Awards dragged on and on. A world geographically a few miles away, but realistically light years from me and mine. We were sitting in the drawing room with our popcorn and our rum-laced sodas when Ajax barged in to tell us he'd been fired. We commiserated and returned to our viewing. But he remained in the doorway, lumpish, staring dully at the T.V. and then at us and then back to the T.V. After a while: 'Hey, you older guys can give me some advice . . . how d'you get rid of unwanted bitches? See, I got this black one. Won't stop bugging me, begging for sex and whatnot. How d'you guys deal with this?' It was a question neither Dr Ron nor I was prepared to answer at this, or indeed any other, moment. Dr Ron made some polite noises and returned to his rum soda; I stuck to the screen. Ajax turned on his heel and thumped off down the corridor. Slam! went his door. A few minutes later the whole house shook, as if by earthquake. Then Ajax rushed in and announced, 'Hey, hey, hey! Give me your blessing – I'm gonna apply to the Sheriff's department for a job as a deputy! They're begging for us in the *L.A. Times* classified section!' What could be worse than Ajax fully-armed and in my house? I told Ron, later and quietly, that I'd get rid of the lug by raising his rent. Dr Ron smiled politely; he had more important matters on his mind.

Over the next month my long-time guide and mentor started work on his exit operation. He applied to a Virginia university for a place as a student/teacher(English grammar and American history), and was accepted. If he graduated, his old Virginny rich relatives would, he said, grant a tidy annuity allowing him to move to England and seek out that cottage in Dover or Bath. Soon he was busying about in my garage boxing up his belongings – all those books on great cities and cultures, all those male porn magazines and movies, all those oils and unguents. As he worked he sang wild Wagnerian selections, loudly and too cheerfully. I was terribly sad.

One night I saw a policeman coming through the front gate. Beefy licked him. 'You're looking at a trainee deputy sheriff,' said Ajax. The uniform certainly fitted his brutish form. I congratulated him – and told him I was raising the rent. 'No problem,' he replied and wrote me out a cheque with one of the many pens lined up in the top pocket of his blue uniform. 'Next week I'll have the gun.'

At this point I felt the need for a strong drink in a faraway place. So I headed for the Far East Terrace, the piano bar where Chas had met the woman who lived with the ventriloquist, you remember? Here I was in luck; they let me sing a whole medley of Al Jolson songs and the Chinese barman kept buying me piña coladas. Also, the lady pianist told me that the new cocktail waitress, Olga, considered me to be a 'tasty dish'. In the dark of the bar Olga and I looked pretty appetizing. We kept it that way, for the time being.

After her work, around 2 a.m., we sat in a corner booth and checked each other out. Olga was German and still had a very pronounced accent; she was the mother of two teenage boys. She was also quite hungry, and so was I. Eventually we made a date. In no time at all she was visiting me, on her night off, at Alameda Street.

Dr Ronald was all over her from the moment he heard her name and voice. 'A German from Germany!' he said as he paced the drawing room floor, waving a cigarette (he only smoked when excited). 'My own name, Bund, is of course Bavarian – and middle, not high ... I once lectured a Panzer fraternity group, in German, on the occasion of their annual reunion in 1969 ...' Olga, a strapping fraulein with tightly pressed blonde curls and aggressive breasts, joined

Dr Ron in spirit. The United States could do with a new Hitler right now – today's youth needed discipline badly. 'Especially mine own brrraats!' Dr Ron tipped an imaginary hat and excused himself: 'I have to prepare my American history – a tedious and squalid tale – for an imminent scholastic career. Good luck to you both – a worthy coupling, if ever I saw one!'

When Olga and I returned from the Oirish place, stoked with food and wine and ready for violent sex, we found Ajax in uniform, lazing on my lounger, scooping great gobs of ice-cream from an enormous tub, and swallowing, whooping, hollering, clearing his throat and talking to himself in his normal manner. The T.V. flickered some silly game show. I made a mental note to move the set into my bedroom, tomorrow or the next day.

Still, the din from Ajax and the T.V. covered up the screams of ecstasy from Olga as we waged our sex war on the bed. 'Pleeessss, pleeessss – oh, fire it, fire it!' she commanded, a Rhine maiden in the North African campaign. Of course, I obeyed with pleasure. Her aftershock convulsions almost tossed me off the bed. 'Six or seven times haf I org-gazzummed. Tanks, tanks!' and she rolled over and was soon snoring like a trooper.

With the help of a glass of wine and a Valium I knocked myself into sleep . . . and the wrong part of Dreamland. Tommy and his gang had stripped the house of everything. Even Beefy had gone. As I stood in this half-way house to hell I heard Tommy laughing at me from somewhere. I woke up because Olga was biting my thigh. 'You haf skin texture of teenager,' she said. I tried to think up a return compliment but failed.

What with Ron's frenzied packing and Ajax's assorted noises I was quite relieved when Olga invited me over to her apartment for a night of 'messink about'. First we dined out stoutly at a North Hollywood hofbrau called The Old Stein, situated in a mini-mall between a dry cleaner's and a video store. No windows let you know what was inside: twisty, curvy, rusticated wood everywhere, and beer steins on every flat surface; leather trousers galore hanging from the low ceiling. Olga knew everybody in the steamy crowded room, and they all knew her. Course after course of heavy food was thudded on to our table by mine host, a jolly old sport from Silesia called Barney; a gypsy trio strolled around, playing Viennese waltzes, German marches and 'Happy Birthday To You'. Olga announced that I was a famous singer and the crowd clapped me into performing. I must have had too much of the hock because I went and sang 'Hitler Has

Only Got One Ball'. Although there was a certain amount of applause a widespread elderly woman in peasant costume biffed up and hissed, 'You have insulted a personal friend of mine!'

Eventually, tight and swollen, we staggered into Olga's modest apartment. Half an hour's polite perusal of her family album (lots of wartime snapshots of uniformed relatives), and then at last she steered me into her bedroom and on to the waterbed. Oh! A life on the ocean wave! We were thrashing and floundering and rolling around and she was 'pleeeesss-pleeesss'-ing when all of a sudden the room filled with harsh light. Disengaging myself, I lay on my back undulating and looking around. Leaning against the wall by the door, arms folded, a knowing smile playing on full lips, was a muscular boy in bikini underpants. Nodding, he said, 'Looking good, man, looking *real* good.' Olga bounced off the bed and strode over to the louche youth, whose heavy-duty wedding tackle I now noticed. Snapping the elastic in his underpants she said, 'You're s'posed to be back on base.' 'Hey, easy, Mom – I got my own special furlough. You know . . . to make more of them movies for Skivvler. The ones that pay the rent.' Skivvler – I'd heard that name before: the pornographer friend of Dr Ron's, the man with the Christmas decorations sideline business. Small world – but I didn't pursue the subject because the boy went on to describe the real purpose of his visit. 'I aim to settle a few scores with Skivvler. Fer screwin' up my life, fer ditchin' me in the dirt. Yeah – I got a gift fer that fudge-pounder and fer the fake doctor who writes his scripts!' And the boy punched a chair flying. Even afterwards as he stood by the door waiting for me to go, his muscles continued to pop in and out and up and down like a robot gone haywire.

I put on my trousers and wished them goodnight.

As I was pulling into my driveway, and morning was breaking, so Dr Ronald was attempting to open the door of a battered old car. He was dressed in his best European clothes, the Tyrolean hat with feather topping the ensemble, and now he was taking a flying kick at the recalcitrant door.

I called out a greeting and he spun round in surprise. 'I was wondering where you were. I'd hate to depart without at least a handshake.' He advanced on me, hesitated a moment and then offered his hand boldly. It was a decent, strong shake. I didn't know what to say. 'Staying with you and being your friend has been an honour,' he said, stepping back smartly. Then I said that knowing him had been an education. 'Too much of it from the street, alas, and not enough from dreaming spires. But now that you have your castle, do try to keep it clean. Get rid of that knave, please do!' Was there a tear in his eye or was it the sun on his contacts? 'Well, off we go to new pastures in my chariot from Rent-a-wreck!'

I continued waving till the spluttering, jerking vehicle had rounded the corner on Alameda Street and Santa Rosa. For a while I stood still in silent homage; then I turned round to face the plug-ugly knave.

Breakfast was laid out at the dining-room table – orange juice, steaming coffee, eggs and bacon. Beefy was eyeing the spread with envy. What on earth? I found Ajax in his room, in silk pyjamas, lying on his stomach on the carpet, watching T.V. He must have moved it back. A cartoon of flat jabbering figures chasing each other was making him bellow and cough. I asked how he could bear such drivel when there were so many good books in this house. At least, there used to be. 'Cartoons are educational,' he replied, spinning round, standing up and facing me fair and square. I was suprised by this sudden articulateness. 'Cartoons show us the real America. They're a metaphor. Understand cartoons, commercials and sport, and you'll understand the American people. Try it!' I was dumbfounded. 'Oh – and I made you a real good breakfast. Enjoy!'

I hadn't the nerve to ask him to leave, but I laid my plans for the future. I would put out the word that I had rooms to rent for normal, reliable, preferably married people. The new boarders would, by force of numbers and example, cut Ajax down and into a shape more suitable for civilized society . . . and if he refused to become a responsible member of my mini-society, then he could get out. Meanwhile I would spend my days in the air-conditioned comfort and safety of the Huntington Library, completing my book on Irving Berlin.

Through my old recording studio connections I met a just-married couple who were only too pleased to be offered a lodging. Troy and Cassandra, fledgling sound engineers and a handsome young couple, took over the Tommy/Dr Ronald Memorial Room. They were as keen to make a success of my house as they were of the Hollywood world just over the hills. 'Good morning, sir! And how are we today?' was Troy's jovial and tireless greeting. Cassandra offered to let me guest at their healthy evening meals, provided I was ready and washed by 7 p.m. As for Ajax, he was bemused, then confused, and finally stupefied. He took to wandering around the house and garden, clearing his throat and sighing, closely followed by Beefy. The latter seemed to love him.

Life with Ajax came to an end one Sunday morning just before

Christmas. Cassandra was cooking up a 'gourmet brunch' for Troy and me; we were all in the kitchen in our underclothes and I must say Cassandra cut an enticing figure – slim in the right places and fleshy in the right places, bottom and breast sticking out sportively – while Troy seemed to have been born to wear Calvin Klein underpants because he filled them so well (Troy had told me quietly, 'What's mine is yours in this house – we both so love you!'); when Cassandra dropped some bacon rashers I crouched down to pick them up and she joined me on the floor. As I say, we were all in underwear. 'Is it so cold this morning?' she whispered as we worked with the bacon. 'Your nipples have gone very hard. Like they're having an erection.' 'Cassandra! Don't be gross!' said Troy from the breakfast nook, in mock shock. 'Soh-wee, so veh-wee soh-wee!' sang Cassandra, pouting and sucking on a rasher of bacon, standing with one hip much higher than the other. 'Shall Cassandra go to her room?' 'Naw – here's Daddy's punishment for you!' And he went over and crushed her to his chest, working his buttocks as in intercourse. Beefy sidled up and licked them both, just to complete the happy picture.

But then in lumbered Ajax, wearing a smart blue suit and a striped red-white-and-blue tie. His eyes were bloodshot and there was deep, dark stubble on his chin. Troy withdrew from his love clinch; Cassandra returned to tending the frying pan. Beefy, tail wagging madly, padded up to Ajax.

He cleared his throat and made his speech. 'You guys all know I was to be a deputy sheriff. But, for certain reasons, I am tendering my resignation to the police academy.' How had he learned to be so articulate, so clear-spoken, so fast? 'I'll be returning to Oklahoma, my home state, there to start life over again.' A dramatic pause. He swivelled his gaze. 'But you can all be certain – and mark my words – that I will be back and I will be something *very*, *very* special!' We all agreed.

Then we got down to business. I bought some of his belongings – the bed and the rug – but I had no interest in the frilly lace curtains he'd put up in his room, nor in his collection of silk pyjamas. 'O.K. I'll give them to my girl. She's been up all night, crying and carrying on at my sad predicament.' The presence of this girl was news to me but I kept quiet because, at last, it really seemed like Ajax was leaving us.

He nodded to each one of us and left the kitchen. We got down to our brunch. Beefy was uncertain as to where his loyalty lay, but when the bacon left the pan he quickly joined our side.

Ajax never said goodbye. After brunch we all went for a hike in the hills and when we came back he had gone. I was quite sorry, surprisingly. Now I worked out that in all the time he'd been my lodger I'd never once socialized with him, never chatted with him, never eaten with him. All that he'd left was a bed and a rug. I had refused his frilly curtains.

'He left some other souvenirs,' said Cassandra. She had volunteered to clean out his room and the job had taken up most of the evening. Now she was standing next to me as I lay on my bed watching the ceiling. 'For your inspection,' she said, tipping out on to the bedspread the contents of a plastic trash bucket. I examined several stolen library books, an envelope stuffed with final demands from collection agencies, and a gift-box of super gossamer condoms. 'He also left a big fat cat,' added Cassandra, flopping down sexily next to me. A big fat cat? How did I never know about this extra being in my house? 'He kept his window open and the cat just jumped in and out. I guess his black girl-friend did the same thing.'

The cat and the girl and the open window! Extra rooms and soaring new floors and right at the top, in the clouds, is a stained wooden dormitory crammed with young strangers having a party. Tommy is standing at the end of the beds, by the open window, hands on hips, head thrown back, laughing.

*

The staff at the Huntington Library welcomed me back and issued a new reader's card. They assigned a new workplace, a bleak cell-like room with nothing on the walls but white paint and the death mask of William Blake. I worked well and steadily; at the end of each page, even if in mid-sentence, I would leave the cell and go for a stroll in the art gallery, losing myself in therapeutic paintings like 'After the Storm' and 'The Blue Boy'. Three pages a day, five days a week. I even encountered Irving Berlin in my dreams. Time raced by and the writing soothed me. KROQ dropped my show, but KCRW, national public radio, offered me an afternoon slot and I accepted because an hour a week playing old songs in Santa Monica complemented my life with Irving. What about sex as recreation? What about Olga?

She soon tired of me and announced that she had turned her attentions to Barney, the jolly Silesian owner of the hofbrau. 'We haf more in common – and I get half the restaurant,' she explained. What care I? A new radio show attracted new fans – and these were intellectuals compared with my old KROQ listeners. There was Carefree Sturgeon who was into I Ching and the East, but had time for me. 'If only you'll adjust to the relationship. . . . Do you want to fuck now? O.K., I'm prepared. Tell me when you've finished, it's your mind I'm after.' A fine romance! She left me for a blue collar worker, 'an airhead hunk but he makes a *great* salad'. Then there was Mandy who loved my show when I played Al Bowlly – 'He's *SOOOOO* sexy, like he has a phallus in his throat.' By this time I had discovered Sterling's Steak House and I liked to test out my new friends by seeing how they reacted to my new-found club. Mandy failed the test – she said the music was 'corny' and the plastic tablecloths 'unsophisticated'. Nevertheless, after a few drinks, she agreed to let me come back to her house and watch a video of Prince Andrew's wedding. 'I'm crazy for British history and isn't Andy sexy?' After the wedding tape we listened to Al Bowlly and soon we were making ourselves more comfortable in the bedroom. She had splendid melon breasts. We were both over forty and most grateful. But we were also, outside of the bedroom, completely incompatible. She loved baseball and hated ragtime. I loved onions, she didn't. In the end she wrote me a kiss-off letter, in fountain pen and a splendid script. Here are some extracts: 'I have a recurring anger about male attitudes and you seem to exhibit them all. . . . Men are not generous, giving, loving people. . . . I am impressed by caring and sharing. . . . You never listen to what I say . . . .You are narrow in your attitudes and you generalize, and this is extremely dangerous for women, minorities, countries, youth – in fact, everyone but upper-class white men who enjoy power and protection. . . . I am sorry to be so harsh but realities are realities.'

Mandy's letter spoiled the whole day and then the whole week. I had the thing photocopied and showed it to friends for their comments. Most were full of sympathy, but Witham, from London, wrote, 'Every word is true, despite the style.'

At this point I gave up attacking on the sex front. Life was full enough, what with Berlin and the boarders. All day I worked in my Huntington cell, conscious that William Blake was invigilating through his death mask. After work, back at the house, there was always an exciting life whirling around me. Troy, for example, noting the empty back bedroom, suggested I rent to his brother Max, a rock'n'roll roadie, and Max brought in his girl-friend Kimberlee, a supermarket check-out person, and they brought in a red-haired biker who was promising them lucrative work in the rapidly expanding acoustic tile business, and the biker had two pit bulldogs, real killers, and I told him to keep them in his truck in the driveway because, I explained, inside the house they might eat up Beefy. And yes, said the red-haired stranger, those dogs could swallow Beefy like a frankfurter but whatever's right, man, keep cool and feel my hair, run your fingers through the stuff, see how thick and tangled it is, that's because I work real hard, harder than them niggers next door, all they do is drum and piano-whammy and they cain't play worth a shit – but *I* explained as how their father, a quiet man, had told me his kids were practising gospel music, and the red-haired stranger said gospel shit, my fuckin' eye, and stomped off to his sleeping-bag on the back patio where he kept a portable T.V. which seemed to show nothing but vampire movies, and where he seemed to be very interested in tending my garden until I discovered that he and Max were growing marijuana plants which I begged them to stop doing because that could jeopardize my status as a resident alien. Huh, said the stranger, isn't this s'posed to be fuckin' lotusland out here, let me tell you about the dogs and cats I run over regular in my truck, you wanna see the video I have showing people being executed and killed while robbing or driving or flying, it's real cool . . . .

I asked Max to get rid of the stranger, as my Christmas present. Max said he'd try. I want him to be gone when I return in January. O.K., O.K., take it easy, kick back. One night I found a matchbook under the lounger and inside the flap was scribbled: 'Your boy-friend is A DEAD MAN.' Max said he knew nothing about a matchbook.

We celebrated my departure for London by dining in the kitchen off Sloppy Joe's, a mucous mince-meat in a squidgy bun. Hey, said the red-haired stranger, this is better than canned spaghetti, and Max said it was a banquet for him and Kimberlee because all they usually ate – morning, noon and night – was sandwiches. Yeah, well I'd rather have a sandwich, said the stranger, hurling his Sloppy Joe on to the kitchen floor and stomping off to his truck where we later heard him teasing his pit bulls.

Next year life changed for the better: I had a pond built and I met Regina.

*

The pond, in the front garden, was the opposite of the hot tub at the back. In all these years I had never learned the knack of operating the hot tub so that bubbles burst and water raged. But my boarders – and lots of strangers – were masters of the art, and when I was away in England great hedonist parties were held in the tub and much stuff of life had, after the action, settled layer upon layer, year after year, building towards the brim. Chas had been fascinated by the sight and wondered aloud about the pair of rubber frog's feet lying nearby. I told him they'd belonged to Fred.

And now, in this bright new year, I intended to deal with the muck in the back, a viscous sludge-fudge, a primeval ooze of evil. For my plan was to get back on the right track, even if it was to be straight and narrow.

So the creation of the pond began with the nailing down of the hot-tub lid. 'You're an oddball,' said the pond builder as he nailed. Then we went round to the front garden and he dug a pit, kidney-shaped. It was a clear day in January, a day for Cubbing on the Downs. Every now and then I'd help him arrange the rocks and stones and pebbles around the PVC-lined pit; the trick was to hide the black plastic. Mostly, though, I left him alone while I read a book about ponds: 'A pond is a small body of still water, artificially formed. It is not a natural pool or a tarn or a mere. It is a pond – the creation of Man.'

The builder let me hose in the water. Then, while he lunched, I drove over to Hanley's Water Gardens and asked the man what kind of pump and power generator (and so on) I'd need in order to operate a fresh, clean fish-pond. The man was furious. He fixed me with his ice-blue eyes and, with his upper lip, he rotated his Kaiser moustache. 'Don't be fooled by no fucking water-filter company! All you need is two sets of lilies facing each other like in a Mexican stand-off. Mother nature will take care of the rest and your fish will thrive like there's no tomorrow. *Eco-system*! Goes round and round like life and death and re-birth and shit!' I was so grateful I almost asked him what direction *my* life should take.

In the afternoon the builder and I slowly, gently lowered the trays of lilies into the pond. The water turned a muddy brown. 'In a short time the eco-system will establish itself and photosynthesis will begin,' said the book. I paid the builder and he said goodbye and wished me luck. 'In the open water habitat are located large free-swimming animals. This is the home for strong swimmers or small drifters. In the bottom zone there is a very different life living off the ooze.' I went to Steve's Pet Shop on Lake Avenue to buy some fish.

The sun was going down when I poured into the pond my bagful of fish – goldfish, feeders, breeders and strange fish with sets of razor-back fins and little wings and big lips and stalk eyes, prehistoric things. Off they darted every whichway, and at once they were lost in the lilies and brown unknown. But when I tossed in some fish flakes they shot back up and ate gratefully.

It was almost dark when I placed a pagoda in the middle of the pond, crowning it with a scale model of the Moot Hall in Aldeburgh, Suffolk. Then I pulled out my beach chair and sat and mused. Moonlight was sleeping on the still waters. And the fish were asleep on their first night. Beefy hobbled out (he'd been having trouble with his back legs lately) and joined me. I was looking into the dark water but I knew he was looking at me, reaching the real one. And there we sat together and could have gone on like this for ever and ever.

Part Three

Into Hollywood!

A few days later, as June began, I had the unfortunate fight at Sterling's Steak House in Santa Monica. The following morning found me meditating into the pond while my boarders went about their bathroom functions. Then we took a look at my diaries to see how an Englishman could find himself in this position. Now, I would like to lead you through the rest of the day, a time when I was trying yet another assault on Hollywood to see if I could carve out for myself some kind of niche in show business.

But first . . . a little background. For there were Englishmen in Hollywood right from the start, and perhaps there are lessons to be learned.

*

1890, tea-time: Arthur Farquar, the famous British travel writer, pulled up his donkey and consulted his pocket compass. If he was going due south-west in this arid San Fernando Valley, then he would reach the village of Hollywood by about 6.30 p.m. The right time for an aperitif with his pen pals Mr and Mrs René Blondeau of Cahuenga House. An armed man on a tower, guarding some blessed wheatfields, was shouting through a megaphone in that rude American style that the writer had already noted. The new book was tentatively called 'By Donkey Through Southern California'.

The Blondeaus kept fine wines, and they liked to mention this. Twenty years ago, Louis had brought over some vines from his native Normandy, and now there were some who opined that the Blondeau chablis could rival any wine from snooty Northern California. The ex-French couple served up their wines, together with sensible steaks and chops, at the Cahuenga House, better known to Hollywood folk as the Blondeau Tavern, corner of Sunset and Gower.

Originally, René and his lady wife had come to America as merchants in high-class perfume. Like so many folks, the couple had been lured by railroad literature advertising the warm joys of the Southland and soon they were living out West, and soon they had purchased a seven-acre lot for use as a retirement home. 'This is truly the Riviera of

190

the West,' the realtor had said, flicking his toothpick to indicate the promise around them. 'With every tick of the clock the value of this land is rising.'

At first the Blondeaus had tried chicken ranching and ostrich farming, but finally they settled down to running a tavern, with René sidelining as a barber. Mrs Blondeau liked to regale customers with stories of how bothersome the bobcats and coyotes had been, how they had once seen a mountain lion . . . and how certain elements were getting too high-falutin'.

For example, take that professional Frenchman, Paul DeLongpré, working to get a street named after him. His mansion on Prospect (later renamed Hollywood Boulevard), with its elaborate gardens and galleries – and DeLongpré's flower paintings for sale – had become a tourist attraction. As part of the tour Paul, fully-smocked and wax-moustached, would appear and start lecturing in an affected accent. At other times he could be seen cycling round the empty sub-divisions of Hollywood, ostensibly in search of rare flowers, silk bandana keeping out the dust, and always followed by an eager crowd of out-of-towners; and always they'd end up at the DeLongpré place, where they'd buy paintings and chicken dinners.

Over a steam beer, Mr Blondeau beefed away to a tired and dusty Arthur Farquar. There was no aperitif. Oh well, thought the writer. Meanwhile a docile Indian led the donkey round for shoeing at the blacksmith, one of two Devonshire men, recent immigrants to the land of the lazy afternoon. 'And speaking of snobs,' said René, 'please don't get friendly with those Wilcoxes if you like me at all.' 'Pourquoi?' asked Farquar indifferently – he was watching the last rays of sun painting the Hollywood hills an imperial purple while the sky behind went deep azure, a thrilling, almost theatrical effect.

'Why?' shouted Blondeau, rising to his feet. 'Because though the Wilcoxes may be our founders they are giving me hell about selling liquor and not going to church. Besides, they hob-nob with DeLongpré!' 'Steady on, old man,' said Farquar. But later, in his bedroom at the tavern, he made a note to do some research on this little community. Trouble in paradise, that sort of thing. . . .

On 1 February, 1887, H. H. Wilcox, a crippled mid-Westerner, fierce prohibitionist and ardent churchgoer, had filed a rectangular-gridded tract map with the county recorder: 'Hollywood'. How he loved to sub-divide, wielding his metal divider like a knight with a lance! Hollywood would be a Christian utopia, plotted and platted and planted with decent folks – like Kansas, only much better. Hollywood would come to set the moral tone for Southern California. The very air held something evangelical. Perhaps there would be a universal rebirth, here on the edge of the civilized world!

'English, are you? Well done!' said H. H. Wilcox on meeting 'always-on-the-job' Arthur. 'You must know Colin Barber, the English-born homesteader who has named his San Fernando settlement of Chatsworth after the Duke of Devonshire's ancestral seat back in the old country?' Arthur didn't know him, but he was pretty sure the fellow hadn't been to a public school. Colin, indeed! Still, Wilcox offered to sell Arthur some choice real estate – he'd get it free if he could show a church affiliation. Arthur said he'd think about it, but certainly he'd stick around, gathering local colour, breathing deeply the clean, intoxicating air of this frostless belt. Clean and intoxicating too, he noticed, were the local children, sons and daughters of erstwhile mid-Westerners. Firm of step, with exquisite toss of head and bend of neck and shoulders. Their skin was clear and smooth, their bodies almost hairless.

Was it the climate, the food, the moral atmosphere? Arthur was on his way to becoming a devoted Southern Californian.

Next year H. H. Wilcox died and two years later his widow married Philo J. Beveridge, realtor, promotor, Elk, Mason and later a charter member of the Knights Templar Commandery of Hollywood. Arthur moved in and after telling the couple of his writing credentials and family connections – and after buying one of Beveridge's choice properties – he was made one of the triumvirate. A nice group they made, wheeling round the dusty village in their carriage, inspecting the subdivisions. The Beveridges felt sure, they told their friends, that Mr Farquar would, through his writings, encourage the right sort of person to come make their heaven in Hollywood, the Kansas of the Coast.

By 1903 there were more than a thousand inhabitants and the decision was made to incorporate. Hollywood village became a 'City of the Sixth Class'. The new council passed laws: no more than 2,000 sheep to be driven down (the newly titled) Hollywood Boulevard at one time; no slaughterhouse, glue factory, gas-works or tannery. And no liquor sales.

No liquor sales! Luckily old man Blondeau had passed away a few months back but his sprightly widow was most annoyed. What now for their roadhouse with its fine wine list and steam beers? She pleaded with Arthur, a pillar of the community, to intercede. But it was no use, he advised. One cannot run against history. The spirit of Hollywood was against strong drink and this city was a city of the future.

*Anyway, Arthur had no wish to upset the apple-cart. He was en-
joying life on the edge of the world where cosiness mingled with coyotes
and often gorgeous youth. His diaries were full of social activities:
'Saturday: The new Vine Street runs right through Senator Cole's
vineyard. That's progress, I suppose. Strolled on to the Cole ranch in
the afternoon – in time for a few holes on their golf-course. Senator's
cows do a good job keeping the grass short. Had a sumptuous après-
golf tea at the clubhouse on Willoughby and Vine. Decent dance in the
evening, string band. Had to send for the sheriff – Jack Everett, the
hardware-store owner – to round up a drunken Indian who'd strayed
into the clubhouse. No jail as yet – so Sheriff Jack, unsalaried and un-
armed, locked the redskin up in the spare bedroom of his house. On
the way home I passed the derelict Blondeau Tavern. Mrs B., a recluse
these days, lives up near Western Avenue.'*

*Arthur's articles, written under the sponsorship of the C. E. Tober-
man Company, Hollywood real estate developers, tended to be more
general. There were numerous references to drooping pepper trees,
stately palms, and voluptuously contoured hills.*

*All through the U.S.A. were spread the stories of a golden life on the
West Coast. On cold, miserable days in New York, another Englishman was fond of lapping up Farquar's stuff over breakfast: David
Horsley, one-armed and determined, ran a motion picture company
called Centaur, in partnership with his brother Bill. By 1911 he had
reason apart from escapism to be keenly interested in these Southland
stories.*

*The movie business was blooming but there were some who wanted
to keep it to themselves – a closed shop, a trust, a monopoly. Like
many small companies, Centaur's cameras used the Edison patent
'loop' system . . . without having the rights. These were expensive
rights and only big boys like the Vitagraph Company paid up. Albert
Smith and J. Stuart Blackton, the two Englishmen who owned Vitagraph, were in cahoots with Edison and the rest of the gang that made
up the Patents Trust.*

*Now the Horsley brothers hadn't left hidebound Britain to flounder
in yet another restricted market. Here in America surely anything
went? Freedom was divisible! It wasn't easy, though, getting their slice
of the pie, and skirmishes were not uncommon. Cameras somehow got
smashed; even blood was let. So Arthur's Far West, with its perpetual
sunshine and its proximity to Mexico (in case of trouble), looked
tempting. And Al Christie, Centaur's chief director, was always complaining about the lack of authentic Western locations around Staten*

Island.

So David Horsley and Al Christie took the train to Los Angeles. En route they met a theatre man who advised them to go see his friend Frank Hoover, the photogravure man, because he knew all about Hollywood light conditions. Mr Hoover, corner of Hollywood and Gower, was also in realty. 'Let me show you some choice lots,' he said. At Sunset and Gower they ran across the widow Blondeau who told them her old, old story. Al Christie said he had a hunch. 'Then play it,' said Hoover. By Sundown the movie men had leased the tavern plus a few backyard acres, which included the barn where Farquar's donkey had once rested.

Within weeks their new company, Nestor, was producing one-reel movies of such clean, clear photographic quality and such authentic background detail that the Eastern companies were jealous. Hollywood was also far away from the law. Within months, fifteen film production companies had set up shop in and around Hollywood.

'The Trust's in town!' said Al to David one day. 'Round up some cowboys and let's pay those boys a visit,' said David.

Among the companies settling in around Nestor was their old enemy Vitagraph. At first they'd tried a studio in Santa Monica, near the ocean, but the fogs were too much. Eventually a suitable location was found at Prospect and Talmadge, not far from Nestor. But there was no need for strong-arm tactics. Vitagraph was finished with old man Edison – a hopeless stick-in-the-mud, not progressive in business, hardly an American in manner. To hell with the Trust – all Vitagraph asked for was a piece of this bustling Coast action. 'What part of England are you from, anyway?' asked J. Stuart Blackton of David Horsley. Vitagraph was famous for its filming of such classics as Romeo and Juliet *and* Uncle Tom's Cabin, *and J. Stuart liked to be referred to as 'Commodore' because he'd once had that position at a New York yacht club. He also knew about wine.*

David and Al wised to Blackton's classiness and called off their cowboys. 'They'll like you here,' said Al. 'Where d'you go to school?' said David. 'Eton House Collegiate School.' 'No need to be exact out here, chum,' said David. 'Just say Eton.'

Genteel Hollywood, the pioneers, went into shock over the antics of the movie people, who were not all of the best type. 'Gypsies' they called them, and their film barns and sheds were 'encampments'. Commodore Blackton encouraged the word 'studio' for its fine art connotations. Fine arts had been around a long time and so would high-class motion pictures be. At the moment, despite the Commodore, the movie people were acting like brats. . . .

Suddenly a boulevard would be found all hosed down, slick and shiny. Next thing autos would race down and then skid all over the place. Mrs Wilcox-Beveridge's friends were amazed. Then you'd see armies of many nations marching in turn down Hollywood Boulevard to do battle in some ex-lemon grove. The cowboys were a real problem. A rowdy bunch, thrown out of real ranch work by the closing of the frontier and the shrinking of the range, they'd hang around street corners waiting for a picture call, teasing the local Mexicans and spitting and whooping. On Saturday nights they'd gallop Hollywood Boulevard, firing off their guns. Hollywood businesses took to hanging out signs saying, 'No Dogs or Actors'.

In August, 1914, Mrs Wilcox-Beveridge thankfully died. The worst was to come. A few years later, with America entering the Great War in Europe, Philo J. Beveridge, not a well man, was awakened at 6.30 one Sunday morning by a loud rapping on his front door. His servant opened it to a fearful-looking pirate, peaked cap on backwards and whip in hand. Out of the side of his mouth, the pirate asked whether they'd mind if him and the boys 'shot some flashes and pick-ups' in their front yard for a 'society picture'. As he spoke, he peeled off $5 bills.

When Mr Beveridge told his friend the Senator, the latter shook his head and pointed to an advertisement in that Sunday's newspaper: 'Thirty women with lapdogs wanted. Arrive at 17.45 N. Cahuenga, 7 a.m. Friday'. The Senator tapped his friend's knee. 'There's money to be made from these movie people, though – Will Beesemyer is about to sell his swell ranch up at Hollywood and Western to a man called Fox who strongly resembles a Hun.'

Meanwhile, what of Arthur Farquar? He had found good work in the new line called 'press agentry'. Feeding the outside world colourful stories about the activities of filmland, combating the excesses of the cheap and lurid fan magazines. He had, for instance, been instrumental in setting up the idea of 'The Little Mother Of The Movies': Hollywood had become inundated with youngsters from every state seeking stardom and the problems of white slavery and rental sex had arisen. Arthur, with the financial blessing of Paramount Pictures, sent 'The Little Mother', a stunning girl named Anita King, out on a mid-West tour in a long motor car to warn of the dangers lurking in Hollywood. 'Stay back home,' she begged.

Hollywood, in the Twenties, grew up and out. The Toberman Company, Arthur's old employers, promoted into existence some of the most impressive structures to line Hollywood Boulevard – the Egyptian Theatre, the Chinese Theatre, the El Capitan Theatre, the Hollywood Roosevelt Hotel, the Hollywood Masonic Temple. Charlie Toberman could always be found, of a lunchtime, holding court at Musso & Frank's, oldest restaurant in Hollywood (founded 1919). And there were kosher restaurants and stores; a synagogue, too. Meanwhile the boulevards were filled with beautiful legs, torsos and profiles, as well as giants, dwarves, hunchbacks and trained dogs.

The Hollywood Boulevard Association, under the direction of a 'Colonel' Baine, organized in 1927 the first Santa Claus Parade. Down the street came live reindeer and 'Wampus baby stars', while from the sky fell a snow of painted cornflakes, dropped by aeroplanes. 'Colonel Baine,' said the city, 'is a living definition of a real citizen.'

Arthur was spending a good deal of time at home these days, reading and pondering. He took on less and less press agentry work, even though the demand was increasing. He still liked to explore Hollywood but one day he got lost. He couldn't even find the site of the old Blondeau tavern. So he retired to the nearby Oriental Café for a smoke and a tea. Who should be there, fooling with a bowl of chili, but David Horsley! He was disgusted to see that Horsley's short-sleeved shirt blatantly revealed its owner's arm stump. He'd never been social with Horsley, but now he felt a certain kinship. They exchanged pleasantries and then, quite abruptly, Horsley said, 'Let's go to Buddy Squirrel's Nut Shoppe – don't forget the two Ps and the E – and view the weird people. Hollyweird – that's what this place is these days!' Having nothing better to do, Arthur went along.

In the Nut Shoppe, on Hollywood Boulevard at Las Palmas Avenue, they examined the new crowd over hot nut sundaes. Grotesques mingled with pretty boys and girls. 'What happened to your studio?' said Arthur. Horsley shot him a sour look and dug into his sundae. 'View that!' he said, nodding in the direction of a dark and hairy midget dangling his legs from a counter stool. 'What breed is that, I ask you? You wanna know what happened to Nestor? The Hebrews ate us up. You know – Universal Pictures, those pushy bastards from Eastern Europe, old-clothes dealers and bagel hole-makers.' Arthur pursed his lips. He remembered that Horsley had once been a poolroom operator. 'Let me tell you something,' continued the film pioneer in a stage whisper. 'We English are inventors, creators, foolish dreamers. But today the name of the game is exploitation and distribution. Oh, what the hell! I always thought movies were junk anyway. I'd rather be a banker or a colonel.' Arthur must have been giving him a *pained expression because he savagely added, 'Don't pretend you got a skunk under your nose! I know a snob when I see one – but you haven't any monopoly on breeding any more. We got Russian dukes here now, trying to make the business. And up at Mary Pickford's place they try out long words on each other every night at dinner. Why, Chaplin eats dictionaries!'*

When talkies came the British pioneers were no longer players in the movie business game. They had been aced out by sharper players. But there was work for Britishers with crisp Empire accents and so they sailed in and settled down, forming cricket teams. As for Arthur, he moved out of Hollywood and into the desert, where he spent the rest of his days ruminating about civilization.

In the Seventies, when Michael Caine and Rod Stewart were repre-senting the British flag in movieland, L.M.S. Farquar, writer nephew of Arthur, was on Hollywood Boulevard doing research for his latest travel book. In Darkest Teenland. *One hot afternoon he sparked up a conversation with a crop-haired youth in a string vest who'd been lounging around the Gold Cup, a notorious rent-boy café on the corner of Hollywood and Las Palmas. According to his uncle's notes, this was where once had stood Buddy Squirrel's Nut Shoppe. 'In-teresting irony when one juxtaposes the old name with the new function of this site,' were the last words written in L.M.S. Farquar's notebook.*

In August 1978, bits of the travel writer, plus his notes and under-pants, were found scattered in the desert not far from a Palm Springs golf-course. No arrests have so far been made.

Years ago Sir Cedric Hardwicke, over in Hollywood to appear in a film, observed from his hotel window, 'Neither the things that grow nor the people seem to have any real roots. Only at night, when heavy dew softens the shape of everything and lights gleam delightfully across the hills, does Los Angeles develop a strange kind of deceptive beauty.'

*

I thought we might start our tour by dropping into the Mountain View Cemetery. It's at the end of my street and quite near the cross street we need to take to get to our first stop, the Pasadena Y.M.C.A. The Mountain View's a perfect spot for meditation before our dive into L.A. life, and it's also convenient for walking Beefy. You will re-member from the previous chapter that this cemetery dates back to the 1880s when Altadena was becoming famous as a twilight garden for old folks and invalids. Now it is well within a black ghetto.

The creamy brochure tells us that 'closely woven into Man's innermost being has always been the abiding hope of eternal life.' Of course, some of us try to get immortality by publishing books, releasing records, making movies. What do these headstones tell us? That we are not alone here on the edge of civilization in this wailing and shaking new melting-pot. In this Altadena cemetery are the names of many great makers of modern American life: A Kellogg (cornflakes), an Armour (tinned meats), a Stetson (baked beans, not hats), a Studebaker (cars) and a Van Nuys (pioneer family of the San Fernando Valley). We are not alone, we are part of history. Beefy loves these headstones. I'll put him on the lead now and we'll leave this place of quietude. Listen to the lyrics of the rap song thudding out from a beat-boxed passing jeep: 'Don't mess with us, you stupid flea/We IS – an' we ain't never not gonna BE!!!' Absolutely no concern about mortality. Unburdened by the past.

Into the Honda and on to the road! On Los Robles Avenue lovely shade trees with a husky, rusky bark form a canopy, a guard of honour, as we roll on down this pleasant street. Such neat and trim and upright houses, with white picket fences and sweeping green swards and shady sun-porches, and built in so many different styles – from fussy Victorian gingerbread through Jazz Age stucco bungalow with red-tiled adobe roof to Fifties Fountain-Blue Riviera with white rocks and pebbles glued to the roof! This is democracy at work in all 57 varieties, homes in no particular social or aesthetic order, all coexisting peacefully! What stranger passing down this deserted street could know that its inhabitants are a racial hot-pot? Greeks, Italians, Armenians, British, Kansans and Iowans, and African-Americans are just some of the tax-payers lining Los Robles Avenue. Never have I had a discouraging word said to me in these parts.

Radio has a different message; we will listen. My favourite shock station, K-TALK, right now has two 'Defense Group' spokespersons – one black and one Jewish – slugging it out while the anchorman stays silent, no doubt considering ratings. 'Coke-eating and rap-shouting – that's all you people ever do! That and complaining! Hey, you want to know something, my friend? Lincoln freed the slaves a long time ago!' the Jewish spokesperson is saying. 'Why, you cock-er-roach!' booms the black spokesperson. 'All Jews do is exploit and control, exploit and control. Crouching behind every hurdle we African-Americans leap over is a little Jew with a fork, trying to stick it to us!' 'You call me Jew-*ish* not *Jew*, when you're talking to me!' 'You call me an African-American!' 'Can you give me a preview of what you people want to be called next week?' The anchorman steps in at this point: 'Let's take a call. . . . We have Fatima from Orange County on the line.' This gives the spokespersons a chance to unite in attacking an Arab.

Careful here, we must slow down, looking right, looking left, looking right again. Once, at a green light on this junction of Los Robles and Mountain, I wasn't looking right and I was broad-sided by an elongated old auto driven by a Rastafarian. My Honda, shunted across the junction, slammed into another car which had been lawfully crossing in the green, and we all ended up in a tangle. The Rastafarian told the black motor-cycle cop, 'My brakes went poof!' 'I understand where you're coming from, I understand!' said the cop. I thought I saw skid-marks under the Rasta's auto, but I decided to come back later when the smoke had cleared. That evening, about 7 o'clock, I was inspecting the skid-marks when stones rained around me. Little black boys from behind a picket fence were lapidating in the moonlight. When I told Mr Goldsmith, my neighbour the businessman/preacher, he shook his head and slowly rolled, 'That is a bad part of town, very bad, yes, indeed. Go carefully, don't stop!' Have I told you this story before?

We are safely through the junction and crossing Villa, where wait dozens of Mexicans hoping to be picked up for any sort of work. Here comes Harry, a harmless local idiot, moving slowly up the sidewalk, spinning like a top till he reaches the foothills, long hair streaming, a Woodstock image; he does this every day. Hi, Harry! *Los Angeles village*. Turn to the right on to Walnut, punch the button for a change of station. The rock DJ has a contest going: 'If you fell asleep and didn't wake for a thousand years – what would be your first question? Kathy from Torrance. . . .' 'Where am I?' 'Great! Way to go! . . . Scott from North Hollywood. . . .' 'Seriously . . . which religions have survived? That's what I'd ask, seriously,' 'I like that. Good direction! Craig from Canoga Park. . . .' 'Is Elvis alive?' 'Now you're joking. . . . Donna from Bellflower. . . .' 'Where's the bathroom? Oh, and . . . where's my American Express card?' 'Cease and desist, children! I guess you just can't face up to this type of reality!'

At the Y.M.C.A. we leave Beefy guarding the Honda and we march in through the lapidarian entrance marked, 'Established 1911. Boys' Entrance'. I have to start my day in this way – popping the pecs, getting pumped up, working off the rage accumulated every yesterday. I've never talked to anybody here in the last few years. The place is falling apart, cockroaches are getting bigger and bolder; long gone is old Charlie in his straw hat and striped blazer who used to offer aftershave and all manner of notions from his counter, he gave shoe-shines as well; in those days there were fat pillars of the community chomping cigars as they sat in the whirlpool reading the *Wall Street Journal*. Nowadays the 'Y' is populated by us narcissists and our weights and mirrors.

But this morning, as we climb the stairs, there's the sweet and manly sound of barbershop harmony. That must be the 'Y's Men' at their Glee Breakfast in the Community Room. Peep in and glimpse these sober businessmen, readying for today's marketplace, soon to face the fax, singing 'I'll Get By', complete with verse, sitting at a table strewn with paper plates, pancake pieces, toast crusts, syrup bottles and little plastic preserve pots.

In the main gym Oscar, a big black ex-policeman, is telling a dumb-bell man in stentorian tones how to solve the problems of the world and L.A. 'A little discipline is what we need.' Another man enters, a big Greek bruiser. 'Wooo-woooo! It's like a morgue in here!' And he plugs in his huge radio and turns it up high. On the air another rock DJ is asking a listener, 'Would you let me share your toothpaste?' 'Well, yeah, man.' 'Your dental floss?' 'Well . . . OK, but . . .' 'Your underpants?' 'Hey, man! Are you some kinda fag? I came out to Hollywood for fresh air and freedom and I don't want no fuck-ing. . . .' Go to commercial. Music of the wide-open spaces, big sky, big country, bank of Wells Fargo.

A stinging shower, a brisk towelling, and we're ready to face the world and another stab at Hollywood fame. But first, breakfast – a great American meal, eaten at a coffee shop where the cup is ever full. We'll stroll to breakfast, window-shopping on our way: the Holly St Bar and Grill – used to be a funeral parlour – tomatoes with real old-fashioned tomato taste, white linen tablecloths, too up-market for us. . . . The Café Sixty and Dessert Factory, a too chic help-yourself bumper-sandwich place, also offering eggs benedict in a croissant, very messy, not today, think you'll prefer something more traditionally American. . . . The Olde Towne Café, run by two friendly Taiwanese sisters, offering specials on a blackboard outside, chicano pork chops and eggs, with pasta and salsa. . . . Birdies, a Café and Muffinery, with blackened catfish as the 'Catch of the Day'. . . .

We're in Pasadena's historic Old Town, now being restored, as high-rise office buildings soar around. Take in the Hotel Green, much used in movies, a riot of cupolas, towers and finicky filigree, echoes of Araby, erected in 1903 by Colonel Green of Altadena, the patent medicine king; these days the old eccentric building is called

Castle Green, pricey apartments. Here's what you'll enjoy: The Rose City Diner, all done in chrome and tile, Fifties style, Doris Day and Jerry Lee Lewis on the jukebox and pix on the wall of Rose Queens of long ago, lots of teeth and flared skirts, booths of pink plastic, masses of chrome, a vintage Mobilgas pump in front of us. Our waitress is blowing bazooka bubble-gum; they give you a free sample with your bill. Please give your order. Eggs any style. Don't make a to-do like Chas Sprawson, just answer quick. I'll walk you through the options: scrambled, over-easy, sunny-side up, poached, soft or boiled. Then you have hash browns and a choice of toast, bagel, English muffin or bran muffin, blueberry biscuit or loganberry biscuit. All dishes have three triple-A jumbo farm-fresh eggs. 'I know you,' says the waitress at me. 'You have a serious problem – you like your coffee after your juice.' When the food comes she'll order, 'Enjoy!', an expression borrowed from Jewish-American life. Meanwhile, listen to the table talk around us. Men in blue shirts with work tools dangling from their great big belts and walkie-talkies that keep crackling out messages about drains in need of repair. 'What's new, Jack?' 'York, Jersey, Hampshire, England.' Funny, very. A know-all oaf rotomontading about how he knows all these big-name rock record producers, but when he gets up to leave you'll see his belt is stuck with screwdrivers, penlights, pliers. One time a bum had the cheek to ask me whether I was living at the Y.M.C.A. There's the woman who tells the world about the predictions of Nostradamus. 'The big quake's coming so spread the word!' Lest you think that the Rose City Diner is only patronized by bums and blue-collar workers, take a look at the table to your right: well-dressed business-women, grey skirts and blue blazers, planning a function. 'Should we have a belly dancer?' Gales of laughter.

'Enjoy!' Eat as much as you can. I'm going to read the papers.

Sometimes I find a discarded copy of one of those supermarket tabloids, and these are good as a starter. A few weeks ago *The Star* had this headline: 'SPACE PROBE SHOWS PICTURES OF HEAVEN – DEAD PEOPLE SEEN ALIVE IN BEAUTIFUL PARKS'. Most of these tabloids are edited by expatriate Brits who used to work for the tabloids of Fleet Street. If you want the British papers you can get them, only a day late, at a shop a few blocks away. Sometimes I buy the *Daily Mail*, but it's usually full of small-time native stuff like: '40-MILE JAM ON M.1'. Los Angeles local news is lots meatier. We'll skip the best-selling *Los Angeles Times* – a great whale of hundreds of pages, the colour comes off on your hands;

today's front page has a picture of June flowers in the Huntington Gardens – and get straight to the dripping blood of the *Herald Examiner*. Ignoring the Lebanon headlines, we'll turn to page three and the latest local gang news:

There's an increase in the use of Uzis and AK-47 semi-automatics. New spray-gun techniques make up for the crude marksmanship of the past. More than half the victims are innocent bystanders. Black and Chicano gangs are being joined by new ethnic gangs: Filipinos used to be organized in disco-dance groups, but now they're in gangs specializing in extortion, narcotics and plain theft. Samoans and Tongans are fighting in gangs. Says Sheriff's deputy Jerry Kaono, 'In five to seven years the Samoans will be as hard as the blacks. The parents have lost control. The church has lost control. They don't go to bingo on Sundays. Now it's "Let's party."' When Hong Kong goes Red Chinese, then L.A. will get a whole mess of Chinese gangs. Only the Japanese, a more assimilated group, are free of gang violence. . . . Listen to this: they've convicted a gang member who took part in the rape of a mother; she was dragged into an alley, raped and raped, and then dumped in a trash receptacle where a burning Christmas tree was tossed on top of her. Since then a hand, a foot and both breasts have had to be amputated. But they got one of them. I could kill them all, couldn't you? Still, I'd better be careful – listen to this headline, it's closer to home: 'FAMILY MAN ARGUES OVER LOUD MUSIC, IS BEATEN TO DEATH BY TWO'. And this: 'PART-TIME GARDENER FATALLY BEATEN AFTER CAR BREAKS DOWN IN SOUTH CENTRAL L.A.' – he'd strayed into the ghetto on his way to buy milk for his girl-friend's three children, and he was found on his back in a vacant lot with a metal bar lodged in his head. Meanwhile in North Hollywood: a year-long feud among three sets of neighbours, revolving around a parallel parking squabble, escalated into a shootout ending in death for a mother and son and serious head injuries for three others. And up in Elysian Park: a Cambodian husband, tipped off by a neighbour, raced home to catch Cambodian wife and her Cambodian lover lying on the master bed watching porno videotapes. With his gun he slayed them both. 'The moral of this story,' says the homicide detective: 'If you're going to watch dirty movies, don't watch them at home.' In downtown L.A. on Skid Row, a man living on the street stabbed a passer-by to death: 'He knocked over my beer bottle.' Now I've spoiled your breakfast and you'd like to be getting along to Hollywood and the sights.

But one last item – a column in the Classified Ads: 'WIN BIG

MONEY AND PRIZES'. My girl-friend Regina has urged me to enter a T.V. game show to, sort of, keep me in show business and perhaps make a pot of gold. 'DIVORCED COUPLES – Still Talking To Each Other – Win Cash Prizes! Call Michael. . . .' Here's the ad she recommended: 'CAN YOU HOLD A TUNE, CATCH A MEMORY? Sing That Golden Oldie To A Pre-Recorded Track And Win Big Money! The Sing-Along Show, K-BOX, Hollywood.' . . .

Watch out, watch out! Duck under the table! That dark-faced man with the unkempt beard and bib overalls is shouting at us all, spiralling and stretching out his arms, wild broad gestures. I thought he was a weirdo the moment he walked in. He may have a gun, one out of five have guns here. Lay low and listen. . . .

'Folks, I want to invite you to a meeting of the Pasadena Heritage Society tonight! In the library! We have to get together to save this city from the iconoclasm of property developers! Act now or we lose our culture! There'll be light refreshments! Do come!'

*

Beefy is tearing around inside the Honda, front to back, back to front. Stop it! We'll be with you soon. But before we embark on our freeway journey I want you to observe the special light of Southern California, the light the world hears so much about. Let us pause here, even here in the Pasadena Y.M.C.A. parking lot.

Los Angeles is famous for its luminescence. Over the years writers have remarked on the dramatic scene-shifting and atmosphere-altering caused by this lighting – marvelling at its softening of mountains into endless ripples or cloudland shadows or purple haze (Aldis E. Sage), or repulsed by the picture, produced after heavy rains, of the once-romantic Hollywood Hills now stark nude and vulgar, transmogrified into a Welsh slag-pit (L.M.S. Farquar, who added, 'Did I come all these miles just to see this?'). Nathaniel West, sinking down in Hollywood proper, wanted the unnatural hell-hole to burn itself into oblivion. But Aldous Huxley, testing mind-altering substances up in the Hollywood Hills, believed that the constant sunlight illuminated the gloaming of his failing eyes. For Raymond Chandler the sun was 'as empty as a headwaiter's smile'. For me the Kleig light waits for 'Action!' when suddenly a muscle-bound Mr Nature L.A. will hurl down meteors or throw up a hot dinner from below, and then both superstars and those of us who wait in line will quake and tremble with fear and there'll be no more talk of ball-games. The Apocalypse waiting in the wings keeps me ever on the alert. The norm is so tedious – the light switched on all day, no real changes of season, sun-razoring, relentless and pointless. 'Another beautiful Southland day!' announces a weather-person.

This morning none of the above applies because the sky is grey and overcast. What a relief!

Off we go, plunging down into the Ventura Freeway (the natives refer to freeways by number, but I like to name things). Now don't start moaning about how we're all auto-dependent out here – *I* know, *we* know; something like 50 per cent of us believe that cars have ruined Los Angeles, but we're not about to give them up; most households have two, upper income homes have at least three, top of the wish list is Mercedes, followed by Jaguar; I know all this stuff because when I'm locked in steady stream freeway density I'm able to read the paper while rolling with the flow. Please buckle up, we're not in England.

I'm really quite comfortable in my car; she's like a moving cloister. With the air-conditioner humming and some genial music playing, I can do creative thinking in this quality time. Working on new songs or reflecting on old friendships, devising ways and means to destroy my enemies.

Out into the stream we sail, nice landscaping on your left, rainbirds spray to keep all verdant, notice different kinds of trees. . . . On our left is a man with a cellular phone keeping tabs on his office and wife, waving hands, shaking head, in his own little world, picking nose as he listens to stocks. Alone. . . . In a bashed-up truck is an army of Mexicans, raggle-taggle, smiling and dangling their legs. They're on their way to mow and blow, janitoring in wealthy gardens, speaking Spanish all their lives, glad to be away from home. Together. . . . Together too are station wagons on their way to Disneyland, taking kids to clean adventure from a land across the Valley, land of newly-built dream homes – Woodland Hills and Wild Horse Canyon, Calabasas, Thousand Oaks, once so dusty, now so brilliant, featuring artificial lakes and riding rings and gourmet markets, all secured by guarded gates.

Wave when you're waved to. We've had a series of freeway murders lately. For flashing bright headlights, throwing out a can and cutting him off on the Riverside Freeway, a Corvette driver pumped shotgun lead through the front side window of the offending Ford. The passenger was killed, not the driver. A grandfather, taking some of his clan to a birthday party, wouldn't give way to two men in a truck as they all climbed a lonely ramp up to the freeway; they chased him for miles till in desperation he swung his old Cadillac off the high road and down into a place called Sunland, a place he didn't know. In a dead-end alley they blew off his head in front of his screaming grand-children. . . . 'You're going too slow!' shouted a pick-up truck to a girl in a Mazda. She died of her wounds a few days later.

Shrinks are conducting driver 'rage therapy' sessions – over the phone if you wish. Stay cool, they say, don't antagonize, turn on a radio station with a cool wash of violins, never challenge a truck; these killers are childhood-arrested, they go straight from the feeling mode to the acting mode, bypassing the all-important thinking mode; these fits of rage may be neurological, therapeutic drugs may be of use in some cases. . . .

See that bright yellow Subaru? The car that was tailgating us for ages and now is pace-racing beside us in the middle lane? Weren't you paying attention? Look at him, he's a killer, mark my words! Neat Beatle hair and shrimp moustache, curling lip and jaw jutting out, white-shirted and with his jacket hung up behind – a super-com-muter, no doubt, making over $60,000 a year, wishing for a Mer-cedes, dormitoring in a dream house up in the mountains 100 miles from here where there's a pine-covered ridge behind and a lake below, and trees to hug and kids to hug, and when he gets home at 8 p.m. there'll be an ice-blonde skeleton to hand him a glass with rat-tling ice-cubes and to fill him in on Little League. He'll be stressed-out, burned-out, bummed-out, he'll be sticky and shaking, he'll be spoiling for a fight. He's had four hours on the road today, but it's all worthwhile because the distant mountain dream house is far, far, far away from the crime, the rotten schools, the foul air and – let's face it – the unattractive and threatening ethnics of L.A. proper. Look at this man carefully . . . he's the most dangerous type on the freeway, he's the killer. And I'll bet he doesn't have George Formby on his car stereo.

Turn on talk-radio, perhaps we should be in touch with today. An old B-Western comic sidekick is describing a show-biz charity ban-quet he attended last night: 'The high point was when Johnny Cash stood up and said, "I defend *your* right to burn the flag and *my* right to carry a gun." See, with that gun Johnny can come and blow your brains out!' Punch up a station to the left of the dial, where sit the more intelligent stations – like the one I do a show for, KCRW in Santa Monica College: 'Next – music from Borneo, Zambia, Ethio-pia and Bechuanaland, all on compact disc. . . .' And the music goes round and round, a ring shout, an endless electronic beat pattern loop taking us nowhere, keeping us calm, displaying the circular nature of African culture. . . .

Jesus Christ! I never saw the biker, never meant to cut him off! He's giving me the finger, he's arching his back, he's coming to get me! Off the Ventura and on to the Golden Gate, heading for the junction with the Pasadena. Is he still following? No ukulele case to threaten him with, telling him I'm fully armed; no albums, cassettes, or CDs of my work with which to fob him off. Off the Pasadena and on to the Hollywood, racing along but he's still on our tail. Swerve down at Gower St, go right on Franklin . . . I've got an idea and I think it might work.

Slowly through the wrought-iron gates of the hedge-shrouded mansion. A circular gravel driveway in front of a red brick Queen Anne classical. Reminded of Bryanston. Here comes the biker – but here come the big boys, muscular, stern-faced, marching in step. 'Can we help you, sir?'

The biker is not interested in Scientology the way we are. We're very keen and we're English and we're just visiting. The biggest Scientologist gives the biker a glare and, with a hitch of his leather trousers and much gunning of his bike, off roars our enemy. Let me handle this. . . .

It only cost us two hardback copies of L. Ron Hubbard's *Dianetics*. The signed glossies of Ron on his boat were free. Nice mansion, beautifully preserved. The Scientologists are buying and preserving a lot of old Hollywood, as you'll see. They do good work for charity and for disasters, etc. . . .

This Denny's Coffee Shop – part of a chain – will give you a bit of the flavour of old Hollywood. We're sitting on the site where Hollywood, the cinema city, was born: Gower Gulch, corner of Sunset and Gower, where once cowboys and Indians hung around waiting for work in the Westerns made by the studios around here. 'Poverty Row' they called the area. Try the carrot cake – with ice-cream. Why do waitresses always interrupt me when I'm talking? So . . . Gower Gulch has been transformed into a modern shopping plaza with frontier town façades: 'Assayer 1885' and 'Lil's Boarding House'. Beneath the façades there's, respectively, a pizzeria and a sushi bar. Never had sushi? Nor have I and I don't intend to. The Denny people have done a creditable job at whipping up a 'good old days' ambience: in front of you is *The Far Frontier* starring Roy Rogers and Trigger; behind you is Tim McCoy in *Two-Fisted Law*.

Here's the scenario: I have to meet the horror film people first, and after that it's the audition for 'The Singalong Show'; Regina will meet us there. Meanwhile we have an hour to kill, so how about a stroll down Hollywood Boulevard, not forgetting what I wrote about its origins?

As we leave the coffee shop, direct your eyes across Sunset Boulevard. See the featureless block on the corner at Gower? Local C.B.S. television and radio studios, built in 1936 as Columbia Square. What had been demolished to make room for the latest in air-wave technology? Nestor Studios and the remains of the Blondeau tavern! Was there any memory of Arthur Farquar's donkey? Hollywood is not what it was.

There's broken glass around the Honda, but Beefy's there to guard against vandals. The weather's gone from grey to dishwater. Here's an antique telephone pole – could be 1920s – with a new poster stapled across its deep brown trunk: 'A Diasporan Festival of African-American Cultures'. Have I shown you a mini-mall yet? There's a good example across the street. Mini-malls are sprouting on so many corners where once were gas stations. Most are designed Middle East Saladin, terra cotta minarets with streaks of salmon mousse and red plastic signs. We'll read some of the signs: 'Giamela's Subs – Pizza – Pasta'; 'The Red Ribbon Bake Shop'; 'Big Weenies Are Better Hot Dogs'; 'Imperial Kitchen Fast Food'; 'One Hour Foto'; 'Rush Copy & Printing'; 'Hastee-Haste Dry Clean'. What price Buddy Squirrel's Nut Shoppe these days? I love the present when it's past. . . .

And now . . . to Hollywood Boulevard and the start of a grand tour!

*

We three – you and me and Beefy – will walk down Vine Street to what was once the most famous intersection in the world: Hollywood and Vine. Nothing to write home about today – but in the Thirties and Forties the fame was started when radio networks, broadcasting national shows from their Hollywood studios, would have their announcer intone, 'And now . . . from Hollywood and Vine we bring you. . . . !' These days the intersection is dominated by a huge billboard, raised high on steel poles, showing off a painting of a moustached man, pleasant enough, wearing many gold rings and a loose gold bracelet. This is Humberto Luna, an important personality at KTNQ Radio: 'Presetado Por Black Flag'. Beside his face is a painting of an aerosol can with a skull and crossbones logo: '*El Asesino de Insectos*'.

207

But proceed down Vine Street from where we parked the car. I want to take you past Capitol Records, a self-proclaiming structure designed by Welton Becket in 1954, very modern at the time. It's a circular tower meant to suggest a stack of discs as in a juke-box. The roof is crowned with a giant stylus. When the tower was opened Sir Joseph Lockwood, head of E.M.I., the company that had bought Capitol, was asked his opinion as he stood on the pavement. 'Very interesting,' he said. A few years later, in 1965, when I was a rock star signed to a Capitol label, I was photographed for an album cover strolling down this same pavement. In three-piece herringbone suit, detachable stiff collar and deerstalker cap, I was representing the up-market aspect of the British Invasion. My Cuban-heeled, elastic-sided boots were treading the world-famous Hollywood Walk of Fame – three and a half miles of paving-stones, each with galaxy background, big star foreground and a circle within that star showing either a silhouette of a film camera, a microphone, a T.V. set or a needle arm on a disc, depending on the chosen artist's field of fame. Over the star the name is printed, in gold. The day of my photo session I was snapped treading on Beverly Bayne, Joe Penner and Bruce Humberstone. Little did I know that Fate would arrange for Reg Dwight of Pinner to lie in gold on the Hall of Fame as 'Elton John'. But by that time my romance with Hollywood was tarnished. Experience had jolted even me.

Approaching us now is our first clump of tourists. Surprisingly they are not Japanese, but palefaces from the Great American Hinterland. Outfitted in Bermudas (those unbecoming long shorts) and drapey bright shirts. Fat-legged, blue-veined women; stick-legged, Adam's-appled, belly-bursting men; goggle-eyed butter-ball children. Wandering, friendly cows. Video camcorders on red alert. The oldest male tourist points a gnarled fist at the pavement. 'Lowell Thomas,' he says, and after a very brief pause the clump moves on. On the back of the T-shirt worn by the oldest male tourist is the legend, 'U.S. Submarine Veterans' . . . I don't know why I'm being so nasty. . . .

See the Spanish Baroque theatre across the street? Built as the Hollywood Playhouse in 1927, it later became a location for network radio shows and then T.V. In 1964, during the British Invasion, the Rolling Stones were guesting on a T.V. show here. Dean Martin, the bibulous host, showed more respect for the baby elephant act than the Stones. 'Don't leave me alone with them,' he drawled, thus winning the group thousands of fans from coast to coast. In 1975, as a guest on 'The Merv Griffin Show', I sang 'You're In Kentucky Sure As You're Born' with an orchestra conducted by Judy Garland's old music director. Such history gives me a stake in these streets, I feel part of the heritage. The theatre is now called The Palace and is a rock venue. Let's see who's appearing here tonight . . . 'Pop Will Eat Itself'.

Beefy is tugging at the lead. We must be getting along if I'm to make those appointments.

And yet. . . . History keeps leading me back . . . *Hollywood and Vine.* Here we are at the famous crossroads. On the far corner, see that many-storied solid stone building in the commercial neo-Italianate style of the era? Erected in 1927 as the B. H. Dyas department store, a fashion magnet for movie stars. In they'd pop to purchase silks and chiffons and little sports suits. All down Hollywood Boulevard were pleasant elegant pop-in shops for the stars to buy everything from French perfumes to a shoe-lace, from a 50 guinea model gown to a packet of chewing-gum. Some of the loveliest women in the world were to be found gliding in I. Magnin among French handmade lingerie and gossamer stockings; in one cabin might well be Billie Dove getting fitted for a billowy evening gown while next door Lilyan Tashman is taking infinite pains over the lines of her new opera cloak; and then we find Bebe Daniels approving the sports suit she has chosen in her favourite shade of periwinkle blue, while at the counter Norma Shearer is choosing artificial flowers – always popular – and Marion Davies toys with a lovely blue dahlia of cut glass. Everyone knows everyone else . . . there is a sudden loud buzz of conversation and two or three stars dash off to keep some urgent luncheon appointment. Further along the Boulevard we reach the exclusive Montmartre Café: violins are playing for dancing as the maître d', in white tails, shows that upcoming film actor Jimmy Hall (who is laden with gardenias) to the table where sits his lucky girl, showing off her fresh dapple-apple face. Like so many of the women of Hollywood this girl's face was prepared a few doors away at the Gainsborough Beauty Parlour run by Mrs Harold Shawn, better known as the screen actress Edna Flugrath. Her parlour specializes in face-masks made of mud, almonds, eggs and honey. Her regular clients include Anna Q. Nilsson, Laura La Plante and Alice White (when this pretty ingenue is not with Sirdar Bhogwan Eisr Singh, Hollywood's pet Hindu perfume-mixer, a master at matching a star's personality with the right flower).

Hollywood and Vine. The great B. H. Dyas building has gone through many changes. Today there's no department store; instead we have a host of small businesses. Will Windy's Donut-Croissant be here long? In front of the little shop is a bus-stop bench and here a tramp in a long overcoat has made his home. He's fully stretched and grunting with defiant pleasure. The top of his head is covered with dirt, but he's smiling. He strokes Beefy's head. At this point we start our brief walk down Hollywood Boulevard.

I'm glad to see that the Guaranty Building, in a grand granite Beaux Arts style of the late 1920s, is being restored to its former glory. Working men are busy setting up a large metal sign on the roof proclaiming that it is henceforth 'The Church Of Scientology'. A street of contrasts . . . on the next block is a nondescript shack called Fatimas's Chillum – Imported Leather, and then several wig-shops. Wig-shops are popular in this increasingly ethnic area.

Here on our side of the street we pass the Julian Medical Building, originally the Owl Drugstore in 1930, noted for its curved wall and tall pillar. Worth preserving if you like Art Deco. In my rock period I was sent here to have a toothache dealt with, but the dentist wouldn't touch me till he'd seen some cash, which my manager eventually brought round in a briefcase. 'Trench mouth,' said the dentist. 'Quit fooling with groupies.' As he worked in my mouth he hummed 'Alice Blue Gown'. Today the Julian Medical Building houses Popeye's Chicken and Biscuits. A banner announces that they are right now featuring 'Sizzlin' Cajun Gumbo Ya Ya'.

Across the street, down Cahuenga, is the Tick-Tock restaurant, a sanctuary for senior citizens. 'Your fans,' Witham would say as we passed the queue of oldsters on our way to dinner at the hipper Musso & Frank Grill a few blocks further on. Actually I enjoy the Tick-Tock's soft nursery food and the security of the old folk. In the Seventies I used to lunch there with the pioneer vocalist and guitarist Nick Lucas of 'Tip-Toe Through The Tulips' fame. I would grill him on his time as a star of 'All-Talking, All-Dancing, All-Singing' movies, but sadly he never had anything to tell me that I didn't already know. He was much happier on the subject of present-day show business. 'On that job we did last week at the Ford dealership – how much you get paid?'

Now, around Whitley, we run across bumpy rows of one-storey, non-designed packing-case structures of slap stucco, put up circa 1930, very old. They are offering T-shirts, rock posters, heavy metal or industrial or psychedelic gear, designer jeans and drug paraphernalia. The biggest store has a sign saying, 'Akai – Aiwa – Toshiba –

Nikon', but this is high class. All have loudspeakers facing the street, competing for attention like fun-fair barkers. The musical fare that blows – you can feel the strength of the sound – from these steamer-trunk-sized beat boxes is Rap: dustbin-lid clash-bang military rhythm, car-alarm beep-screech melody, Uzi-spray threat lyrics spoken robotically. Demotic culture, rock culture. This is where Bill Haley, the grand square-dance caller, has led us. Or was it jazz that started it? Adopt the primitive at your peril! Let's read some of the wit on the T-shirts: 'If You Don't Like My Attitude – Dial 1-800 EAT SHIT'; 'Club Intercourse – No Dues, No Fees, Just COME.' Here's a painting of a banana-erect dong wearing a condom nightcap at a jaunty angle and saying, 'Cover me! I'm GOIN' IN!!' There are also, of course, the usual posters of Elvis, The Beatles, Bogart and Monroe.

The weather is changing. The sun is breaking through, splashing on to the pale tourists vainly seeking glamour, on to the greasy bikers leaning on their machines as they talk of auto parts and pussy, on to bean-pole punks and long-haired hippies, and a gang of rat-faced wretches with baseball bats. 'Up to no good, I'll be bound!' – the words of Captain Manning come back to me. No use these days. But the youths make way for Beefy.

We'll stop and admire Frederick's of Hollywood, an institution, the purple shop in zigzag moderne with chevron patterning, and a window full of intimate lingerie for the bolstering of marriages. You'll be amused by some of the offerings. Or not. I took an English couple inside once – they were on their first visit to Hollywood – and although the wife giggled at the sexy underwear the husband, who had been head boy at his public school, grew grim-faced with determination. After some time prowling around he made his purchases and presented them to his startled wife: a satin and lace basque in black for the woman with a voluptuous bustline; a semi-corset with underwired cups and light boning and a lycra spandex back for perfect figure fit; plus detachable garters and straps, and also a crotch with zip peep-hole in crushed rose-print satin of teddyette. 'I want to see you wearing that at White Ladies, Godalming.' But she pulled herself together and trumped him by ordering from the 'HIM' department: a non-binding thong in velcro-release solid nylon with an elephant-head pouch which, on pressing the tip of the nose, plays 'Old MacDonald Had A Farm'.

*

211

Almost noon. The show-biz people will be starting to enter Musso & Frank's Grill for power brunches or lunches. We will dine there this evening with my old friend Basil, the English screenwriter (from Part Two). Who knows what stars we'll see! Meanwhile, we pass 'The Supply Sergeant'.

I well remember when I first laid eyes on 'The Supply Sergeant', his plywood cut-out figure – camouflaged, helmeted, and at a crouch – towering over the shack-shop, and me a fallen rock star living alone in a courtyard apartment block just off Hollywood Boulevard. I had left my one room to go out in search of bathroom requisites and frozen dinners. I was homesick for natural green and normal rain. I was even missing cricket and tea . . . which I'd never cared for when in England. 'The Supply Sergeant' did nothing to help.

The present window offers everything a survivalist might need, except guns and ammo. There's dried beef, water pills, khaki suits for boys and – just arrived – a T-shirt showing a helmeted skull saying: 'KILL 'EM ALL – LET GOD SORT 'EM OUT'.

Next, on the corner of Las Palmas and Hollywood, is a nothing building – architecturally. Now it's called Asahi Fast Food and the door is chained and padlocked. In Arthur Farquar's day this was Buddy Squirrel's Nut Shoppe, but the cafeteria didn't last long and over the decades it transmogrified until in the Seventies it became The Gold Cup, the coffee shop where Arthur's nephew met the crop-haired boy. The boys have moved down to Santa Monica Boulevard, by the way.

The fine old nine-storey red brick building we're approaching was built in 1922 as the Christie Hotel by local artist H. H. Christie, but the big bold plastic sign along the front says DIANETICS. A free 'personal test' is offered. Here come the young men from out of the shadows. Pink-faced, fixed-eyed, in white shirts and brown trousers, heavily-armed with literature. . . .

'Do you have only a few people of whom you are really fond? . . . Does emotional music have quite an effect on you? . . . Do you hold on to things for which you have no real use? . . . Are you prejudiced in favour of your own school, college or club? . . . When passing a beautiful child, do you avoid showing interest rather than looking and smiling?' . . . Why me, why me? Show them our copies of *Dianetics*.

See that souvenir shop across the street? That's where the Montmartre Café used to be, an Italian Renaissance palace for the 1920s movie crowd. The pink-faced men are moving back into the shadows of the old Christie Hotel. To the right of the souvenir shop is the

Hollywood Wax Museum, owned at present by a Mr Spoony Singh, and he also owns the cinema we're hurrying past right now – it's the oldest theatre in Hollywood, built in 1913. Mr Singh has plans for this theatre; he wants to turn it into a 'Guinness Book of Records-type attraction.' He says he'll hire the tallest man and the heaviest man and so on. . . . Come along, the sign says 'Walk' – we can get across the intersection at Hollywood and Highland, with eyes-right for a few seconds so you can see the interesting Security Pacific Bank Building with its octagonal neo-Gothic tower and repeated frieze running round the walls: Copernicus is Science, Columbus is Enterprise, repeated . . . Christ! I nearly tripped up. Beefy's going too fast. And there are too many people out now. A carnival of nations, worse than Oxford Street. The sun's brazen. We never get any clouds, it's a pity. . . .

This is prime tourist territory. The Chinese Theatre, 1927, with the handprints, footprints and signatures in concrete of the famous and the forgotten. And the tour buses and tour guides and these appalling tourists pullulating and ullulating. . . . I can't stand it any more. Come over to the next block, to C. C. Brown's famed ice-cream parlour, home of the original hot fudge sundae. Blast! Not open yet. Lazy bugger! Look inside – see the open family Bible and framed family photos round the wall and round the cash register. . . . Nothing much else to see down this end of the Boulevard. The vacant lot on our right – red dirt and beer-cans – was filled with the grand wedding-cake splendour of the Garden Court Apartments until recently. When opened in 1919, the Garden Court was the last word in modern luxury – suites with oriental carpets and grand pianos and real oil paintings, all the flavour of the best from Old Europe. Now the lot waits for redevelopment. Constant motion is the rule in these parts. . . . On the next block we have a Greek Classic-style building, but is it old or new? Can't tell. Must look it up in the calm of the Huntington Library. A fresh sign in bright plastic is being tacked to the front wall by a spotless workman: 'THE L. RON HUBBARD LIBRARY'. Below the lettering is a full colour picture of the smiling skipper himself, yachting cap nicely perched, cool azure ocean in the background. . . . *Dianetics* promises success in life, if read correctly. I must be off to my appointments now. . . . You're on your own . . . please take very good care of Beefy. . . . Meet you back at the Honda in a couple of hours.

*

You didn't miss much. The horror movie meeting came first. Nick Supino runs a company called Nick Supino Pictures, Inc. He specializes in films of sex and action. When we first met he told me 'Understand – I'm a film buff, but you got to start somewhere. I was a distributor in New Jersey.' He nodded at me and then waited to let this fact sink in. 'We got a unique situation. We need an opening title song and a closing credit song. They say you're campy and affordable. Give me some soft bread to contrast with the blood and body bits of the sandwich filling.' We agreed on a modest budget and a few days later I delivered him two songs – 'In Hollywood!' and 'Come And Make Your Heaven In L.A.' – recorded in a friend's garage. That was last week. Today I was supposed to pick up the other half of my money and maybe watch the editors match my songs into 'Horror House'.

Nick Supino Pictures sits behind the Boulevard in a narrow alley of no name. The chipped old brick round the door is the kind of unreinforced masonry we're told will be the first to tumble in the next earthquake. A yellow-streaked plastic strip above the door announced that this building was available on a 'Dollar-A-Day Leasing Plan'. A business card stuck in the doorbell said 'Nick Supino Pictures, Inc.' in Italian script. 'The bell don't work,' said a homeless person sitting in a shopping basket nearby.

The urine smell had even got into the office . . . maybe it started there. But as I got nearer to the secretary it got swallowed up by a sweeter smell, like wino breath in the morning. 'You like it? It's designer brand.' Her breasts were bigger than her head and she wore a mini-skirt made of some crinkly Christmas gift-wrap material. She was sitting on a filing cabinet admiring her fingernails from afar. I looked at the lurid posters taped to the wall.

'Whaddya think? *Dead Men Don't Walk* or *Zombies Don't Cry*? Same picture, different marketing. One's horror, the other's terror.' A fat figure was silhouetted in a doorway; an arm and a finger gestured me in.

'There *is* a difference between terror and horror,' he said. 'I was at film school.' I sat on a bean-bag in his office. The stuffy little box of a room was filled with scripts and film cans and old fast-food cartons. I couldn't see Supino's desktop because of the hills of paper, but I had a good view of his head: his face was round and orange, his hair was rust-coloured and tightly-curled, like a black's. When he talked his hands flew about like a hyperactive semaphore signaller. 'These offices are strictly temporary. Remember that!' A phone rang and he

214

took it from the floor. 'Listen,' he screamed at it, 'tell that asshole I'll hang him by his heels if he don't deliver!' The secretary sashayed in with some papers in one hand and, dangling in the other, a long slice of pizza. 'Whasssamatter? Don't I feed you girls enough at the house? Not you, you cocker-roach!' He clapped the phone into its cradle and slipped the ensemble into a pocket of his cardigan. I liked it that he wore a cardigan, especially in such clammy weather as today's. He grabbed the papers from her and started at once to sign them up against the wall. Then he handed them to me. 'Contract – we see you right here.' The copy paper was wet and smelled like a hospital. 'We'll have new technology soon, you wait!' He spun around the room, a vaudeville ballet dancer. 'All this is transient! Who wants decor? I want *product*!' He gestured me to the window and we looked down at a clutch of blacks deep in animated discussion in the alley. 'That's one world. And in Beverly Hills and Newport Beach there's another world. Never the twain shall meet! The successful live in sealed cars, sealed estates, sealed offices. Guarded and gated from that slime below. But that slime is growing and creeping, killing books and good music. That slime needs product and I intend to give it to 'em in buckets of blood and gore and dripping sex organs! Then I too can go seal up with those fuckers in Beverly Hills and Newport Beach!'

He continued his talk as we jolted along Hollywood Boulevard in his car, heading for the editing studio. We were going in the opposite direction to Beverly Hills, soon in a neighbourhood of Asian cafés and adult book-stores and mini malls. 'Piece of the pie is what I want. That's all *they* want too – the blacks, the Third Worlders, the Asians. Even you Englanders.' There was a powerful sour smell in the sports car, but I couldn't identify it. 'The Porsche needs work, I know. But it's window-dressing, see? You understand – you're a bit of a self-salesman. . . . All those books you gave me – I'll scan 'em on the john. Don't be hurt – I only read when I shit but I can spend up to two hours or more shitting so feel good!'

The dubbing studio was in a street corner mini mall next to a Thai fast-food joint. It wasn't really a studio – just a big acoustic-tiled room with audio and video equipment and a skinny old man in a baseball cap riding the stuff. I knew the name – he'd been a Sixties one-hit wonder like me – but we didn't reminisce. We were grappling with the beast of the present; some of us had dreams of gated estates and champagne jacuzzis. As for myself . . . I was just so glad to be working in show-biz again.

215

Supino flopped down on a leather couch and started banging his head against the wall. '*Zombies Don't Cry! Dead Men Don't Walk!* Which is it, for Chrissake?' 'Vot iss wrong vitt *Horror House*?' said a guttural voice. A stooped and silver-haired man with one empty jacket sleeve emerged from a hole in the wall. His good arm was zipping up his trousers. Supino banged his head so hard he slipped off the leather and into the shag carpet. 'Klaus! I'm talking about the voodoo rock musical, not the stalk-and-slasher!' I introduced myself to the old gent and was thrilled to realize that he was Klaus Zwimmer, the German director of countless B-pictures of the Thirties and Forties. 'Be happy, Klaus,' said Supino from the floor. 'We're all buffs here! Run the picture, Artie!'

A T.V. monitor perched on top of an 8-track recording console showed us a snowstorm followed by a lot of lines and then a grainy and weakly-coloured picture of a bearded man in a leisure suit, tied to a tree. Suddenly his lower torso was torn away and red mush gushed out. 'Not now! Not now! Run the top of the pic! I wanna match the Englander's song!' said Supino.

My song, 'In Hollywood!' is one that I wrote years ago – shortly after Dr Ronald Bund had revealed to me a darker side of Hollywood Boulevard: 'Down on the Boulevard Saturday night/You've never seen such a colourful sight/But make sure that you roll up your windows real tight/In Hollywood!' Supino's thinking was to lay my vaudeville number, riddled with ukulele, at the top of the picture. 'We gotta ease into the red meat. . . . Let's splice an instrumental before the vocal. . . .' Klaus Zwimmer exchanged glances with Artie the engineer. 'But *mein lieber*!' said Klaus. 'Ve vill haf two minutes off nuttin' but music und titles!' Supino hit the side of his (own) head with the palm of his hand . . . and *I* leaped into the breach!

Off the top of my head I suggested I pretend to be a 1930s movie-town tour guide who, in megaphone voice, would welcome everybody, off camera, like a commentator, to Hollywood, land of dreams. . . .

'Go for it!' said Supino. 'And submarine sandwiches all round!'

I love pressure. I love this kind of work. In no time at all, on the back of my contract, I wrote out the tour guide's speech. It was full of purple prose about roses and rainbows and bright nights and Klieg lights in the Dream Factory. While Supino busied himself with the sandwich-ordering the veteran director and I worked on my interpretation in the recording booth. 'Giff me much sincerity – only phoney it up!' Tape was rolled and Klaus Zwimmer – who had directed countless singing cowboys as well as a few Tarzans – conducted me with a ballpoint pen in his good hand. I felt the first take was fine, but Zwimmer wanted it again . . . and again . . . and again. After twenty takes or so, Supino barged into the booth and said, 'O.K., Klaus – you made your point. Let's eat!'

We were awarded submarine sandwiches filled with spiced Italian sausage, grilled onions and lots of tomato. Supino already had tomato on his face, shirt and trousers. Zwimmer made a gesture with his silk handkerchief. 'I know, I know,' said Supino, throwing away the tiny heel of his sandwich. 'But such matters are trifling. It's the picture that counts!' He pulled out a big metal comb with long jagged teeth and chopped it slowly through his tight Negroid curls. 'You may stay for the sound-effects dubbing.' But it was time for my singalong show try-out. 'You may return here – if you so wish.' As I got up to leave, Zwimmer tapped my knee. 'You did vell. Von time I made Colonel Tim McCoy do von hundret unt eight takes off pullink hiss gun from hiss holster!'

*

The T.V. game-show try-out was hopeless. They played me the tape of the tunes, but I didn't recognize a single one and so I couldn't singalong. Me – a supposed expert on popular music! At school I had never learned anything about the Renaissance or Shakespeare or Beethoven. Instead I'd chosen a field that everyone else was ignorant of: despised pop – 'The debased street music of the vulgar,' said folklorist Cecil Sharp. I'd worked and I'd worked in my chosen field and then, around the late Sixties, I'd sat back and rested. I knew my pop from Stephen Foster to Elvis Presley. I could relax and be consulted for fees.

But here I was standing at a podium with flashing lights behind me and a girl with a clipboard smiling in front of me . . . and backing track music that bounced and ponged and clashed and meant nothing to me except annoyance at the Y.M.C.A. when I'm trying to exercise quietly and this stuff keeps interrupting. 'Have a stab,' said the clipboard girl.

Over the tape I made a short statement – but expressed in stentorian tones – to the effect that a show purporting to embrace popular music should certainly contain songs from the Golden Age, songs made famous by the likes of Al Jolson, Ruth Etting, Whispering Jack Smith. . . .

'Thank you,' said a deep voice over the studio speakers. 'We're a

217

contemporary adult music format on "The Singalong Show". We're talking current market pop – Springsteen, Bon Jovi, etc. We might slip in a Stones number. . . . We want to thank you for taking time out to visit us. . . .'

As I stumped off, the clipboard girl caught up with me. 'Your girl-friend was in earlier for a try-out . . . Regina? Yeah. She did well – she has a lovely voice and you should be real proud of her. She speaks so well of you.'

Back at the studio they were getting into pizzas and beer. Even Zwimmer had food smears on his face. 'Ve are gettink zonked,' he explained. The tearing in half of the leisure-suit man had been dubbed with appropriate sounds, as had the sequence of the teen girl impaled on the railing and the decapitation of the Siamese cat. Now they were running a scene where the biker girl, in only a thong, falls down the stairs of the old mansion to her death. *Close-up*: eyes stare glassily, tongue sticks out stupidly, blood pours from mouth, breasts still quiver.

After the umpteenth running of this sequence Supino finally called a halt. 'Something's wrong!' he shrieked, crushing a beer-can round his chipolata sausage fingers as a percussive exclamation point. 'It ain't working!' Then he moved towards the wall for, I assumed, some more head-banging.

I seized another opportunity.

Heading him off on his walk to the wall, I stood in front of him and made my pitch. I said that as the biker girl tumbles to her death and her head hits the banisters over and over . . . well, there ought to be a loud *ker-runcccching* sound as her skull gets crushed. 'We already got that effect on the track,' growled Artie. 'Then let's hear the fuckin' thing!' said Supino. Artie shoved the console knob up a few inches. I looked doubtful. 'Give it the full cock-sucking ker-runcccch!' ordered Supino. Artie shot me a killer look and shoved the knob up to max. 'That's it!' Supino screamed. 'The bitch is strawberry jam in a chicken pot pie!' Then he grabbed me and held me by the shoulders. He smelled sweet. 'Listen. You aided in the creation of something good. Give yourself a pat on the back.' I started to speak, but he waved me shut at point-blank range. 'Listen. You learned a fact of motion-picture life. You wanna know what that is?' I opened my mouth, but then thought better of it. 'You learned that . . . IT'S THE SOUND THAT CREATES THE FUCKIN' FURY!'

Timing's important, too. I stayed too long after my moment of glory. I told Supino that if he wanted my services in any of his other productions he shouldn't hesitate to call on me because I could write any kind of music for him, I could write screenplays too. . . . He snapped the elastic on his parachute pants, stopping my flow. 'Let's get this matter straight, shall we? You helped us out at the last minute in a unique situation. A *unique* situation. O.K.?'

*

We've walked Beefy round the block and now it's time for our dinner with Basil at Musso & Frank's. We're round the side of the old restaurant now – a block of un-reinforced masonry, the cement overflowing from the red bricks looks like white icing on a carrot cake. *I've taken lots of topographical notes.* Glad we have Beefy with us, because he clears a path through the jungle clumps of riff-raff that infest these streets. *Threatening ethnics.* Are they really? They've never threatened me . . . but you read about their violence in the papers and you see it nightly on T.V. Did you see that bum who just passed us? He was wearing Bugs Bunny ears. So many tramps these days that I've stopped giving them money. You could spend your whole life giving away your property, and I'm not Jesus. The other day an old crone with masses of thick white hair stopped to panhandle me, telling me she'd had a two-thousand year-old baby who'd died at thirty-three, but I gave her a dollar because she was holding her grandson's hand and that touched me. The encounter took place right here outside the front of Musso & Frank's.

Regard the front. A historic landmark ringed by the disorder of today. Mind you, the decor isn't aesthetically noteworthy but I like it: the crazy-paving slab-stones on either side of the front door – same as Sterling's Steak House – are correctly described as 'Ski lodge rustic Fifties moderne' according to an architect friend of mine. But Musso's is much older than the Fifties. It's the oldest restaurant in Hollywood, opening in 1919 when all the movie stars patronized it; and in the Thirties the writers came in, Fitzgerald and that lot; these days you find rock people too – all sheltered and sealed off from the swirl outside. I saw Streisand coming down the aisle one night. Let's put Beefy in the car and then make our entry. It's hipper to come in from the rear entrance, by the parking lot, but I'm not famous and they charge too much for parking.

*

God, how I wish I was famous again! It makes dining out so much easier. All these successful-seeming people in loose-fitting clothes milling around the sloping clerkly desk, sucking up to the grizzled

219

varmint of a maître d' so as to get the right booth or banquette in the right dining room – the one on our left. Very important to be on the left, the one on the right is for the tourists, but the maître d' always puts me there when I'm not with Basil. Of course, Basil's not here yet – *typical*! Has to be fashionably late. Meetings at the studio, etc. You'll see – he'll make a grand entrance from the back and as he walks down the aisle a procession will form . . . waiters and maître d's and chefs, fawning along in step. If we could get through these bastards I could show you the historic aisle and the booths and banquettes – I couldn't tell you if that's Brian de Palma or Martin Scorsese or neither – they all wear beards and bush hats. . . . I love those semicircular red banquettes and also the little brown wooden booths – so dark and comfortable, I'd like to have one of each in my house. They have a coat-and-hat stand too, a nice period touch. If you're alone – as I sometimes find myself – you can dine without embarrassment up at the counter, reading or listening or watching the chef as he pokes at chops and steaks in the open fire. I usually have macaroni au gratin because it's inexpensive and I like it, and anyway I can't have it when I'm in Basil's company because he thinks I'm making a point about being a failure. Or about how he's borrowed so much money from me that I've become impoverished. Where is he? He'd better have a good excuse. Solid old American food is served at Musso's – chicken pot pie, steaks, sauerbraten and potato pancakes, corned beef and cabbage – served by surly old waiters. If you're Basil, you're on first-name terms with them. If you're Basil, you get a good table immediately. He told me his secret once: 'It's simply because – unlike you – I tip well and have done so ever since I first came to Musso & Frank's.' Dining out is Basil's life . . . he writes screenplays so's he can indulge in this characteristic local participatory art. Sometimes he gets a sensation even before his fork has been sucked of its load. Often there are bits of the load that spill off on to his clothes (but he wears very casual outfits) or stick to the sides of his mouth, or get spat in my direction (for he is a tireless raconteur of 'inside' movie trade stories). Perhaps I should tell him about the stray food, but I'm frightened of losing the last of my English friends over here. He's getting awfully fat, too. Has trouble sliding into a banquette. He says he should invest in a pair of chopsticks and then he'd eat slower and perhaps less. But Curlew Worthington has carried a pair of chopsticks for years, and he's actually fatter than Basil. You remember Curlew? The film director and Art Nouveau collector who is offended by my Hawaiian curtains? Well, I dine here with Curlew every now and

220

then, but he has some annoying habits – for example, he *will* keep interrupting me to moisten his lips with his tongue and bug out his eyes at some youth he's spotted. It's always a weight-lifting lug, somebody I wouldn't notice. 'Ah,' he said recently after I complained, 'but now you understand why *I'm* a film director and you're not. You see – I'm *outward-directed* and you're *inward-directed*.' So bloody inward-directed that I didn't order first and thus Curlew got the last loin of pork special and I had to make do with filet of sand dabs – mind you, sand dabs are better than those disgusting prehistoric fish-lips-in-rice that Basil insisted on ordering for us when we last visited Chinatown; as Curlew and I sat with the other film folk around the rotating circular table watching the heads and tails and eyes of lightly-boiled animals merry-go-rounding past us, we exchanged glances because we knew that Basil was paying his share of the dinner out of money that we had loaned him – after that special telephone pleading that Basil does so expertly with his rumbling-low, non-regional classless British accent; he swears the 'four-figure deal is only a phone call away from the green light at Paramount'. While Basil was talking up a storm and tucking into boiled fish-lips and the glazed canvas side of a Peking duck, Curlew – loyal pal that he can be – patiently but deliberately explained to me that as a film industry outsider I couldn't be expected to know of the terrible humiliations that creative artists such as he and Basil have to suffer at the slimy hands of fool executives, but perhaps now I'll understand that some of the boiling poison inside Basil can be . . . can be . . . calmed, cooled? Evaporated away? Can be . . . got rid of by a good dinner of . . . of fish-lips, if that was necessary. 'Speaking for myself,' said Curlew, pulling himself together again, 'when I am harassed by barbarian movie executives I go home and redecorate a room.'

The aisle has cleared! We can see all the way down to the back entrance where the stars appear from and, hopefully, Basil. Years ago, when I was on dining terms with Christopher Isherwood, we were sitting in a party of half a dozen at the big banquette up at the front when who should make a boisterous appearance at the back entrance but Tennessee Williams, costumed in a white linen plantation outfit and a broad-brimmed sombrero, supported at the armpits by blond beach-boy types. 'Chris! You old bugger!' bellowed the playwright. There was a dramatic silence as the three characters made their way downstage towards our banquette. Then: 'Tennessee . . .' replied the writer wanly and a little reluctantly for he had been in the middle of a yarn about pre-war Berlin. What happens to me as a rule is that no

221

sooner have I commandeered the floor when a waiter barges in to take our orders and afterwards nobody asks me to resume my performance. . . . All right, I'm getting maudlin – let's take a walk down the aisle and soak in some ambience. Grungy men with foxy women. How do they do it? Curlew insists it's all a matter of money. Look at that rumpled cretin with hair sticking up in vaselined spikes! And the girl's all over him! A bald man says to a strawberry blonde, 'I'm beginning to feel at ease in our relationship,' and she replies, 'Love to plug into your brain!' See that couple working out their bill with a pocket computer in solemn silence? Silent too is the party of four at the next banquette – because they're poised at that exciting moment of grace when, with loaded plates set before them, they can appraise the food before digging in. Next, two stiff-backed men in boys' clothes. The older one's coughing fit has the younger one horrified – pursed-lipped, goggle-eyed, tips of his fingers pressed hard together. . . . This next table's more like my handwriting: a fat old man smoking a big Havana. Basil was smoking a big one here only the other night when up comes an emaciated wimp in wispy New Age clothes and dumps a plate of roast duckling right in front of my friend. Says the New Ager, '*You* polluted it – *you* consume it!' What a world! Ah . . . here IS Basil! A bit plumper, perhaps, since last week. Head shaved and gleaming. A cashmere sweater with no shirt underneath. And dating a tall red-headed woman in a vintage tuxedo and shocking pink jeans. I suppose we'd better respond to his signal, but one of these nights I'll make him come over to me first. That waiter just shoved me – it's the one Basil calls Juan. . . .

The situation's getting out of hand. Basil never said Curlew was joining us, and I can't stand this fake cockney media man with him who probably went to Bedales or Dartington Hall. I asked Basil, in the lavatory, if he knew which school and he hissed, 'What does it matter?' But it *does* matter because I like to get things straight. Basil *did* agree to tell me the ghastly type's name: Jake Hodge. I hate his skinny black leather tie and his cowboy check shirt and his long neck and his dry cant-drawl about how you can only understand America by studying her soap operas and commercials. And the creature's only been here a couple of days! Listen to him: 'So Quentin at *The Observer* said pop over and do a sort of sour piece about Hollywood – put on your Dennis Potter cap – and of course I knew what he meant 'cos they love such stuff when it's a wet summer – "Dada In La-La Land" or "Down In Clown-Town" – and already I'm getting good vibes just being at the Château Marmont which is such a hoot with bloody great billboards hovering right over the French Normandy roof and the spirits of Garbo and Belushi oozing out of the walls . . .' 'You *must* meet my dear friend Hercules de Brisco,' interrupted Curlew. 'He's a witch, you know, and he has his very own coven in West Hollywood . . .' Hodge jammed two fingers into his temple. '*Excellente*! West Hollywood has a gay mayor, do it not? Perhaps you can slip me into a bath-house for some local colour before they're all gone. . . .' It was clear that Hodge had the floor but then, suddenly, the red-head girl broke in with, 'I hear the fags have some kinda deal called "Cocks Across The Continent", and the idea is to form a coast-to-coast daisy chain butt-fucking for famine relief.' There was a terrible pause . . . but it was quickly filled by the chatter and clatter from the Musso & Frank dining room. 'I'll see about our table,' said Basil. Curlew cleared his throat with a long *aaaaaaaaagh* and took the floor: 'There's a most amusing new restaurant that *everybody's* talking about. Roddy called this morning to tell me about the heavenly white fish *interwoven with oysters* – his very words, I swear – and *flecked with orange* – again I quote. When he got on to the rabbit sausage in aspic, I cried, "Stop! I'm drooling!"' The redhead, obviously high on something, started to speak but Curlew kept the floor by emitting another, and much louder, *aaaaaaaaagh* which let him get back into his act: 'I simply *have* to treat myself to a nice dinner because I've been so down lately – missing an important party due to double booking, and then Beverly invited me to dinner on condition I bring Anne Baxter or Claire Trevor and – can you believe it! – both are out of town touring in dinner theatre. Still, we had an amusing time this afternoon at the "Whatever Became Of?" reception. Freddie Bartholomew failed to show, but Baby LeRoy was rumoured to be present – you enjoyed it, didn't you, Jake? – material for the film. Remind me to introduce you to my dear friend Bella Rasputin, daughter of the mad monk – she's a channeller, you know, and she's recently located a dead Victorian boy in the guest bedroom I just had remodelled – quite an attractive child, she says – *aaaagh* – the restaurant we're going to has young stand-up comedians as waiters instead of the usual out-of-work actors, and the pizza apparently is spectacular – they raise their own baby lamb and vine-ripened tomatoes – and the desserts are worth dying for! But I'm taking no chances. . . . ' He flourished a long, thin silver case. 'I'm bringing my most difficult pair of chopsticks!'

*

So here we are at Curlew's restaurant. I did ask Basil – on your behalf – whether instead we could dine at Morton's. It's very glitzy – the current club for the movers and shakers of show-biz, owned and operated by Peter Morton, the Englishman who started the Hard Rock Cafés – and it's so chic they don't have a sign outside. Jack Nicholson eats up at the bar. . . . But Basil nixxed the suggestion. He said he was at Morton's only last night – a charity banquet for Ethiopian famine relief. How much did that set him back? 'Peter and I are old chums from way back, so the evening was complimentary.'

Here we are at Art Pescora's. Battleship-grey, steel rods and concrete, huge searchlights criss-crossing the West Hollywood sky. Latino valet parkers, in satin Art Pescora bomber jackets, waving us in with flashlights like we were aircraft. And now we're all stuck in the crush of the bar where the rock'n'rap music makes Basil's turn at monologue impossible to follow. So I'm gazing up above at the grey steel girders and the grey metal air extractors, the twisting tubes, and the tilted T.V. monitors beaming down garish-coloured pictures of black men batting and boxing and huddling, and I'm catching gobs of prattle: '. . . We had noodles and spinach for breakfast, but the waiter poured cheese in my raspberry tea. . . . An impossible arrangement when both lovers insist on being dominant and male. . . . I sold Columbia on the story in one sentence – sex rivalry in the fireworks industry. . . . I always, but *always*, bring my own sparkling water. . . .'

*

The time has come for us to start our journey westward, returning to where we began. I couldn't stand that man Hodge and in the men's room I told him so and then I started stuttering. So we left the restaurant and now you and I and Beefy are ascending on to the Santa Monica freeway, which so many call the Ten. The freeway is a lovely thing tonight, a ribbon of smooth pavement, straight as an arrow, ready to fleet us over trouble and let us off at friendly homes as far away and over the hills as Rancho Cucamonga or Point Mugu.

But tonight we are travelling west. Fairfax a mile or so, Robertson further – signs in white letters on pleasant green background. The landscape slips by like a cartoon-film chase – bushes and peppers and lollipop trees – a stately row of waving willows. (Thoughtful urban planners.) The Honda connects with the pavement so naturally, thumping and sighing and whistling and creaking. (The normal high-pitched ringing in my ears has gone.)

224

There's traffic all around us, flowing quite freely, friendly faces centred in a world of their own. Above and across us chatters a police helicopter, keeping the peace with a piercing white light. Further up are jumbo jets and satellites and space-ships – artefacts connecting, bringing sense to the nothingness of space with its dust and gas and no ukuleles. From microcosm to macrocosm – but now back to sludge. . . .

Beneath us, travelling west too, in concrete tubing, is a gurgling, spitting, wrestling river of hot sludge. From the lavatories of rich and poor and middle-of-the-road – yes, but I'm thinking tonight of my restaurant friends and the fruit of their lives. I'm imagining their legacy as it fights its fiery way through underground pipes down to the sea. I'm seeing a sludge-stew of duck sausage mousse, baked lobster with drawn butter, saddle of rabbit with Dalmatian sage, quail eggs with caviar on a pizza crust, fire-roasted chili pasilla with goat-cheese and Balsanic vinegar and pesto, finished off by sherry trifle and chocolate 'suicide' cake.

The fighting continues till at last the great green Pacific is reached, and there the ragout is slowly discharged, to be walloped by the surf. Then, like crimes hushed-up, the legacy slides to the ocean bed, thickening the blanket of sewage built up through the years. For a once-featureless subterranean plain is now a firm landscape of hills and dales and little winding pathways, created by new forms of life such as the *parviluvina* clam and the *capitella* worm. Perhaps some day these creatures will find their way into the cuisine of Los Angeles – and so life goes on and on and round and round. *Arrows and circles*.

At the interchange of the Santa Monica and San Diego freeways we have a choice: left for San Diego and the Southern Hemisphere, right for Sacramento and the Great North-west. But the Third World is already arriving in L.A. and the New World up north – a snow-white land of tree-hugging, self-congratulation and constant harping about the intoxicatingly clean air – is not my idea of interfacing with the future.

No . . . we will keep right on till the end of the Santa Monica freeway. Just before the road turns at the beach we will exit and make our way to Sterling's Steak House where we started this story. A light sea breeze will greet us and Beefy will take his place with the other dogs at the great wooden front door. Once inside I will make amends and there will be singing and dancing all night long. And the circle will be joined.

225

Epilogue

A few weeks later Sterling's Steak House closed down because the lease had run out. Regina and I attended the farewell party. Dick Gimbel and I played a duet – cornet and ukulele. We all swore allegiance to the music and to each other. That was 5 July, 1987.

Next year, after months of intensive and noisy erasure of our old world, there opened on that site a restaurant so chic, so expensive and so exclusive that only those in the know knew its name. Four successful French chefs, so the papers say, take turns commuting from Paris in order to prepare transcendent pizza. There is no music to speak of.

On 1 October of that year, at 7.42 a.m., I was shaken awake by a 6.1 earthquake. Its rumbling seemed to say, 'You bloody fool, you bloody fool, you bloody fool!!' But the giant could not be reasoned with. My first concern was for Beefy; however, he came rambling into the bedroom during the aftershocks, wagging his tail, unconcerned. I made him stand next to me in the corridor under the main doorway. Troy and Cassandra, Max and Kimberlee joined us, laughing. We were all naked but nobody was interested. There was no damage to the house. Some copies of my novel *LotusLand* had fallen from a bookshelf. But 'terra firma' had lost its meaning for me. The authorities said that the 'Big One' is yet to come and could be arriving any day.

The first person to phone me after the quake was Regina. We had been seeing an awful lot of each other lately. She always pointed out the best side of life. I had started to teach her some songs. The following year, on Easter Sunday, she sang, 'All I Do Is Dream Of You' with my band at a brunch-and-dance. I introduced 'Altadena Lane', with extra lyrics mentioning both her and Beefy.

Next morning I found Beefy's noises hard to bear. For several weeks he'd been overdoing the harrumphs, but now he was groaning too. I shut him outside in the garden, but he pushed his way back in through the doggie door even though I'd shut it tight. When I scolded him he held up a paw and gave me a look. I made an appointment with his vet, Dr Shackleford.

The X-rays showed dark spots around his heart and lungs, probably cancer. Who's in charge of this evil? I was to take him for tests at another hospital and return him tomorrow. He seemed so bright and well the next morning. Just before entering Dr Shackleford's I decided to give Beefy a short walk. He tugged me into a dark corner of an industrial block next door. I sat him down and ordered him to get better.

That afternoon I was lying on my bed having a telephone interview about my Irving Berlin book when a beep told me somebody was trying to get through. I asked the reporter to hang on a second. 'This is Dick Shackleford. I have bad news. We just lost Beefy.' They were draining the cancerous fluid when his heart gave out. 'I'd like to do an autopsy.' Of course.

I marched around the house and garden, crying out and cursing God. It was a terribly sunny day. . . . Then I threw away his big sack of special avocado-based dry food and all his rubber balls except the red one with the bell inside. I also kept a lead. When I called Regina and said his name I broke down and cried. For the first time in ages. We stayed the night at the Santa Monica house of a Sterling's friend. I dreamed that Beefy's double was romping up and down the many floors of my house, chasing the red ball.

Dr Shackleford left a message on my answering machine: Beefy had a very rare cancer called mesotheliona – he spelled it out – which is associated with asbestos and smoking. Steve McQueen, the movie actor, died of it.

Over the next few days I kept finding balls I'd forgotten about, behind chairs, under my desk, under my bed. Hairs remained on the sofa and my bedspread. I framed two colour photographs of him and set one in the drawing room and one by my bedside. And then I began seeing Beefy in every dog everywhere. . . .

Out of the blue Jack Wontner called up to invite me to dinner. He was sympathetic about Beefy and I suppose he was trying to help when he said that we're all – humans and animals – just types, and there's plenty more where we came from and probably a few models of me living around the world – and certainly several in Britain. I thanked him but I didn't believe a word. I felt certain of my own inexorable self.

Within days of Beefy's death I invited Regina to come and live with me. She accepted and was soon brightening up the house. But the lodgers fell into disarray: Max and Kimberlee split up and left without a word or the rent; Cassandra cried a lot and Troy grew sullen – eventually they filed for divorce and left. My boarding-house/boarding-school was no more.

In June 1989, following a great afternoon conducting my dance band – with Regina singing 'I Don't Want To Walk Without You – she and I dined at a Mexican restaurant in Pasadena. During the second margarita we got engaged. And now, in 1990, we are married and live in the house on Alameda Street. Of course, it's cleaned up and ready for visitors.

Here's what I wrote for the *Old Bryanstonian Yearbook* – don't you agree it marks the end of the journey?:

I. WHITCOMB (Salisbury House, 1959). It is high time I put pen to paper and told of the changes in my life. Since my last entry – which extolled the virtues of crime and vice in Hollywood – I have mended my ways and joined society proper. My contemporaries will be interested to learn that I have settled down to become a married man, even here in Southern California! Seriously, though, my wife and I would be delighted to see any OBs passing through – they can be assured of a decent meal and a clean bed and much, much hospitality.'

THE END